SURPRISED BY THE POWER OF THE SPIRIT

This is the most persuasive answer I have ever read to the objections of people who say that miraculous gifts like healing and prophecy are not for today. The book is solidly anchored in the Bible and written by a skilled interpreter of Scripture who knows the objections from inside out. If you already believe in these things, this book will renew your faith and your love for Jesus, and help you guard against abuses. But if you don't believe these gifts are for today, be prepared to change your mind—and maybe your life!

—*Wayne Grudem*
Professor of Biblical and Systematic Theology
Trinity Evangelical Divinity School

Like many of the rest of us, Dr. Jack Deere came kicking and screaming from his cessationist position. This is the clearest presentation of a theology of miraculous gifts I have ever read. I'm going to urge every cessationist I know to wrestle with Jack Deere's brilliant presentations. This book is among the first in the new paradigm in church life.

—*Ralph Neighbour, Jr.*
Touch Equipping Stations, Singapore

Here is a timely book, which should cause a degree of (good) discomfort to Pentecostals and cessationists alike, calling the former out of their smugness and Spirit-talk, all too often without experienced reality, and the latter to recognize that their case is predicated almost altogether on their *experience*—or lack thereof—of Spirit life. This is narrative theology at its best—at once confessional, testimonial, and biblical. The reader, too, is in for a surprise.

—*Gordon D. Fee*
Professor of New Testament, Regent College

One of the most severe historical setbacks to the full manifestation of the kingdom of God in the U.S.A. was Benjamin Warfield's *Counterfeit Miracles* published seventy-five years ago. Jack Deere's new book, more than anything I have seen, has all the potential for neutralizing Warfield and his followers and opening the body of Christ to the full power of God's Holy Spirit. It is truly a landmark book!

—*C. Peter Wagner*
Fuller Theological Seminary

In my opinion, Jack Deere's book *Surprised by the Power of the Spirit* is 'must' reading for all Bible-believing Christians. I am convinced that this book will inspire, challenge, and bless every reader. I wish with all my heart I could place it in the hands of every conservative evangelical.

—*James Robison*
Life Outreach International

A dramatic turning point came in Jack Deere's life when the Spirit of God took him by surprise. Sovereignly, God took charge of him, just as he did to Saul the Pharisee, to Augustine, the profligate, and to John Calvin, the 16th-century humanist. Dr. Deere's book describes that turning point and examines its biblical foundations. It is a book whose time has come.

—*John White*
Psychiatrist and author

This book is a real barn burner. Through fascinating stories, a fresh look at the Bible, and a theology of passion and power, Dr. Deere assaults the traditional Protestant position that the miraculous ministry of the Holy Spirit has ceased. Dr. Deere allows no neutrality. You are either with him in his quest for more of the Spirit's miraculous powers or against him. The book calls for a response, one way or the other, not a reaction.

—*Bruce K. Waltke*
Professor of Old Testament, Regent College

Simply written, brilliantly argued, Dr. Deere's thesis is, in my opinion, irrefutable. It will win the day. It will convince those who are open and many who are not.

—*R. T. Kendall*
Minister, Westminster Chapel, London

Surprised
by the Power of
the Spirit

JACK DEERE

KINGSWAY PUBLICATIONS
EASTBOURNE

ISBN 1 84291 270 4

09 10 11 12 Year/Printing 19 18 17 16 15 14

KINGSWAY COMMUNICATIONS LTD
Lottbridge Drove, Eastbourne BN23 6NT, England.
Email: books@kingsway.co.uk

Printed in the USA

Contents

APPENDICES

For Leesa,

Who is this that grows like the dawn,
As beautiful as the full moon,
As pure as the sun,
As awesome as an army with banners?

(Song of Solomon 6:10)

Acknowledgments

I don't know how any author could have a better experience with a publisher than I've had with the people at Zondervan. At every level their skill and kindness have been overwhelming.

In particular I wish to thank Dr. Stan Gundry, who has overseen this project from start to finish with a remarkable degree of patience and expertise, and also my editor, Jack Kuhatschek, whose considerable talents have significantly improved this book. I am also grateful to Joyce Smeltzer, Dr. Samuel Storms, and Professor Wayne Grudem, all of whom read the manuscript in its entirety and made many valuable suggestions. Thanks are also in order to Lara Gangloff, who typed the manuscript and whose unexcelled secretarial and administrative skills helped to bring this book to completion.

I am indebted to my wife, Leesa, who not only gave me valuable suggestions and corrections for the book, but who also served as an inexhaustible source of encouragement to me during its writing. Finally, I must thank three wonderful teenagers, Craig, Scott, and Alese, who with exceptional patience and understanding endured an absentee father during the final stages of this work.

SHOCKED AND SURPRISED

1

The Phone Call That Changed My Life

In my most undisciplined fantasies I would never have dreamed that a single phone call would alter the course of my life—and not just my life, but a number of others in my circle.

Before that phone call I knew where I was going. My life was both comfortable and secure. I was in control and liked it that way. Most of the time I felt I knew what God was doing. But by the time I put the phone down on that cold day in January of 1986, all of that changed abruptly. I was no longer certain of where I was going and what I was doing, and I was beginning to wonder if I really knew what God was doing.

As it turned out, my life would never be the same after that phone conversation. I would never again feel the comfort and security that comes from thinking you are in control of your life. Granted, that is a false security—I know that now—but it does feel good to be under the spell of that illusion. Had I known the pain and the trauma that lay ahead of me, I might never have picked up the phone. But then, as the words of a popular country western song say, 'I would have missed the dance,' and that would have been the greatest pain of all.

I was the most unlikely candidate in the world for the 'joke' that God was about to play on me. I was just completing my tenth year as a professor in the Old Testament department at Dallas Theological Seminary. I was entering my seventh year as one of the pastors at a Bible church in Fort Worth that I helped to start. The previous fall, I had just returned with my family from a year-long study leave in Germany. It had been a wonderful year, and I was excited about returning to my teaching and pastoral duties.

My main passion was teaching and preaching the Word of God. I believed the most important thing in life was to study God's Word and that most of our needs—or at least our most important needs—could be met through studying the Scriptures. If they could not be met in that way, then we were in trouble, for I had embraced a theological system that didn't leave God much room to help us in other ways. The God I believed in and taught about wasn't as involved in our lives as he had been in the lives of New Testament believers. At the time that didn't bother me very much because I thought *he* wanted it that way. I thought *he* had made the changes. To be sure, I thought God answered prayers, but only certain kinds of prayers.

For example, I knew that God no longer gave the miraculous gifts of the Spirit. There was no need for them; we had the completed Bible now. Of course, God sometimes did miracles. After all, he is God, and he can do anything he wants. It is just that he didn't do them very often. In fact, he did them so rarely that in all my years as a Christian I could never point to one healing miracle that I was confident was the result of God's power. I had never even *heard* of such a miracle! Nor could I point to one in history that was properly documented after the death of the apostles. The one exception was conversions, which I believed then and still believe today are the greatest of all miracles. Other than conversions, the closest thing in my experience to a miracle were answers to prayers, especially those for financial needs, which sometimes seemed too specific to be left to mere coincidence.

This absence of New Testament miracles in my experience didn't bother me, however, because I thought God was the one who initiated this change. I was confident that I could prove by Scripture, by theology, and by the witness of church history that God had withdrawn the supernatural gifts of the Holy Spirit.

I was also confident that he no longer spoke to us except through his written Word. Dreams, visions, inner impressions, and the like, reeked of a subjectivity and an ambiguity that nauseated me. I cringed when one of my students came up to me and said, 'God spoke to me and . . .' Hardly anything could provoke a stern rebuke from me as rapidly as the statement, 'God spoke to me.' To me those words implied that whatever communication was about to follow had the same authority as the written Word of God. That was not only presumptuous, it seemed blasphemous! I loved to heap ridicule on people who said God spoke to them.

As you might guess from what I have said so far, I was not the kind of believer who was looking for 'something more.' I didn't need any healing miracles from God. My family and I had always enjoyed good health, and on those rare occasions when we needed a few stitches or a little medicine, our family doctors were more than adequate. Our congregation was also young and strong, and we had very few deaths in the seven years of our history. Divine healing just wasn't high on any of our priority lists.

I certainly didn't need God to speak to me with any of those subjective methods he used with the people of the Bible. After all, *I had the Bible now*, and I was one of those few people who also had exceptionally good theology. No, neither I nor my circle of friends were looking for 'something more' from God. If I had any problems at all, it was just figuring out how to give more of myself to God.

My wife had a different view of things than I did. In fact, if there is a human reason why I should have gotten that phone call, I would attribute it to my wife's prayers for me. Leesa is one of those rare people who *live* the Christian life rather than talk about it. She would rather spend an hour praying for you than two minutes rebuking you for some obvious sin. Though she didn't say so at the time, she felt that I needed something more from God.

During the year we lived in Germany (1984–85), she would go on a two-hour walk every afternoon in the little mountains of the Black Forest. When I asked her about her walks, she told me that she was praying. I never asked her what for, and she never told me, but she was praying for me. Over the years she had watched my passion for God slowly drying up like the reservoirs in Southern California during a draught. I wasn't conscious of losing any passion for God. I thought I had just grown up. But she was concerned that I had become complacent and self-satisfied. And she saw my attitudes as an enemy of God's calling on our lives. Humanly speaking, I will always feel it was Leesa's prayers that moved God to cause a man on the other side of the country to pick up a phone and dial my number.

Late in the fall of 1985, the leadership of my church decided we would have a spring Bible conference. After an elder meeting, as the chairman of the elder board and I were walking to our cars, he asked me whom I would like to have as a speaker for our spring Bible conference. Without hesitation I replied that I would like to ask Dr. John White, the British psychiatrist and Christian author. He had written about fifteen books at that time, all of which my wife and I had read.

He was my favorite popular author. I was absolutely sure he would do a wonderful job as our conference speaker. I knew from his writings that he held the Word of God in high esteem, that he was intelligent, that he was immensely helpful in the practical areas of Christian living, and I thought I had found clues that he, too, was a dispensationalist. (In fact, it did turn out that he had a Plymouth Brethren background.) We had been using his books for years in our Sunday school classes. The chairman of our elder board immediately agreed with my suggestion.

The next day he called Dr. White's publisher to find out how we might entice him to come to our church. The publisher told him that most likely Dr. White would not accept our invitation because his schedule was already full for the next eighteen months. The publisher said the only chance we had of getting Dr. White would be if we asked him to speak on a topic he was currently writing or researching, since he did not like to speak on things he had already written about. The publisher gave us a few other hints in approaching Dr. White, but not much encouragement. Our chairman sent an invitation through the publisher, but in a short while we received Dr. White's polite letter declining our invitation.

For some reason I was not yet ready to give up. I wrote Dr. White a personal letter asking him to come. Just a few days after I wrote that letter, I received the phone call that altered the whole direction of my life and ministry.

The phone call was from Dr. White. I was shocked that he had called, and even more shocked that he had called so quickly after receiving my letter. He said, 'Hello Jack, this is John White. I want to thank you for inviting me to speak at your spring Bible conference. I think I may be able to work it in. What would you like me to speak on?'

Armed with my insider information, I replied, 'Oh I don't know, how about something you are writing or researching now?'

'Well, I am working on a book on the kingdom of God. How does that sound?'

'That's wonderful! We love the kingdom of God around here.' I thought to myself, *Great, we'll have a prophecy conference. We'll talk about different views of the millennium—or maybe different conceptions of the kingdom and differing theological camps.*

Then I added, 'Now you and I both know what the kingdom of God is, but I will have to give a report to the elders about the different lectures you intend to give on the kingdom. We would like four lectures for the weekend. How would you like to divide them up?'

'When I think of the kingdom of God,' he replied, 'I think pre-eminently of Christ's authority. If you want me to give four lectures, I think they would go something like this. The first one would be Christ's authority over temptation.'

'Right,' I said.

'The second one would be Christ's authority over sin.'

'Good.'

'The third one would be Christ's authority over demons.'

Hmm, I thought to myself, *Demons? Well, I guess there must be demons around somewhere. There certainly were a lot of them in the first century. (Where would they have all gone anyway?) And I am sure that if demons are still around, Christ must have authority over them. This was going to be an interesting lecture, even if it wouldn't have much practical relevance.*

I said, 'Well. . . sure . . . O.K.'

'The fourth lecture would be Christ's authority over disease.'

'*Disease!*' I exclaimed, trying to restrain the tension in my voice. Certainly I had misheard him.

'You didn't say *disease*, did you?'

'Yes I did.'

'You are not talking about *healing* are you?' I almost spit out the word 'healing.' I had such a disdain for anything that had to do with healing.

'Well, yes I am.'

I could not believe my ears. Until just a moment ago, I was sure Dr. White was a sane person, a biblical person, and an intelligent person, and now he was talking about healing!

He's a psychiatrist, I reasoned. Perhaps he is just using 'healing' to refer to some kind of psychotherapy. So I asked, 'You're not talking about *physical* healing are you?'

'Well, I wouldn't limit it to physical healing,' he calmly replied, 'but I am including physical healing.'

'*You're kidding!* Surely you know that God's not healing any more and that all the miraculous gifts of the Spirit passed away when the last of the apostles died. Surely you know that, don't you?' I had never met a person that I regarded as intelligent who didn't know these things.

At this point Dr. White didn't reply.

I thought, *Well, perhaps he is a little weak in this area; after all he is not a trained theologian, he's just a psychiatrist.* I took his silence to mean that he was waiting for me to prove from the Bible that these things didn't exist anymore.

So I said to him, 'We know that the gift of healing has passed away because when we look at the healing ministry of the apostles we see that they healed instantaneously, completely, irreversibly, and that everyone they prayed for got healed. We don't see this kind of healing going on today in any movements or groups that claim to have healing powers. Instead, what we see in these groups are gradual healings, partial healings, healings that sometimes reverse themselves—and many people that don't get healed at all. We know, therefore, that the kind of healing that is happening today is not the same kind of healing that took place in the Bible.'

'Do you think every instance where the apostles prayed for someone is recorded in Scripture?' Dr. White asked.

I thought for a minute and said, 'Of course not. We only have a small fraction of their ministry and of Jesus' ministry recorded in the pages of the New Testament.'

'Then might there not be a case where they prayed for someone, and they didn't get well, and it is simply not recorded in the Scriptures?'

I had to concede that he was right because the Bible doesn't record every instance of the apostles praying for people. There might have been times when they prayed for people, and they didn't get healed.

I realized that Dr. White had just caught me in an interpretive error. I had used an argument from silence. That was something I carefully taught my students not to do. When the subject of the gifts of the Spirit came up, for example, a student might say, 'You don't have to speak in tongues to be spiritual because Christ never spoke in tongues.' I would ask, 'How did you know Christ never spoke in tongues?' The student would reply, 'Because the Scriptures never tell us he spoke in tongues.' I would immediately correct that student, reminding him that you cannot use what the Scriptures *don't say* as proof of your view. For example, the Bible does not tell us that Peter had children, but we're not justified in concluding from the Bible's silence on this point that Peter was childless. That is what is meant by an argument from silence.

Yet I had just used an argument from silence with Dr. White, and I was embarrassed.

I was still quite sure that I was right, however. I had four more biblical arguments lined up and ready to go, but I thought I should be more careful this time. I didn't want to get caught in another mistake.

My next argument was going to be that at the end of Paul's life he couldn't heal Epaphroditus (Phil. 2:25–27), nor Trophimus (2 Tim. 4:20), nor Timothy's frequent ailments (1 Tim. 5:23). I thought this proved that the gift of healing had left the apostle Paul, or that it was in the process of leaving. But now I thought, *What would I say to this argument if I were taking Dr. White's position? I would just say that these three incidents prove that not everyone the apostles prayed for got healed!* That one hit me like a bullet from a .44 magnum. My second proof was no proof at all!

As I quickly examined the next three arguments I was about to use, I found something wrong with each one of them. In most theological debates I had taken my opponent's side and examined very critically all of my arguments from my adversary's perspective to find loopholes or weak points. But my belief that miraculous gifts had ceased had never seriously been challenged before. I had never needed to examine these arguments that closely because everyone in my circle accepted them as true.

I was still sure that I was right, but I was exasperated to find something wrong with each of my arguments. So I just blurted out to Dr. White, 'Well, have you ever *seen* anyone healed?'

'Oh yes,' he replied in a calm, quiet voice. He wasn't going to argue with me. He had nothing to sell me. In fact, I was the one who was trying to get him to speak at our church. He just said, 'Oh yes,' and offered no examples.

Taking the offensive again, I said, 'Tell me your most recent spectacular healing.'

'I'm not sure what you mean by spectacular, but I will tell you two recent healings that have impressed me.'

He then told me about a young child in Malaysia who was covered from head to toe in eczema. The eczema was raw in some places and oozing. The child was in such discomfort that he had kept his parents up for the previous thirty-six hours. The child was behaving so wildly that they had to catch him in order to pray for him.

As soon as Dr. White and his wife, Lorrie, laid their hands on the child, he fell fast asleep. Within twenty minutes or so of their prayer, the oozing stopped and the redness began to fade. By the next morning the child's skin had returned to normal and was completely healed. Dr. White told me a second spectacular story of bone actually changing under his hands while he prayed for someone with a deformity.

After I heard these things, I thought, *There are only two options. Dr. White is either telling me the truth, or he is lying to me. But he is not*

deceived. He is a medical doctor. In fact, he had been an associate profes-
sor of psychiatry for thirteen years. He has written about hallucinations.
He knows the difference between organic illness and psychosomatic illness.
He is not deceived. He is either telling me the truth or he is intentionally
deceiving me.

I thought about that for a moment. What did he have to gain by deceiving me? He wasn't asking to come to my church; I was asking him to come. Furthermore, everything about his manner reflected the Spirit of the Lord Jesus. I was convinced that he was telling me the truth. I was convinced that God had healed the two people he talked about. But I was also still convinced that God was not giving the gifts of the Spirit any longer and that there must be another explanation for the healings.

So I said, 'Well, Dr. White, I believe what you are telling me is the truth, and I would like you to come to my church and give those four lectures, even the one on healing.'

'There is one more thing we need to discuss, Jack. If I come to your church, I wouldn't just want to talk about healing, I would want to pray for the sick.'

'Pray for the sick! You mean *in the church?*' I was flabbergasted. My mind raced ahead to alternatives. 'Couldn't we just get a lame person or a blind person and go off to a back room where nobody would know about it and pray for them there?' I was sure that if we prayed for some sick people in front of the church, they wouldn't get healed, and it would destroy everyone's faith.

'Well, we can work out the details when I come,' he replied, 'but I wouldn't want to just talk about healing without being able to pray for some of the sick people in the church.' He said this very gently, but I knew that if we would not let him pray for the sick in our church, he wouldn't come.

I took a deep breath and said, 'Well, Dr. White, I really do want you to come and give those four lectures, and you can even pray for the sick people in my church, but it's not just up to me. The other pastors and elders have to agree to this before we can make this invitation official. I am not sure how they are going to respond to this suggestion.'

'Oh, I understand, Jack. I understand your fears, and I understand their fears. If after this you all decide to withdraw the invitation, I won't be offended at all. I will just take that as the Lord's will.'

We said good-bye, and I went immediately from that conversation into an elder meeting.

At the beginning of the meeting I announced to the elders and other pastors that I had some good news and bad news. The good news was that Dr. John White had reconsidered our invitation for our spring Bible conference and had decided to accept it. Everyone was happy at that news. 'What's the bad news?' they asked.

'The bad news is that he wants to give some lectures on healing and to pray for the sick in our church.'

'You're kidding!'

'That's what I said to him.'

For the next two hours we talked back and forth about the advisability of Dr. White doing this conference in our church. At the end of our discussion, as each of us gave our final opinions, one of the men said, 'This conference could split our church.'

My last word on the subject was, 'I think we ought to have the conference even though it could split our church. Look at it this way. We started this church with just a handful of people. If our church splits, I suppose we could start another church with just a handful of people if we needed to.' As it turned out, God used even that kind of arrogant insensitivity on my part to accomplish his purposes in a number of our lives.

The conversation with Dr. White and the subsequent elder meeting took place in January of 1986. We decided unanimously to invite Dr. White and hold the conference in April, even though we were sure that the miraculous gifts of the Holy Spirit had ceased.

I spent a good deal of time from January to April studying the Scriptures to discover what they said about healing and the gifts of the Spirit. The first time I had studied the Scriptures on these topics, I had not studied them with an open mind. Godly and brilliant men told me that the Bible taught that the gifts of the Spirit had passed out of existence with the death of the last apostle and that God only spoke through his written Word today. They did not tell me, in so many words, that God was not healing anymore, but they led me to believe that healing was a rare thing and not a significant part of the ministry of the church today.

When I had studied the Scriptures, therefore, it was not really to discover what they taught about the gifts of the Spirit or what they taught about healing, but it was to gather more reasons why God was not doing those things today. But from January to April of 1986, I questioned all my cessationist arguments in the light of scriptural teaching.[1] This time I tried to be as objective as I knew how.

By the time our conference took place in April, a radical reversal had taken place in my thinking. My study of Scripture convinced me that God would heal and that healing ought to be a significant part of the church's ministry. I was also convinced that the Bible did *not* teach that the gifts of the Spirit had passed away. None of the cessationist arguments were convincing to me any longer. I still did not know if the gifts of the Spirit were for today, but I was confident that you could not use the Scriptures to prove they had passed away. I had also begun to believe that God could speak apart from the Scriptures, though never in contradiction to the Scriptures.

These were cataclysmic shifts in my understanding. But my thinking had not changed because I had *seen* a miracle or *heard* God speak to me in some sort of supernatural way. I had no such experiences. I had no dreams, or visions, or trances, or anything that I could identify as supernatural beyond my conversion experience. This shift in my thinking was not the result of an experience with any sort of supernatural phenomena. *It was the result of a patient and intense study of the Scriptures.*

Almost against my will, I now believed that God was healing today and speaking today. I still had a significant revulsion toward the gift of tongues. Even if that gift were for today, I didn't want any part of it! And I did not want any part of what I thought were common abuses in the charismatic or Pentecostal movements.

So I found myself believing one thing with my mind, but with my heart I wasn't quite sure whether I wanted these things in my life or in the life of my church. I knew, however, that if the Scriptures taught that God's healing and speaking should be significant in the life of the church, we *had* to pursue them even if we didn't desire them. These were the conclusions I had reached by the time April arrived and our conference was beginning.

2

Surprised by the Holy Spirit

As I drove to the airport in April to pick up Dr. White, I was tense with anticipation. My months of studying Scripture had given me a new openness to God's power, and I sensed that I was about to embark on a new stage in my Christian life.

Because of some misinformation about Dr. White's flight schedule, it took me almost one-and-a-half hours to find him. I finally saw him standing on the curb in front of one of the terminals.

After a short drive and a pleasant conversation, we arrived at the church. The sanctuary was filled to capacity. I felt pleased at the large turnout—but also a bit apprehensive. I knew people would respond well to most of Dr. White's lectures, but I worried about his upcoming talk and 'demonstration' of healing.

The first three sessions went as I had expected. But on Saturday afternoon, Dr. White gave the last lecture, the one on Christ's authority over disease. There were approximately three hundred people in the audience on that day. After a time of questions at the end of his lecture, he invited people to come to the front of the church for prayer for spiritual or physical needs.

I thought one or two people might respond. Instead, approximately one-third of the people in the room literally rushed down to the front of the church. Some of the pastors and the elders also came down to the front to help Dr. White pray for these people.

I could not believe what I was seeing. People I knew well, who seemed so in control of their lives, were on their knees crying and asking for prayer. I recall one very wealthy woman confessing that she didn't feel loved by anyone except her husband. She asked for prayer that the Lord might remove the barriers she felt around her. I remember another very strong man on his knees confessing that he was eaten up by jealousy over some of his friends' successes and his lack of success. It seemed like people were hurting all around me. I was perplexed and mildly repulsed.

My first reaction was to label this as emotionalism. But emotionalism means that someone has whipped up our emotions through some form of manipulation. In this case, we had just heard a very unemotional lecture on healing, followed by a somewhat bitter question-and-answer session in which some of my friends had said some very unkind things to Dr. White (who, by the way, never lost his temper or gave an unkind reply in return). And then, at the conclusion of that question-and-answer time, Dr. White had given a very matter-of-fact invitation, with no music or emotional plea, to anyone who wanted prayer. How was I to account for the tears, the confessions, and the almost shocking honesty that was happening now?

Had I been a better student of revival history at the time, I would have understood that this very thing had happened on numerous occasions during periods of revival, when the Holy Spirit had fallen on a church or a city. I didn't know it, but the Holy Spirit had just fallen on my church! It was as though God himself took the cork out of the bottle and gave people permission to express all of the pain that had been bottled up inside them for so long. The honesty and courage it took to confess their sins and their pain was actually an indication of the Spirit's presence among us that day.

I wasn't sure how much I liked all of this—but the worst was yet to come.

A very articulate and intelligent lady I had known for a long time came up to me as I was standing at the front of the church. She asked me and another elder to pray for her. This woman was very well educated, very noncharismatic, and she had come out of the same religious background as I. She had an amazing heart for God, spent long hours in prayer, and was a gifted Bible teacher. Yet for many years she had suffered from fears and depression.

What was at the root of her problem was a strong desire for the approval of others. It could almost be termed a 'lust after the approval of man.'

It wasn't that she lusted after men, but that her desire for people's approval was actually controlling her life.

'Would you pray for me?' she asked.

The other elder and I began to pray for her, and absolutely nothing happened. We knew it and she knew it. She thanked us and walked away. I turned to pray for some more people with about the same rate of success.

A few minutes later, I noticed that she was standing in line to talk to Dr. White. I walked over to her about the time she began to tell Dr. White her story. Since I did not seem to have much success in praying for people, I thought I would listen to Dr. White pray for her to see if I could learn anything.

'O.K., let's pray for you then,' he said to my friend.

When she bowed her head, it was more like she hung her head in shame. Despair seemed to be all around her, fueling her pain. Like a gentle father, John White put his hand under her chin and lifted her head. 'Look up,' he said, 'you don't have to do that any more. You are a child of the King.'

I was mesmerized by this. I thought, *That's a nice touch. I have to remember that line—'Look up, you are a child of the King.'* At this point I was still assuming that technique and formulas were the keys to healing. Mercifully, I would be delivered of that assumption shortly.

Then he put his hand lightly on her shoulder and said, 'Lord, I bring your servant Linda [not her real name] into your presence now in the name of Jesus Christ. She doesn't feel the affection of the Lord Jesus Christ for her. Let her feel in her heart how much Jesus loves her and likes her.'

When I heard Dr. White say this, a light went off inside me. I thought, *Of course that is why she has lusted after the approval of others. She doesn't feel in her heart the affection Jesus has for her. If she really felt loved by God, the approval of others wouldn't be nearly so important to her.*

Then Dr. White prayed, 'And Lord, if there be any darkness here manipulating this pain, I pray that you would make it leave now.'

When he said those words, Linda's head began to go up and down, and she began wailing. She could not stop her head or the wailing. I had never seen anything like that before! It was as though those sounds had a physical force in them. When I looked at her, it was as if she had lost consciousness, or at least the control of her body. I sensed a tormenting presence around her.

Almost everyone in the auditorium was shocked by what was happening. I had never seen a demon before, but I was convinced I was looking at the work of a demon that very minute.

'In the name of Jesus, I command you be at peace now,' Dr. White simply said.

And when he said that, everything stopped immediately. He was not going to allow her to be humiliated by an evil spirit before all those people. Later my friend was prayed for in private so that the evil spirit was dealt with and sent away. Today Linda ministers very powerfully in teaching and healing prayer.

As I watched all this happen to her, why was I sure an evil spirit was at work? Because this woman would never act in public like that or do anything that embarrassing. She had no charismatic background. There was no possibility for any of this to be learned behavior. Later she told me that a force had 'come up' and gripped her, and that she was powerless to stop it. Only the name of the Lord Jesus brought it under control.

While I watched her being tormented, I thought of all of the wasted years she had spent in Christian counseling without having any significant improvement. She had followed spiritual directions from her pastors and sometimes even received judgment from her pastors. Even though she prayed and read her Bible faithfully, she had not shown a great deal of improvement, and here was the simple reason; there had been a demonic power behind much of her depression and fear.

I felt tears running down my cheeks as I realized the damage arrogant pastors like myself can inflict on the Lord's children. Sometimes we are so sure we know the causes of a person's pain or depression. If they would just follow our little spiritual prescriptions, they would get better. When they try to take our advice and do not get better, we get angry with them. I thought of all the bad advice I had given this dear woman, and of all the years of professional and pastoral counseling she had endured. I realized how foolish we pastors and counselors had been. You don't 'counsel' demons out of people. Nor do demons come out when a person takes your advice and becomes more disciplined. Demons only come out by the power of the blood of Christ. Until John White came along, none of her pastors or counselors had had the discernment to realize what was the root cause of Linda's afflictions, so Linda had 'suffered much at the hands of her physicians.'

At that very moment, for the first time that I can be certain, the Lord spoke to me. I heard these words not audibly, but just as clearly as audible words, 'You're a deceiver and a manipulator, and you're just playing at church.'

Just looking at these words in print makes them sound so harsh, but they weren't harsh on that day. What I heard was not a condemnation, but an invitation. Somehow I knew I was at a crossroad in life, and that the way I responded to that voice would set a whole new direction for my life. I would either be moving closer to God or away from him. I simply said, 'Yes, Lord.'

That simple, 'Yes,' was the beginning of my learning again what it means to become like a child in the kingdom of God. Not only do we have to become like little children to *enter* the kingdom of heaven (Matt. 18:3), but we have to continue in the humility of a little child if we want to *progress* in the kingdom (Matt. 18:4). When I said, 'Yes,' I was agreeing with God's assessment of my character and ministry. I had just crossed the threshold of a repentance that would become so profound that it would eventually break the chains of some of my most arrogant prejudices about the Christian life and ministry. However, I did not feel any heavy chains falling off at the time. Instead, I felt like a little child whose Father was about to show him a better way.

The next morning was Sunday. I woke up in a state of shock. Our church had been visited by a demon! I wondered what that would do for Sunday's attendance. But more than that, I wondered what kind of strife and divisions might arise because of it. The more I wondered, the more fear I felt creeping over me. I wasn't so sure I wanted this new ministry of praying for the sick in our church if it meant people were going to get emotional and demons were going to manifest themselves.

Then I did something a trained theologian is never supposed to do. I sat down on the couch, opened up the Bible *at random*, and began to read. I knew better than to do this. I had made fun of people who expected God to speak to them out of a random passage, a sort of 'Bible roulette.' I should have taken out a concordance and looked up all the passages on fear, but I didn't. I just opened the Bible and asked God to speak to me.

The passage I opened to was Luke chapter eight, and my eyes fell immediately on the twenty-sixth verse. That, of course, is the story of the Gerasene demoniac. I read the whole, wonderful story of how Jesus cast a legion of demons out of a man and how that man returned to his right mind. Then I came to verse thirty-seven, 'Then all the people of the region of the Gerasenes asked Jesus to leave them, because they were overcome with fear. So he got into the boat and left.' I was on the verge of doing just what the Gerasenes had done.

In great mercy the Lord Jesus Christ had visited our church. He had sent the Holy Spirit to prompt confession and to uncover hidden demonic power in order to strengthen and heal us. And now I was on the verge of asking him to leave because I was afraid of how some people might respond. I repented immediately and asked the Lord to forgive me. I told him that anytime he wanted to deal with a demon in our church, he had my blessing.

After the conference was over, all of the elders and pastors agreed that we should start praying regularly for the sick in our church. At the conclusion of our services we simply invited anyone to come forward who wanted to receive Christ as their Savior or who wanted prayer for spiritual, physical, or financial needs. We had no intentions of becoming charismatic.[1] We simply wanted to fulfill the biblical commandment of James 5:14–16:

> Is any one of you sick? He should call the elders of the church to pray over him and anoint him with oil in the name of the Lord. And the prayer offered in faith will make the sick person well; the Lord will raise him up. If he has sinned, he will be forgiven. Therefore confess your sins to each other and pray for each other so that you may be healed. The prayer of a righteous man is powerful and effective.

We let our church know that from now on we would be applying this passage in our services and also in our private counseling appointments. From now on, the elders and the pastors of the church would be willing to visit homes whenever called on and would pray for the sick in their homes. Of course, we had always been willing to do this, but now we actually *encouraged* people to obey this text. We also let them know that when they came in for counseling, we would be happy not only to counsel them but also to lay hands on them and pray for them according to the New Testament model.

Shortly after we started praying for people in public in our services, a lady in our church named Ruth Gay called me. She told me she had an aneurysm, and that on Wednesday she was going into the hospital for a second angiogram. (An aneurysm is a swelling in a blood vessel so that the walls of the blood vessel become stretched and thin. The danger is that the walls of the blood vessel may burst, resulting in the death of the person.) On Thursday they were going to operate in order to repair the aneurysm. She asked if we would come to her house on Monday night and pray for her. On Monday night, Leesa, Joyce Smeltzer (the wife of John Smeltzer, one of our pastors), and I went to Ruth Gay's house to pray for her. Ruth was living by herself and had been estranged from the rest of her family. She was lonely, depressed, and frightened over her impending surgery.

When the three of us entered her house on Monday night, we could actually feel the gloom surrounding her. We talked with her for a little while, and then we laid our hands on her head and asked the Lord to take her aneurysm away. We prayed very calmly, specifically asking God to supernaturally heal her aneurysm. We didn't rebuke any demons, or shout, or work up any religious excitement. We didn't pray for the Lord to guide the doctor's hands. We asked the Lord to use his own hands to touch this blood vessel and take away the aneurysm.

None of us heard the Lord speak directly that night, nor did we see any overt supernatural signs or manifestations. When we left the house, however, we all had a sense that the Lord had healed

Ruth. We didn't say this to her, but nevertheless we thought we sensed his presence there. On Wednesday morning I received a call from Ruth. She had just come out of her second angiogram. Her voice was so weak I could barely hear her. She said, 'Jack, I have been healed!'

'What?'

'I have been healed!'

'You're kidding!'

'No, it's true. The aneurysm is gone.'

'What did your doctor say?'

'He said I have been healed. A nurse just came in this morning and told me it was a miracle.'

'Did you ask your doctor how he could explain this?'

'He can't explain it. He told me that aneurysms never go away. They have to be corrected by surgery. I asked him if he had ever seen this before, and he said, "Never." He said, "I have no explanation for it, you have been healed."'

This was the first medically documented healing that happened in our church. God had shown great mercy to one of his children who was lonely, depressed, and frightened. We continued to pray for the sick in our church, and we saw other healings—some physical and some emotional. We also saw some demonic manifestations, although not in a public service again.

During my new adventure with the Lord, I had first been surprised by the Scriptures, and then I had been surprised by the Spirit. But this was only the beginning.

3

Signs and Wimbers

When I first made contact with Dr. White, I did not know that for the previous seven months he had been living in Anaheim, California, and attending John Wimber's church. John Wimber is the pastor of Vineyard Christian Fellowship in Anaheim and is the leader of the 'Vineyard movement.' After my initial conversation with Dr. White, he told me all this.

It didn't mean anything to me at the time because I had never heard of John Wimber or the Vineyard. For several years I had not been reading any of the popular Christian magazines, all of which had done reports on Wimber and the Vineyard, nor had anybody discussed him in my presence.

Dr. White told me about Wimber, and he seemed to feel very positive toward him. He told me that if I ever had the opportunity, I should try to meet Wimber and talk with him about healing. Dr. White said that he could verify a number of significant healings that had taken place in Wimber's ministry. After Dr. White left our church, I heard that Wimber was coming to Fort Worth in about two weeks. He was to speak at Lake Country Baptist on the far-west side of Fort Worth.

I decided to go hear him on a Thursday night, but I didn't feel comfortable about visiting a Baptist church that had gone swimming in this new movement called 'The Third Wave.' Some of my friends had also warned me about John Wimber. They had heard that some very weird things went on at his meetings. Just to be on the safe side, I took about ten people from my church with me. That way, if things really did get weird, I would have some witnesses who could confirm that I had merely gone there to evaluate, not to participate.

We arrived late and sat on the back row, right next to the door (just to be safe). People had already begun to worship. They were singing, and some of them were raising their hands, but nothing strange was going on. After about thirty minutes of singing, the pastor, Jim Hylton, a well-respected and sought-after speaker among Southern Baptists, introduced John Wimber. Wimber announced that he was going to speak on the kingdom of God. I said to myself, *And I am going to follow* **every word you say** and evaluate it by the Scriptures.

Twenty minutes into his message, I found myself agreeing with everything he said about the kingdom. Actually, I could have given that same lecture in one of my classrooms at the seminary, and no one would have raised an eyebrow. What is more, I found myself genuinely liking this man. What he was saying was true, and he was saying it in an entertaining way. He was also very honest about his own flaws. There seemed to be little pretense in him. After an hour or so, he finished his lecture and announced it was 'clinic time.'

I thought, *Clinic time? Oh, this is where it gets weird.* Wimber announced that he was going to ask God to show him what the Holy Spirit wanted to do in the remainder of this meeting.

'Right now I have no idea what direction we are supposed to take, but I believe the Lord will show us what he wants to do tonight. I am going to ask the Holy Spirit to come now,' he said.

Ask the Holy Spirit to come? Where is that prayer in the Bible? I wondered.

It bothered me when Wimber announced that he was going to use a prayer that wasn't in the Bible. It didn't bother me when I used prayers that weren't in the Bible. But somehow it seemed wrong for Wimber to do it. Maybe I felt he had no business talking to the Holy Spirit. He should have been talking to the Father through Jesus by the Holy Spirit. At least that is the formula some people believe is the only biblical way to pray.

Or maybe I wondered how he could ask an omnipresent Spirit to 'come.' Yet those who wrote the Psalms asked the Lord regularly to 'come.' I don't really know why; it just bothered me.

Or maybe Someone was bothering me—a frightening thought! I tried to dismiss that idea by telling myself that the Holy Spirit was a gentleman who didn't go around scaring the Father's children, especially the ones with flawless theology.

I was still bothered.

Apparently others were bothered by that simple little 'come Holy Spirit' prayer, because even John Wimber sensed a general uneasiness in the audience. He interrupted his 'clinic time' to admonish the audience.

'Listen, I am going to ask the Holy Spirit to come. You don't have to be afraid of demons or the Devil now. When you ask your heavenly Father for the Holy Spirit, he doesn't give you snakes or scorpions.'

Everyone seemed to be calmed and assured by those words.

Then Wimber added, 'The only demons that are going to manifest themselves are the ones you brought in with you.'

With that last little joke everyone seemed bothered again, even the ones with flawless theology.

He did finally ask the Holy Spirit to come, and then he was silent. So was the audience.

About a full minute later, he looked up and said, 'O.K. I think I know what the Lord wants to do tonight. He has given me some words of knowledge for healing.'

Presumably that meant that God was communicating to Wimber that he would heal certain people in the audience that night. I had never been in a service like that, and I didn't know what to make of it.

Wimber said that God wanted to heal people with back pain. Quite a few peole came down to the front of the church to be prayed for by teams of church members rather than by Wimber himself. After a few minutes he said, 'There is a woman here who has severe back pain, but you haven't come forward yet. Come forward; I think the Lord will heal you right now.'

When I heard these words I thought, *That is incredible.* By now my study of Scripture had led me to believe that God would speak to us in order to give us warnings, guidance, and directions, but I had never seen anyone outside of Scripture get something so specific from God.

I know, now, that Wimber was merely illustrating 1 Corinthians 14:24–26:

> But if an unbeliever or someone who does not understand comes in while everybody is prophesying, he will be convinced by all that he is a sinner and will be judged by all, and the secrets of his heart will be laid bare. So he will fall down and worship God, exclaiming, 'God is really among you!' What then shall we say, brothers? When you come together, everyone has a hymn, or a word of instruction, a revelation, a tongue or an interpretation. All of these must be done for the strengthening of the church.

God had given Wimber a revelation about someone in the audience he wanted to heal, so that not only that person might be touched, but the whole body might be edified. I thought, *This is incredible. This is just how Paul said church was supposed to be.*

But no one came forward.

I thought, *Poor John Wimber. He was doing so well when he was just talking about the kingdom. If he hadn't tried this clinic stuff, this meeting would have been a success tonight.* I felt embarrassed for him and also disappointed.

Wimber did not seem to share my embarrassment or my disappointment. He announced a second fact about this woman. He said, 'You went to the doctor several days ago, you have had this pain for years. Please come forward.'

This was one of the most incredible things I had ever heard. It was like one of the prophetic narratives of the Old Testament.

But no woman got up and came forward. Now the tension was mounting significantly in the room.

Wimber seemed to be praying for a few seconds. Then he looked up at the audience and said, 'Your name is Margaret.' Then, with a grandfatherly smile, he added, 'Now Margaret, you get up and come up here right now.' About halfway down the center section, next to the aisle, Margaret got up and began to walk rather sheepishly toward the front.

I thought that this was the most amazing thing I had ever seen. This was just how the apostle Paul said it should happen. There was awe and conviction in the room. But before Margaret made it down to the front of the church, a wave of skepticism and disgust came over me. I said to myself, *What if he paid her to do this. What if she's Margaret on Thursday night here in Fort Worth, Texas, and then on Saturday night in some other city she is Mabel MacClutchbut, walking down to the front of the church carrying an envelope with two malignant tumors she coughed up?* And I said to myself, *I don't believe this is true.*

At about the same time I had begun to doubt this whole process, the man sitting next to me, whom I had known for fifteen years and who was also in my church, exclaimed, 'That's Margaret my sister-in-law!'

Mike Pinkston's sister-in-law, Margaret Pinkston, went down to the front of the church that evening after being called out specifically by John Wimber. And when several adults prayed for her, she was healed of a condition she had had for years. I knew that family, and I knew there was nothing fake about that healing. This really was a graphic illustration of New Testament church life as revealed by the apostle Paul in 1 Corinthians 14.

You will never guess who was the first one in line to talk to John Wimber after the meeting was over! Leesa and I had a number of questions we wanted to ask him about the events of that evening—about healing and about revelations from God. John was so kind to us, answering our questions patiently and even giving us some on-the-spot instruction as we watched him and others pray for people that evening. I had a theoretical biblical knowledge regarding healing and the revelatory ministry of the Holy Spirit, but Wimber had a practical knowledge and experience in how these things actually work.

It was a fascinating evening, one I shall never forget. It was the evening when our friendship with John and Carol Wimber began, a friendship that would eventually lead to our working together for four years.

During the remainder of 1986 and 1987, John Wimber and I became close friends. Leesa and I went to several Vineyard conferences during that time. We continued to learn more about healing and the present-day ministry of the Holy Spirit, both in the Scriptures and in practical experience. My friendship with Wimber and my growing interest in the supernatural ministry of the Holy Spirit eventually led me to resign from my church and resulted in my dismissal from my teaching position at Dallas Seminary. Before I left Dallas Seminary, however, I met another man who would also be divinely used to alter the course of my life. His name is Paul Cain.

In the fall of 1987, during my last semester at Dallas Seminary, I had helped George Mallone start the Grace Vineyard in Arlington, Texas. In September when George and I were in Kansas City for a conference, Mike Bickle, pastor of the then Kansas City

Fellowship (a large church of about three thousand people), had told us about the ministry of Paul Cain. As a young man in the late 1940s and early 1950s he had played a major role in the healing revival of that time. Mike told us many fascinating stories about alleged supernatural incidents that had surrounded his birth, his life, and many New Testament-quality miracles that had occurred in his ministry.

In 1958 he had become so disgusted with the corruption and abuses that had become common in the healing movement of which he was a part, that he left that movement. Over the next twenty-five years he voluntarily walked into relative obscurity, pastoring a couple of churches for a short while and then doing itinerant ministry. Occasionally he still spoke at large gatherings, but this was much rarer than in his earlier ministry.

Mike said that Paul was a treasure house of historical information about all of those who were reputed to have had great healing power in the 1950s. He knew virtually every person that had been prominent in that movement. He had seen the good side and the bad side of that movement. He had watched men, gifted by God, start out well and end badly, and he had watched a few— very few—remain uncorrupted throughout that whole time.

When George and I came back from Kansas City, we called Paul and asked him to have lunch with us. It was true; Paul really was a treasure house of knowledge about all of those personalities and events that happened during that time. We asked him questions for nearly two hours. Over the next year Paul and I became very close friends. We shared many meals together and talked often on the phone. During this time I had never heard him preach or teach, nor did I see him use his revelatory gift for which he had been famous in his early days.

Then in September of 1988 my family and I were preparing to leave Fort Worth, Texas, and go to Anaheim, California, to join John Wimber in ministry at the Vineyard Christian Fellowship in

Anaheim. During that time, Paul Cain and I shared our first meeting together.

We were speaking at the Emmaus Road Ministry School. This is a school in Euless, Texas, for training in practical ministry. The school is run by T. D. Hall and staffed by Dudley Hall, Doug White, Jack Taylor, Jim Hylton, and James Robison, among others. Most of these men were Southern Baptists or ex-Southern Baptists who had begun to believe in the gifts of the Holy Spirit. Paul and I were to share the teaching responsibilities for the morning hour during the first week of September.

On the first two days, Paul attended the meetings, but he did not feel well enough to speak. This was a little bit ironic since I was speaking on healing and Paul was supposed to have a reputation for being used by the Lord in healing. But on the third morning I saw something in ministry that would forever alter my concept of the ministry of the Holy Spirit.

Paul had just finished giving a wonderful message and was beginning to pray for the people in the audience. There were about 250 people there that morning. He asked the diabetics to stand. As he started to pray for the diabetics, he looked at a gray-haired lady on his right. He stared at her for a moment, having never met her (or anyone else in the audience for that matter), and then he said, 'You do not have diabetes; you have low blood sugar. The Lord heals you of that low blood sugar, now. I see a vision of you sitting in a yellow chair. You are saying, "If I could just make it until the morning. If I could just make it until the morning." Your allergies torment you so badly that sometimes they keep you awake all night. The Lord heals those allergies, now. That problem with the valve on your heart—it goes now in the name of Jesus. And so does that growth on your pancreas.'

By this time there was a strong sense of the fear of the Lord in the room. People had begun to weep openly as they saw the power of the Lord being displayed and the concern of the Lord for one of his children. Paul continued looking at the woman and then he said, 'The Devil has scheduled you for a nervous breakdown.' When he said this the man sitting beside her, who turned out to be her husband, began to weep. He knew that his wife was very close to a nervous breakdown. Paul said, 'The Lord interrupts that plan now. You will not have the breakdown.'

And then, just as suddenly as Paul had begun to speak over the woman, he stopped and said, 'I think that is all the Lord wants me to do now.' Then he sat down on the front row.

The rest of us were stunned. We had never seen anything like this. I had seen healings over the last two years, and some wonderful healings, but I had never seen anyone called out of an audience like that, unknown to the speaker, and then have four conditions in her body not only identified but pronounced healed.

This reminded me of the revelatory power of Elisha who was able to tell the Israelite king the plans that the Syrian commander had made in his own bedroom. It was also like the apostolic healings in the New Testament, where apostles commanded or pronounced healing rather than praying for healing. We were utterly dumbfounded. No one knew how to close the meeting. The fear of the Lord was so strong in the room that no one wanted to act presumptuously. Finally, Jack Taylor stood up with tears in his eyes and led us all in a hymn.

The woman whom Paul pronounced healed that day is named Linda Tidwell. I have had several conversations with Linda and her husband Jim since that September day in 1988.

Here is what happened in the aftermath of Paul's ministry to her. She went to her doctor that week and was tested. Her low blood sugar was now normal, and her allergies had left immediately. (They had been just as severe as Paul had said.) A heart murmur that she had since her childhood was healed, and the problem with her pancreas was gone. Her depression and nervous condition also left, and over the next few months she lost thirty-five pounds of weight that had been brought on by worry and anxiety. Every medical condition mentioned by Paul had been both accurate and healed.

A year later she told me that one thing Paul had said didn't ring true to her. He had said, 'I see you sitting in a yellow chair.' She puzzled for a long time afterwards. It didn't make sense to her because they didn't have a yellow chair. Then she remembered that before they had moved to Fort Worth, she had painted her rocking chair, which was yellow, black. After awhile, she had forgotten that it used to be yellow. Paul had actually seen a vision of her prior to their moving to Fort Worth, when her allergies were at their worst. Since that time Linda has visited a number of churches in the Dallas/Ft. Worth metroplex, giving her testimony about the wonderful healing God had done for her.

Since September of 1988 I have seen the Lord use Paul in this way literally all over the world. I am not saying this to exalt a man. I believe God is using a number of people like him in many different parts of the world today. I believe that this kind of supernatural ministry is available to the church today.[1] I believe the Lord has given us ways to cultivate this ministry. I also believe there are mistakes the church can make that can hinder this ministry today.

In the following pages I want to share with you some of the things I have learned over the last few years, both in the Scriptures and in practical experience, that may help you learn how to pursue and experience the reality of the gifts of the Spirit without all the hype and abuses that have plagued others who have attempted to minister in the power of the Spirit. I also want to share with you the biblical and theological objections that I had to the present-day supernatural ministry of the Holy Spirit, and the answers that removed those objections for me. Finally, I want to discuss the fears and the hindrances I experienced in trying to minister in the power of the Holy Spirit, and how these have been and are being removed.

SHATTERED MISCONCEPTIONS

4

The Myth of Pure Biblical Objectivity

A psychiatrist once had a patient who thought he was dead. No amount of argument could convince him otherwise. Finally, out of desperation, the psychiatrist came up with a brilliant plan. He decided he would prove to the patient that dead men don't bleed. He gave him several medical textbooks to read and set up an appointment for the following week.

The patient did his homework and arrived at the psychiatrist's office at the appointed time.

'Well, what did you discover in your reading?' the psychiatrist asked.

'I discovered that medical evidence proves that dead men don't bleed,' the patient replied.

'So if a person were to bleed, you would know for certain that he or she was not dead?'

'Absolutely,' said the patient.

This was the moment the psychiatrist had been waiting for. He pulled out a pin and pricked the patient's finger. Immediately a drop of blood appeared.

The patient looked down at his finger in horror and exclaimed, 'Oh, my goodness, dead men *do* bleed!'

We all like to think that we are purely reasonable and objective.

But the truth is, as one person has said, that we often tow our brains around behind us to justify what we already believe.

I was one of those Christians who loved to tell themselves that they do not live by their experience but by the Word of God. My practice and my beliefs were determined by the teaching of the Holy Scriptures—or so I thought. Only in recent years has the arrogance of that kind of talk become apparent to me.

Somehow I must have thought I was an exception to the teaching of Jeremiah 17:9, 'The heart is deceitful above all things and beyond cure. Who can understand it?' What made me think my heart was so pure that I understood accurately my motives for believing and doing the things I did? The truth is, we all have many reasons why we believe and do things, and Scripture is only one of those reasons. Sometimes, Scripture is not even a primary reason for our beliefs or our practices, no matter how much we may protest to the contrary.

The idea that fallen humanity, even redeemed fallen humanity, can arrive at pure biblical objectivity in determining all their practices and beliefs is an illusion. We are all significantly influenced by our circumstances: the culture in which we live, the family in which we grew up, the church we attend, our teachers, our desires, our goals, our disappointments, our tragedies and traumas. Our experience determines much of what we believe and do, and often it determines much more than we are aware of or would admit.

Let me illustrate this for you. It is common for professors of theology to protest that Scripture, not their experience, determines their doctrine. If you ask a Dallas Seminary professor his view of the millennium (the thousand year reign of Christ described in Rev. 20:4–6), he will tell you that he is premillennial. That means that when Christ comes back to the earth, he is going to set up a kingdom on earth and will reign here a thousand years before the creation of the new heavens and new earth. If you ask him why he believes this, he will declare to you that it is the plain teaching of the Scriptures.

If you ask a professor from Westminster Seminary the same question, he will probably tell you that he is amillennial. (Unlike Dallas Seminary, Westminster Seminary does not require their faculty to hold a certain view on the millennium, but the majority of Westminster's faculty is amillennial.) That means there will be no literal thousand-year reign of Jesus on earth between his second coming and the creation of the new heavens and new earth. If you ask him why he believes this, he will tell you that it is the plain teaching of the Scriptures.

Both cannot be right and, in fact, neither may be right. The truth is that both Westminster Seminary and Dallas Seminary have godly, intelligent, and skillful interpreters of Scripture who disagree on quite a few doctrines of Scripture. Yet both sides will claim that the reason they hold their position is because it is the plain teaching of the Scripture! I suspect that this is not the whole truth.

The truth is, if you take a student who has no position on the millennium and send him to Westminster Seminary, he will probably come out an amillennialist. If you take that same student and send him to Dallas Seminary, he is even more likely to come out a premillennialist. There will be few exceptions to this rule. Our environment, our theological traditions, and our teachers have much more to do with what we believe than we realize. In some cases they have much more influence over what we believe than the Bible itself.

Consider the preceding example. Either the amillennialist or the premillennialist is definitely wrong. If the premillennialist is wrong, then no matter how much he protests, his doctrine could not have been derived from the teaching of Scripture because Scripture would not have taught that, assuming the doctrine of premillennialism is an error.

Over the years, I have observed that the majority of what

Christians believe is not derived from their own patient and careful study of the Scriptures. The majority of Christians believe what they believe because godly and respected teachers told them it was correct. I have seen this illustrated in hundreds of ways, but the following is one I shall never forget.

Seminary graduates who want to enter into the doctoral program are required to pass both written and oral examinations before they can be admitted. As a professor, one of my tasks was to help administer these exams along with some of my colleagues.

On this particular day we were examining three young, hopeful, prospective doctoral students. We were giving them the oral exam, the most nerve-racking part of the entrance requirements. In this exam, four to five professors ask the prospective student questions about the Hebrew language, archaeology, other technical fields of study related to the Old Testament, and about his own personal views of theology. The reason for the latter was that we did not want to give our Th.D. degree to a student who held to a theology that the seminary could not approve.

The first student to be examined that day had almost straight A's in his previous seminary training, and he had taught for a year at another seminary. He breezed through all of the technical questions we asked him concerning the Old Testament. The last area in which he was to be tested concerned his theological views. On this particular day, my colleagues and I had decided that I would ask the theological questions.

My first question was, 'What do you believe about the deity of Jesus Christ?' His response was to laugh at me—not a good thing to do during your doctoral examinations! It is better to wait until you get your degree and then mock your professors. I told him that I was serious and was really interested in what he believed about the deity of Jesus.

'Well, I believe in the full deity of the Lord Jesus Christ,' he replied.

I told him it was good that he believed in the deity of the Lord Jesus Christ; we also believed in his deity. Then I asked him *why* he believed in the deity of Christ.

'Because the Scriptures teach that Jesus is God,' he said.

'Good, that is what we believe also. Now tell us one specific text in the Old or New Testament that unambiguously teaches that Jesus is God.'

For the first time during that whole exam the look of confidence vanished from his face. He hesitated a moment and then asserted, 'The deity of Jesus is everywhere in the New Testament.'

'Could you be just a little bit more specific? Tell us one text that teaches his deity unambiguously.'

After hesitating for what seemed like a full moment, he finally blurted out, 'I and the Father are one.'

I told him that it was true John 10:30 did say that, but did that actually mean that Jesus was God? I could say, for instance, that he and I were one, but that wouldn't prove that we were the same, let alone from the same family. Jesus could have meant that he and the Father were one in purpose.

At that point he gave up trying to use John 10:30. He didn't know enough to cite the next few verses that showed clearly that the Jews understood this to be a claim to deity. If he had done that, I would have granted that this passage taught the deity of Jesus, which it does unambiguously. In the end he could not give us one clear passage from the Bible on the deity of the Lord Jesus Christ. Here was a man who had completed four years of Bible college and four years of seminary. He had a masters degree in theology, and had taught for one year at a conservative biblical seminary. Yet he could not produce and defend one unambiguous reference in the Bible to the deity of Jesus!

My next question to him concerned how one gets into heaven. What I wanted him to do was to give us one clear reference to the doctrine of justification by faith alone in the Lord Jesus Christ. This discussion went exactly like the first question. He could not give and defend one clear reference to justification by faith alone in Christ.

When I asked him a third question, namely, what he believed about the miraculous gifts of the Holy Spirit, his confidence seemed to return. Undaunted, he replied that they were not given any longer. Again, his reason for this was that it was the plain teaching of the Scriptures. I asked him what he thought was the strongest evidence from the Bible to support the passing away of the miraculous gifts of the Spirit.

'The Bible teaches that there are only three periods where miracles were common in the history of God's dealings with his people. They were common during the time of Moses and Joshua, Elijah and Elisha, and Christ and the apostles—three periods of two generations each. The next time miracles will be common will be during the reign of the Antichrist and the great Tribulation,' he replied without a moment's hesitation.

'Did you arrive at this position from a careful inductive study of the Scriptures?' I asked.

'That's correct.'

At this point, I knew he was not telling the truth. He did not come to that position from a careful study of the Scriptures. Benjamin Breckenridge Warfield, the Princeton theologian, had popularized that position at the beginning of the twentieth century, with the result that reformed and dispensational theologians have been using it ever since. One or more of us had passed this teaching on to the student, and now he was trying to claim that he had gotten it by careful study of the Scriptures.

His dishonesty was a little more than I was willing to tolerate, so I said, 'Let's see if you can defend that position now. Let's start with chapter one of Genesis and think our way through every chapter of the Old Testament to see if the biblical evidence supports your theory. Remember, we should only find three periods in which miracles are common. What took place in the first chapter of the Bible?'

'That is where God creates the world.'

'How about chapter two?'

'That is the story of the creation of the world with man at the center.'

'Chapter three?'

'That is where the Devil comes to Adam and Eve and tempts them to sin, and God has to expel them from the garden.'

'Are these things miraculous?,' I asked.

'Well yes, but you have to start somewhere.'

'O.K., fine. Chapter four?'

'The first murder,' he said.

'Chapter five is a genealogy. What happens in chapters six to nine?'

'That is where God wipes out the whole earth with the flood and rescues eight people in an ark, on which species of every living animal have been miraculously summoned.'

'Chapter ten?'

'Another genealogy.'

'Chapter eleven?'

'The Tower of Babel, where God comes down and confounds the language of all the families of the earth.'

'So really the first eleven chapters of Genesis don't actually fit your theory, do they?'

'Yes, but that is primeval history; I mean you expect things like that at the very beginning.'

'O.K., for the sake of argument let's dismiss the first eleven chapters of the Bible. At chapter twelve and for the rest of the book of Genesis we move into simple narrative biography. What happens in chapter twelve?'

'God sovereignly calls Abraham to leave Ur of the Chaldeans

and go to a land where he is going to begin a program to redeem the entire world.'

'Anything else strike you as supernatural or miraculous elsewhere in Abraham's life?'

'Well, in chapter fifteen there was that supernatural smoking oven and flaming torch that passed between the parts of the sacrifice Abraham had laid out (Gen. 15:17). Besides the divine conversation in chapter 17, the Lord and angelic beings appear to Abraham in chapter 18 and eat with Abraham. Then there was the destruction of Sodom and Gomorrah, when the heavens rained fire and brimstone on those cities (Gen. 19). Then there was the supernatural birth of Isaac in chapter twenty-one and the encounter with the angel of the Lord as he offered up Isaac on the altar in chapter twenty-two.'

'So, the life of Abraham doesn't really fit your theory that miracles or the supernatural are not common until the time of Moses and Joshua, does it?'

'No.'

'What about Isaac, Jacob or Joseph; anything there seem miraculous or supernatural to you?'

'Chapter twenty-eight—the prophetic messianic vision of the angels ascending and descending on that ladder while Jacob slept.'

'What else in Jacob's life?'

'Chapter thirty-two. He actually wrestles with God, or the preincarnate Christ, all night long. Then with Joseph there are all of those dreams and interpretations.'

So I said, 'As far as the evidence goes, the book of Genesis doesn't fit your theory, does it?'

'No.'

'Now we are at the book of Exodus, and we have already said that Moses' and Joshua's life contain miracles and supernatural occurrences, so let's skip from Exodus through the book of Joshua and come to the book of Judges. Anything in the book of Judges strike you as miraculous?'

He said, 'Well, the angel of the Lord actually appears to Gideon, and there is all that stuff going on with the fleece. Then the angel of the Lord appears to Samson's parents, and there is the miraculous power of Samson.'

'So the book of Judges doesn't actually fit this theory, does it?'

'No.'

'What do you have in the book of 1 Samuel?'

'A prophet whose words do not fall to the ground' (1 Sam. 3:19–21).

And on and on the discussion went. In chapter after chapter the student was forced to list miraculous and supernatural occurrences that contradicted his assertion that miracles only occurred at three points in the history of Israel.[1] The student was forced to admit not only that could he not defend his position, but that the Scriptures actually contradicted it.

After that student left, we examined two more young hopefuls. Both of them did well with technical questions related to the Old Testament, but their showing was almost as miserable as the first student's when I asked them the same three questions concerning the deity of Jesus, justification by faith, and the miraculous gifts of the Holy Spirit. When the last student left that day, I remarked to my colleagues how disappointing the whole experience had been. I said, 'Those students don't believe what they believe because the Bible teaches it; they believe what they believe because authority figures in their lives told them these doctrines were true. They didn't get their beliefs from a careful study of the Scriptures. They can't even defend their beliefs by using the Scriptures.'

One of the older professors said, 'That's true, but I would have to say that today's experience is more the rule than the exception during these exams.'

All of these students came into that exam confident that they believed what they believed simply because the Scriptures taught it, but they were significantly deceived. If that is true in a seminary setting, how much more true do you think it is in a non-academic setting? Experience and tradition determine the majority of what church people believe, rather than the careful, patient, and personal study of the Scriptures.

J. I. Packer writes,

> Nobody can claim to be detached from traditions. In fact, one sure way to be swallowed up by traditionalism is to think that one is immune to it. . . . The question, then, is not whether we *have* traditions, but whether our traditions conflict with the only absolute standard in these matters: Holy Scripture.[2]

Neither Packer nor I are claiming that all tradition is bad. I agree with Packer's statement that,

> All Christians are at once beneficiaries and victims of tradition—beneficiaries, who receive nurturing truth and wisdom from God's faithfulness in past generations; victims, who now take for granted things that need to be questioned, thus treating as divine absolutes patterns of belief and behavior that should be seen as human, provisional, and relative. We are all beneficiaries of good, wise, and sound tradition and victims of poor, unwise, and unsound traditions.[3]

There are many Christians, for example, who believe in the deity of Jesus, but who could never defend his deity from the Scriptures. Although they believe the Scriptures teach that Jesus is God, they did not come to this belief through a careful study of the Scriptures. It is part of the tradition that has been handed down to them by their teachers. In this case, they benefit from tradition because this particular tradition rests squarely on the teaching of Scripture.

However, when our belief systems move beyond the basic fundamentals of the faith (the deity of Jesus, justification by faith, the substitutionary atonement of Jesus, and so on) to things that aren't as fundamental (the mode of baptism, the manner of taking the Lord's supper, or a particular view of the millennium) we are much more dependent on tradition than we realize. In these cases, Packer offers sound advice, 'What we must do, rather, is acknowledge that we are full of tradition, good or bad, to a much greater extent than we realize, and must learn to ask by the light of Scripture critical questions about what we have thus far taken for granted.'[4]

Some, however, fail to acknowledge the significance of tradition and other factors in our environments for determining or shaping our views. Edward Gross asks why there are so many interpretations. His answer is that

> there are two simple reasons why there are so many interpretations: the lack of comprehensive study and the lack of following the simple rules of hermeneutics (the science of biblical interpretation).[5]

Next, he cites three hermeneutical rules summarized by Charles Hodge to the effect that Scripture is to be interpreted in it's grammatical historical sense, Scripture must interpret Scripture and cannot contradict itself, and the guidance of the Holy Spirit must be sought to interpret Scripture.[6] Gross concludes that

> employing these rules will assist us in determining the true sense of Scripture. If Christians would constantly unite a thorough investigation with these simple rules, differences of interpretation would practically disappear.[7]

I am sure there are others who sincerely believe with Gross that lack of study and hermeneutical differences can account for contemporary theological diversity. However, I do not think there are very many skilled theologians or knowledgeable interpreters of Scripture who would agree with Gross.

When I was at Dallas Seminary, everyone on the faculty that I

knew would agree with the three hermeneutical rules summarized by Hodge, and we all believed in comprehensive study of the
Word. Nonetheless, we differed significantly with the reformed
theological position that Gross quotes throughout his book. Did
we dispensationalists not study the Scriptures as comprehensively
as the Reformed theologians with whom we disagreed? Were we
inconsistent in our application of the three hermeneutical principles? The obvious truth is that a lack of comprehensive study of
the Scriptures and dissimilar hermeneutical principles cannot
account for the vast majority of modern theological differences.[8]

Tradition and the Gifts of the Spirit

If you were to lock a brand-new Christian in a room with a Bible
and tell him to study what Scripture has to say about healing and
miracles, he would never come out of the room a cessationist. I
know this from my own experience. Prior to my conversion at
seventeen years of age, I had no training in theology, in the Scriptures, or in Christian history. Immediately after the Lord saved
me, I began to devour the Scriptures. I read them day and night
and memorized them. When I began to ask my newfound Christian teachers about the miracles in Scripture, I was taught that
God no longer did these kinds of things through human agency. I
was taught that the real miracle, the only one that really mattered, was the conversion of the lost. Since godly people whom
I respected told me this, and since I saw no miracles in my own
experience to counter this teaching, I accepted it as true. I gave
myself to evangelism and promptly forgot about praying for miracles or healings.

   This is not a system of doctrine that I would have ever come up
with on my own. I had to be *taught* that the gifts of the Spirit had
passed away. Now, twenty-seven years later at the age of forty-
four, I have had the privilege of being on both sides of this

theological debate. I am absolutely convinced that the Scriptures do not teach that the gifts of the Spirit passed away with the death of the apostles. It is not the teaching of the Scripture that causes people to disbelieve in the contemporary ministry of the miraculous.

There is one basic reason why Bible-believing Christians do not believe in the miraculous gifts of the Spirit today. It is simply this: *they have not seen them.* Their tradition, of course, supports their lack of belief, but their tradition would have no chance of success if it were not coupled with their lack of *experience* of the miraculous. Let me repeat: Christians do not disbelieve in the miraculous gifts of the Spirit because the Scriptures teach these gifts have passed away. Rather they disbelieve in the miraculous gifts of the Spirit because they have not experienced them.

No cessationist writer that I am aware of tries to make his case on Scripture alone. All of these writers appeal both to Scripture and to either present or past history to support their case.[9] It often goes unnoticed that this appeal to history, either past or present, is actually an argument from *experience*, or better, an argument from the *lack of experience*.

I was once arguing with a well-known theologian over the subject of the gifts of the Spirit. I made the comment that there was not a shred of evidence in the Bible that the gifts of the Spirit had passed away. He said, 'I wouldn't go that far, but I know that you cannot prove the cessation of the gifts by Scripture. However, we do not clearly see them in the later history of the church, and they are not part of our own theological tradition.'

This man taught at a seminary that was dogmatically cessationist in its approach to miraculous gifts, but in private conversation he freely admitted that this doctrine could not be proved by Scripture.

He actually mentioned the second most important reason why people disbelieve in the gifts of the Spirit, namely, they cannot find New Testament-quality miracles in the history of the church. The third most common reason for disbelieving in the gifts of the Spirit is the revulsion caused by the misuse, or the perceived misuse, of the gifts in contemporary churches and healing movements.

None of these reasons are ultimately founded on *Scripture*. They are based on *personal experience*. Actually, in the case of the first two reasons, they are based on a *lack* of personal experience.

It is common for charismatics to be accused of building their theology on experience. However, all cessationists ultimately build their theology of the miraculous gifts on their lack of experience. Even the appeal to contemporary abuse is an argument based on *negative experience* with the gifts.

What I am saying, therefore, is that the real reasons for disbelieving in the gifts of the Spirit today are not at all based on Scripture; they are based on experience. In the chapters that follow, I want to look at these three reasons in more detail.

5

The Real Reason Christians Do Not Believe in the Miraculous Gifts

At the close of the last chapter I said that the real reason Christians do not believe in the miraculous gifts is simply because they have not seen miracles in their present experience. Yet no one openly admits that this is the cause of their unbelief. I have had numerous conversations with theologians and lay persons from all over the world. When I ask them why they reject the miraculous gifts of the Spirit today, they usually say that contemporary 'healing ministries' are far different from the ministry of the apostles. I also used to think this way.

When I looked at the healing ministries of Jesus and his apostles, I saw instantaneous, irreversible, complete healings.[1] I also saw them healing the most difficult organically-caused diseases imaginable. People born blind could suddenly see. The lame could walk and even leap for joy. Lepers received soft new skin. Crippled and maimed limbs became whole and strong. The dead came back to life. And fierce storms were commanded to be calm. It seemed as though Jesus and the apostles could heal at will under any conditions.

I had never met anyone who had experienced or even seen healings like these. All the healing reports that I had heard sounded like they were psychosomatic—someone's headache or stomachache went away because their mental stress was relieved. When I did hear a report about a truly organic healing, it could not be verified. Or it was a third- or fourth-hand report.

Since neither I nor those I trusted could verify a truly instantaneous, complete, and irreversible healing like that of the apostles, I concluded these things were not happening today. The gradual, partial, and sometimes reversible healings that could be verified in my experience did not measure up with what I presumed to be the New Testament gift of healing.

At first glance, this reason for rejecting the gifts of the Spirit looks like a biblical argument, but ultimately it is not. At best it is a confession of a *lack of experience*. The argument simply says that *I* do not see or hear of a contemporary ministry that has New Testament-quality miracles. But my limited experience cannot be used as proof that no such ministry exists today.

I believe that God is doing New Testament-quality miracles in the church today, and I believe that he has done them throughout the history of the church. But for the sake of argument, let's suppose that no such ministry exists today. That would still not prove that *God* has withdrawn the New Testament ministry of the miraculous. We would have to know the reason why this ministry doesn't exist today. Indeed, one of the reasons could be that God had intentionally withdrawn this ministry. However, the ultimate reason for the cessation of the gifts could be due to the church's response. It could be that the rise of a bureaucratic leadership has finally been successful in triumphing over 'gifted' individuals within the church. Or their absence could be due to widespread unbelief in the church, or a number of other factors.

How are we to decide? Not by an appeal to what we see or don't see, but rather by an appeal to *the clear and specific teaching of Scripture itself*. And this we shall do shortly, but for now I merely want to make the point that the real or perceived absence of miraculous gifts is not an argument from Scripture, but an argument from experience.

There are also some scriptural problems with the view of healing I set forth above. It is based on two false assumptions about healing in the New Testament.

False Assumption 1: Healing Was 'Automatic'

The first assumption is that the healing gifts of Jesus and the apostles were 'automatic.' By 'automatic' I am referring to the idea that they could heal anyone, anywhere, anytime, at will. I viewed this gift as a permanent possession to be exercised at their discretion. I thought they could do healings or miracles or give prophetic words simply at will.[2]

If this is your view of the gift of healing, I can guarantee that you will never find *anyone* who has the gift of healing. And when you examine the Scriptures, you will have to conclude that neither Jesus nor the apostles had the gift of healing! Even Jesus and his apostles could not heal at will—if by 'at will' we mean anywhere, anytime, under any conditions.

Three incidents in the life of Jesus demonstrate that he was not free to heal at will under any conditions. At the beginning of the story of the healing of the paralytic at Capernaum, Luke writes, 'One day as he was teaching, Pharisees and teachers of the law, who had come from every village of Galilee and from Judea and Jerusalem, were sitting there. *And the power of the Lord was present for him to heal the sick*' (Luke 5:17, emphasis mine).

Why would Luke say that 'the power of the Lord was present for him to heal' if Jesus could heal at any time, under any condition, and solely at his own discretion? This statement only makes sense if we view healing as the sovereign prerogative of God the Father, who sometimes dispenses his power to heal and at other times withholds it.[3]

A second incident is just as instructive. John chapter 5 contains the story of the healing of the man who had been paralyzed for thirty-eight years. He was lying at the pool of Bethesda when Jesus met him. There were many other sick people lying around the pool. This was because there was a tradition that once a year an angel of the Lord would come down and stir the waters of the pool, and the first one in the waters after the angel stirred them would be healed. So the Pool of Bethesda was like an ancient hospital where people brought their friends, relatives, and loved ones to be cared for in hope that they might be the first one in the water to be healed. The point is that when Jesus encountered the sick man that day there were many other sick people lying around the pool also (John 5:3).

Jesus asked the paralytic a question that has been difficult for some to understand, 'Do you want to get well?' (John 5:6). I never understood the significance of that question until I started praying for the sick. I had assumed that all sick people want to get well, especially those who have chronic ailments like paralysis or blindness. But now, after praying for thousands of sick people all around the world over the last seven years, I have found that a number of sick people do not wish to get well at all. In fact, their whole identity is bound up in being sick, and they are literally afraid of the changes that would take place in their life if they were made whole. If you suspect that is true of someone you want to see healed, it is important to counsel with them and identify that problem before you ever attempt to pray for them. In any case, the man in this story never says that he wants to get well, but Jesus does heal him instantly and completely.

Now having done that, you would assume that Jesus would heal the other people there at the pool of Bethesda. On many occasions in the Gospels he heals large crowds of people. Several times we encounter the statement 'and he healed them all' (Matt. 8:16; 12:15; Luke 6:19). Yet on this day he heals only one person at the pool.

Why did he ignore all the other sick people? Immediately after the healing we find Jesus involved in a theological dispute with religious leaders. In the midst of this dispute Jesus answers the question why he did not heal the others at the pool, and he gives us the principle that governed his whole ministry.

John 5:19 says, 'Jesus gave them this answer: "I tell you the truth, the Son can do nothing by himself; he can do only what he sees his Father doing, because whatever the Father does the Son also does."' Jesus only healed one person at the pool that day because his Father was only healing one person. If his Father was not healing, then Jesus could not heal. Jesus was completely obedient to the sovereign will of his heavenly Father for all of his ministry. Jesus could not heal at his own will because he was committed not to do or will anything independent of his Father's will. He always did the things that pleased his Father. This is not an isolated teaching in the book of John; it is a major theme in John's Gospel. Numerous times Jesus says he only does what his Father does, he only speaks the words his Father gives him to speak, and that his teaching is not his but that of the One who sent him (John 3:34; 5:30; 7:16; 8:28; 12:49–50; 14:10, 24, 31).

Incidentally, this principle answers a question I am asked all the time, 'If you believe in healing and you think you have a gift or ministry of healing, why don't you go empty out the hospitals, or why don't you go into the slums of places like Calcutta where you can really do some good?' The answer to that question is that the gift of healing is not automatic; it can not be exercised at your own discretion. The Lord Jesus himself was at an ancient 'hospital,' and he only healed one person there. The only way anyone with a healing gift could have an effective ministry in a hospital or in the slums of Calcutta would be if the Lord Jesus Christ actually sent and directed that gifted person to heal there.

This principle is also a valid answer to the same question when it is asked in a different form. Occasionally people ask why at some gatherings where the sick are being prayed for that the most serious ailments are not healed while some of the 'trivial' ones are. Why on some occasions are words of knowledge given to pray for people with migraine headaches but not for people in wheelchairs? Skeptics of divine healing call this a tragedy and express 'concern' for all those in wheelchairs who were not healed. They mock the healing of 'trivial' illnesses as psycho-somatic.

If the people who are conducting the meeting are not frauds, but sincere servants who are really trying to follow the leading of the Lord, they do not actually have a say in what kind of healings take place or what kind of words of knowledge are given for heal-ings. According to the principle of John 5:19, God decides who gets healed and directs his servants accordingly. It is our respon-sibility to listen for those directions and follow them, rather than to determine who gets healed.

People who mock when God decides to heal 'trivial' cases rather than the 'hard' ones may actually be mocking the wisdom and will of our Father. On the other hand, if 'healers' are adver-tising meetings in such a way as to *promise* that God is going to bring people out of wheelchairs, heal blindness, and so on in their particular meetings, and it does not happen, then there is room for criticism. In the latter case, the discernment, if not the integrity, of those leading the meetings may justly come under question.

A third incident in the life of Jesus conclusively demonstrates that he could not heal at will under any and all conditions. It hap-pened when he returned to his home in Nazareth. The people of his home town were offended at him with the result that, 'He could not do any miracles there, except lay his hands on a few sick people and heal them. And he was amazed at their lack of faith' (Mark 6:5–6). Matthew writes of this same incident that Jesus 'did not do many miracles there because of their lack of faith'

(Matt. 13:58). In other words, God allowed the healing ministry of his Son to be limited, at least on some occasions, by the unbelief of the people. Thus Jesus himself could not heal independently of the Father, at his own will, and under any conditions.[4]

If this was true of the Son of God, how much more do you think it was true of the apostles? When we examine the apostles' ministry, this is exactly what we find. Jesus told the apostles in John 15:5, 'Apart from me you can do nothing.' Jesus had said the same thing of himself, 'By myself I can do nothing; I judge only as I hear, and my judgment is just, for I seek not to please myself but him who sent me.' (John 5:30). In the same way the apostles could do nothing divinely powerful apart from the sovereign will of the Lord Jesus and his heavenly Father. We find numerous illustrations of this principle in the lives of the apostles.

For example, when the Lord uses Peter to heal the lame man at the gate called Beautiful (Acts 3:1ff.), the people stare at Peter in amazement. Peter is horrified to think that the people might somehow credit him with this healing. Therefore, Peter cries out to the people, 'Men of Israel, why does this surprise you? Why do you stare at us as if *by our own power or godliness* we had made this man walk? The God of Abraham, Isaac and Jacob, the God of our fathers, has glorified his servant Jesus' (Acts 3:12–13, emphasis mine). Peter made it plain that this healing was not the result of his own apostolic power or holiness. It was the result of the sovereign will of Peter's heavenly Father.

Who really thinks that Peter could just walk into the temple on any day that he wanted and heal anybody he wanted? Yes, there were extraordinary outpourings of healing power and grace in the life of Peter and the other apostles, but these outpourings were not initiated by the apostles; they were initiated by the sovereign will of their heavenly Father. Their part was to recognize the Father's initiative and obey, but not to originate *any* ministry apart from his direction.

This same principle is illustrated by a miracle in the life of Paul. While Paul was preaching at Lystra, a man who had been crippled from birth was listening to him. Luke said that Paul 'looked directly at him, saw that he had faith to be healed and called out, "Stand up on your feet!"' (Acts 14:9–10). Again, this healing was not something Paul initiated. He saw that the man had faith to be healed and then proclaimed him healed.

This was not something that Paul could do at will. He could only do it when the circumstances were conducive to healing. If God had not granted this man faith to be healed, then Paul could never have pronounced the healing.[5]

On the other hand, there are three negative examples from Paul's life when he could not get his friends healed. Paul couldn't heal Epaphroditus (Phil. 2:25–27); he had to leave Trophimus sick at Melitas (2 Tim. 4:20); and he even had to exhort his dear son in the faith, Timothy, to take a little wine for his stomach's sake and his frequent illnesses (1 Tim. 5:23).

Some people assume that Paul could not get these three people healed because he was not free to use his healing gift on Christians. They assume that the gift of healing was only to be used on unbelievers or in the presence of unbelievers to convince them of the truth of the gospel.[6] If this were the case, why did Paul heal Eutychus, a believer, by raising him from the dead in the presence of only believers (Acts 20:7–12)? Furthermore, the gift of healing mentioned in 1 Corinthians 12:9 is said to be for the *edification of those in the church* (1 Cor. 12:7).

Others have claimed that Paul's failure to heal Epaphroditus, Trophimus, and Timothy was due to God's withdrawal of Paul's healing gift by this time in his life. This is an incredible explanation. Here we would have to admit that miracles had ceased even before the death of the apostles. There is no contextual argument to back up such a suggestion.

In light of the texts mentioned above, it is much easier to

believe that the apostles could not heal at will. They were dependent on the will of the Lord Jesus.[7]

A final illustration of the apostles' inability to heal at will is demonstrated in the case of the epileptic boy. This is especially significant because it occurs after Jesus has *given them power and authority over all demons and over all diseases* (Matt. 10:1; Luke 9:1). Yet they could not heal a demonized boy who was both suicidal and suffering from epilepsy (Matt. 17:16). After Jesus healed the boy, the disciples asked him why they couldn't cast the demon out. Jesus said to them, 'Because you have so little faith' (Matt. 17:20).

It is simply a misunderstanding of Scripture to assume that anyone can heal at will. The apostles' relationship to the Lord and our relationship to him is far too personal for such a mechanical explanation of the gift of healing. Therefore, in our attempt to understand the gift of healing today, we should not be looking for or expecting to find people who can heal at will.

But even with this qualifier, it still seemed to me that the gulf between the healing ministry of the apostles and that of present-day ministries was far too wide for me to accept the present-day ministries as biblical. The quality and the number of people healed by the apostles were far superior to what *I thought* was going on today. It was at this point that I realized the second false assumption about the New Testament ministry of healing and miracles.

False Assumption 2: The Apostles' Healing Ministry Was the Same as the Gift of Healing

One day while I was driving home after teaching a full day of classes, it dawned on me that there had to be a distinction between the apostolic ministry of healing and the gift of healing given to others in the body of Christ.

Here is how I came to that conclusion. First I realized that in 1 Corinthians 12:8–10 Paul is describing miraculous gifts that are given to the whole body of Christ, not just to the apostles. There is abundant evidence for this widespread distribution of gifts. Prophecy, for example, is found in the church at Thessalonica (1 Thess. 5:20), in Rome (Rom. 12:6), in Ephesus (Eph. 4:11), and in other locations throughout the book of Acts (11:27; 13:1; 15:32; 19:6; 21:9). Likewise, the gift of tongues is found in Jerusalem (Acts 2), Samaria (Acts 8:5ff.), Caesarea (Acts 10:46), Ephesus (Acts 19:6), as well as Corinth. Miracles were being done in the churches of Galatia (Gal. 3:5).

This wide distribution of gifts across the body of Christ is what Joel prophesied when he saw the Holy Spirit coming on all people in the last days (Joel 2:28–29). Peter used Joel's prophecy to argue that the gift of tongues given on the day of Pentecost was one of the signs of the fulfillment of Joel's prophecy (Acts 2:16). With the outpouring of the Holy Spirit at Pentecost, there came gifts to the *whole* body of Christ. In fact, Peter says that each Christian has received a ministry gift, a *charisma* (1 Pet. 4:10).[8] This is exactly the same word that Paul used in 1 Corinthians 12 (vv. 4, 9, 28, 30–31) for spiritual gifts, and Paul maintained that all the gifts were operative in the church at Corinth (1 Cor. 1:7). The evidence of the New Testament, therefore, forces us to conclude that the miraculous gifts were not simply confined to the apostles but were widely distributed across the whole body of Christ.

The second thing I realized is that spiritual gifts vary in their intensity and strength. Paul admits this in regard to the gift of prophecy. In Romans 12:6 he said, 'We have different gifts, according to the grace given us. If a man's gift is prophesying, let him use it in proportion to his faith.' There are different measures of grace and faith given with which to exercise the various gifts. Paul himself had a greater gift of tongues than anyone at Corinth (1 Cor. 14:18).[9] Timothy had let one of his spiritual gifts decline in its strength so that Paul had to encourage him 'to fan into flame the gift [*charisma*] of God, which is in you through the laying on of my hands' (2 Tim. 1:6). All of these texts demonstrate that spiritual gifts occur with varying degrees of intensity or strength.

No one has trouble recognizing that the spiritual gifts that are usually viewed as nonmiraculous vary in their strength. Some teachers have a greater teaching gift than others. Luke, for example, draws a portrait of Apollos as a preacher and teacher who was 'mighty [Greek: *dunatos*] in the Scriptures' (Acts 18:24 NASB). Some evangelists have a greater gift than other evangelists, and so on. By analogy we should expect the same thing with the miraculous gifts of the Spirit.

This seems to be the case even among the apostles in the book of Acts. Of the apostles, Peter and Paul are presented as the ones who are most gifted in healings and miracles. Peter's ministry is so extraordinary that apparently even his shadow is used by God to heal (Acts 5:15)! All of the apostles were used to do signs and wonders (Acts 5:12), but Luke seems to single out Peter as pre-eminent among the apostles. When Paul comes on the scene, he is also portrayed by Luke as having extraordinary healing powers, 'so that even handkerchiefs and aprons that had touched him were taken to the sick, and their illnesses were cured and the evil spirits left them' (Acts 19:12). Paul and Peter were the only apostles whom Luke mentions as raising the dead. Even among the apostles, therefore, the New Testament seems to indicate that there were varying degrees of strengths in their giftings.

The third thing I discovered is that, taken as a whole, the apostles are presented by the New Testament as the most gifted individuals within the church. Although I am sure that the apostles received *charismata*, just as others in the body of Christ, the New Testament never describes their healing ministries with the term *charisma*. The miraculous ministry of the apostles is designated by the phrase *signs and wonders*.

What are signs and wonders? In the Old Testament the phrase is most frequently used to describe the great plagues that God sent on Egypt and the subsequent deliverance of his people from that nation (Deut. 4:34; 6:22; 7:19; 23:9; 26:8; 34:11; Neh. 9:10; Ps. 135:9; and so on). In the New Testament, 'signs and wonders' describe the ministries of Jesus (Acts 2:22), the apostles (Acts 2:43; 5:12; 14:3; 15:12; Rom. 15:18–19; 2 Cor. 12:12), and the ministries of Stephen (Acts 6:8) and Philip (Acts 8:6).[10]

The phrase 'signs and wonders' is used to describe an unusual outpouring of the Holy Spirit for miracles. The phrase is not used in contexts where one or two miracles or healings take place. It is used in contexts where an *abundance of miracles* are taking place (e.g., Acts 5:12; 8:7), and those who behold the signs and wonders are astonished.[11] Even a person like Simon, who had been skilled in occult arts, is amazed at the signs in Philip's ministry (Acts 8:13). Signs and wonders occur in the midst of revival in connection with the proclamation of the gospel, and the only people who are said to do signs and wonders, outside of the Lord Jesus and the apostles, are Stephen and Philip.

Here are the conclusions that I drew from these observations. First, there is a distinction between signs and wonders and the gift of healing. Signs and wonders are an outpouring of miracles specifically connected with revival and the proclamation of gospel. The gift of healing is given to the church for its edification (1 Cor. 12:7) and is not necessarily connected with revival or an abundance of miracles.

Second, it is wrong to insist that the apostolic ministry of signs and wonders is the standard for the gifts of healing given to the average New Testament Christian. We have vivid descriptions of the apostles' ministry in signs and wonders, but apart from the ministry of the apostles there are few if any *descriptions* of the average Christian who had healing gifts, or *examples* of how the miraculous gifts operated in the local church.

It is simply not reasonable to insist that all miraculous spiritual gifts equal those of the apostles in their intensity or strength in order to be perceived as legitimate gifts of the Holy Spirit.[12] No one would insist on this for the nonmiraculous gifts like teaching or evangelism. For example, what person in the history of the church since Paul has been as gifted a teacher to the body of Christ? Luther? Calvin? Who today would claim to be Paul's equal as a teacher?[13] I do not know of anyone who would make such a claim for the past or the present. Therefore, since no one has arisen with the gift of teaching that is equal to the apostle Paul's, should we conclude that the gift of teaching was withdrawn from the church? Likewise, should we assume that everyone who has a gift of evangelism is going to evangelize like the apostle Paul? Who has planted as many churches or started as many new works with the depth and the authority that the apostle Paul did? We can admit to varying degrees of intensity and quality in gifts of evangelism, in gifts of teaching, and in other gifts. Why can't we do that with the gift of healing? Or the gift of miracles? Or the gift of prophecy?

We should, of course, expect the healing ministry of the apostles to be greater than that of others in the body of Christ. They were specially chosen by the Lord to be his handpicked representatives, and they were given authority and power over all demons and over all disease (Matt. 10:1; Mark 3:13–15; Luke 9:1). They received a special promise to be 'clothed with power from on high' (Luke 24:49, cf. Acts 1:8). They possessed an authority that no one else in the body of Christ possessed. Paul, for example, actually had the authority to turn someone over to Satan for the destruction of his flesh (1 Cor. 5:1–5).

If we are going to say that the apostolic ministry sets the standard by which we should judge the gifts in Romans 12 and 1 Corinthians 12, we might be forced to conclude that no gifts, miraculous or nonmiraculous, have been given since the days of the apostles! For who has measured up to the apostles in any respect?

Third, we should not draw the conclusion that signs and wonders must have ceased with the deaths of the apostles. Stephen and Philip were not apostles, but they were given a ministry of signs and wonders similar to that of the apostles. And there may have been others in addition to Stephen and Philip.

There is also nothing in the New Testament that would preclude future outpourings of revivals accompanied by signs and wonders. In fact, it is very biblical to long for and pray for such revivals. Consider the prayer of Acts 4:29–30, 'Now, Lord, consider their threats and enable your servants to speak your word with great boldness. Stretch out your hand to heal and perform miraculous signs and wonders through the name of your holy servant Jesus.' If the church were to take this prayer seriously, who knows what kind of outpouring of signs and wonders in revival that God might be pleased to give us?

As I look across the body of Christ, I don't see anyone who has the quality and quantity of miracles that took place in the apostles' ministry. But that no longer leads me to conclude that God is not using people to do miracles and healings today.

In fact, it has been my privilege to be friends with a number of people like John Wimber who are very gifted in healing and miracles. Paul Cain, whom I mentioned previously, is the most gifted person in the ministry of the miraculous that I have ever met. On a number of occasions I have seen Paul visit what I call the realm of apostolic power. By that I mean I have watched him command or pronounce healings, rather than pray for them. I have seen him command spirits to be silent or to come out, and with a single command they have left.

In March of 1990 we were sharing a meeting in Melbourne, Australia, in Waverly Christian Fellowship, where Kevin Connor is the pastor. At the conclusion of the meeting, Paul prayed for some of the people in the audience. He pointed to a man in the back of the audience and said, 'Your right shoulder is separated.' Paul had never seen that man before, and there was no evidence to indicate that his shoulder was separated. In fact, only that man, who happened to be an athlete, and his mother knew that his shoulder had been separated. Paul said, 'Stretch forth your hand to the Lord Jesus, and your shoulder will be healed.' Instantly, as the man stretched forth his hand, his shoulder was healed. And he began waving both of his arms and giving thanks to the Lord.

In June of 1992, Edward and Jewell Levsen of Tustin, California, were attending a conference in Kansas City, Missouri, where Paul Cain was one of the speakers. The Levsen's were retiring and preparing to move back to Iowa. They were feeling that their usefulness to God was either over or would be significantly minimized in their retirement years. Both of them had significant physical problems. Edward had severe arthritis in his shoulders and Jewell had both neck and back problems.

The Levsen's had attended other conferences where Paul Cain had been speaking, so they were familiar with the way the Lord uses Paul's prophetic and healing gifts. Yet neither of them really expected any direct public ministry from Paul.

One afternoon, about a week before the conference, Jewell prayed something like this, 'Father, I know Paul Cain calls out leaders in meetings, but do you ever use Paul to call out ordinary people? I don't ever expect to be called out, but if I am, would you call me Jewell Floyd?' (Floyd was Jewell's maiden name.)

'If you do speak to me through Paul Cain, I want to ask you a question. I have heard what a lot of people have said about women in ministry, but I want you to tell me what you think about women in ministry. I know I am too old to be in ministry any more, but I still want to know what you think about women in ministry.'

A week later, during the conference, the Lord gave Paul a

vision of Jewell and her husband while Paul was praying in his hotel room before the meeting. After the message that evening, Paul looked out across the audience and said, 'There is someone here named Edward. You are from out west and your wife's name is Jewell.' Then when Edward and Jewell stood up, Paul looked at Jewell and said, 'Does the name Jewell Floyd mean anything to you?' Immediately Jewell began to weep, being overcome with the tender omniscience of the Lord.

Then Paul spoke to her discouragement. He said to Jewell,

The Lord said he called you, and it was real back there in Iowa. The Lord called you and had his hand on you. It's not over until its over!

And something is happening to Lisa [their daughter]. Something is happening to your whole family! Your prayers have been heard. And Lisa has been already having an encounter with the Lord for this life-changing thing to come to her.

Let me tell you, you are two people that I talked about tonight who can have dreams after sixty. You are two people that are going to come through and see the glory of God while you are yet alive. And I want you to know that it is not over for you, Edward, and for you, Jewell.

As he looked at Jewell, Paul said, 'You have pain from your neck all the way down to the end of your spine and in your feet and legs.' Jewell acknowledged that this was true. Paul told her that the Lord was going to heal her that night. Then Paul looked at Edward and said, 'I am having a vision of your pain right now. You have almost worn out your shoulder, and arthritis is there from driving something big—it has almost killed you. The Lord is going to heal that arthritis.' Then he looked at Jewell and said, 'I believe you have a birthday in July. The Lord just healed your husband for a birthday present.'

About six weeks later I got a letter from Jewell. She wrote, 'Right after the meeting on Friday night with Paul Cain I felt my neck, and I knew I had a creative miracle in my neck, as the whole muscle structure in my neck had changed! After this I felt so good and healed of the trouble from the nape of my neck and all the way down to the end of my spine. It would take a few pages to tell you what the doctor diagnosed.'

I saw Edward and Jewell in the fall of 1992. They had enrolled in the Emmaus Road Ministry School in Euless, Texas. Both of them were still completely healed from the conditions Paul had called out, and they were filled with a new passion for God in their hearts. They were awestruck over the healing God had given them, but Jewell was just as grateful for the specific answers God had given to her prayer a week before the conference. God demonstrated his tender affection for Jewell by calling her by her maiden name, Floyd, by letting her know that God does call and use women, and by letting her and Edward know that they were not too old for God to use them significantly in ministry.

Both of these examples are near the level of apostolic healing. First, the ailment was revealed supernaturally by the Lord to Paul and, second, the Lord revealed that he would heal these conditions. Paul did not pray for their healing; he simply pronounced it. This type of healing often characterized the ministries of the Lord Jesus and the apostles.

I would like to say that Paul Cain lives in this realm, but that is not true. There are times when Paul prays for someone's healing just like all the rest of us. But there are a number of occasions, and they seem to be coming more frequently now, where he visits this realm of apostolic healing, and there are significant similarities between his ministry and that of the apostles.

Why should we have difficulty believing that the Lord uses people like this today? Why should we have difficulty believing that some people are simply more gifted at praying for healing than others? We don't have any trouble believing that some people are more gifted at teaching, others more gifted at evangelism, others more gifted at administration, and so on. Why should we have difficulty believing the same thing can be true of healing and miracles?

This explanation solved for me the problem of the inconsistency between the apostolic healing model and what I was seeing and hearing presently in the church.[14] If we do not see apostolic healing in the church today, the only conclusion we are warranted in drawing is simply that we are not seeing *apostolic* healing. It does not mean that God is not giving apostolic healing or that he has withdrawn the gifts of healing from the body of Christ.[15]

It is always possible that we may be like Jacob, who had to confess, 'Surely the LORD is in this place, and I was not aware of it' (Gen. 28:16).

The Miraculous Gifts in Church History

If the main reason that Christians do not believe in miraculous gifts is because they have not seen miracles, the second most powerful reason is that some feel there is no evidence for miraculous gifts between the death of the apostles and the present day. If these gifts were to be permanent, how could they be lost throughout church history, or at least for large periods of time?

Let us assume for a moment that the gifts actually were lost. It would not be the first time the people of God have lost divinely given gifts. Sometime after the death of Moses, either the entire Pentateuch or the book of Deuteronomy was lost. It wasn't discovered again until around 622 B.C. during the reign of Josiah (2 Kings 22:8). Think of that, the people of God lost their Scriptures!

For all practical purposes, this occurred a second time in church history when people could no longer read the original Hebrew Old Testament, the Greek New Testament, or their Latin translation of the Bible. It was not until the time of the Reformation that the Scriptures became accessible to people again in their own language. This certainly was not a case of God hiding Scripture from the people but rather the church's neglect of Scripture.

There are other examples as well. One of the most precious teachings ever given to the church is the doctrine of justification by faith alone in Christ. Shortly after the death of the apostles, however, the writing of some of the Apostolic Fathers begins to show that the doctrine of justification by faith was already being perverted (cf. the epistle of Barnabas and the Shepherd of Hermas). Eventually this doctrine was lost and not widely recovered until the Reformation in the fifteenth and sixteenth centuries. Should we explain this absence by assuming that for approximately fifteen hundred years God had withdrawn the teaching ministry of the Holy Spirit or that justification by faith was no longer important to him?

These kinds of examples could be multiplied. Dispensationalists, for example, claim that the early church believed in premillennialism and a pretribulational rapture. Yet they have to admit that both of these doctrines were allegedly lost in church history and were not recovered until the time of Darby in the nineteenth century. How could the church lose something that was intended to be permanent? The church seems to have no difficulty at all in misplacing the Holy Scriptures and foundational doctrines. Why should we believe that the church would have difficulty in misplacing spiritual gifts?

It also needs to be pointed out that this argument from the absence of the gifts in church history is not a biblical argument. It is an argument based upon *experience*. If the gifts were lost in history, the most important question is not *whether* they were lost, but *why* they were lost. Of course, it could be due to a divinely planned obsolescence, as some have argued. (When we study the purposes of miracles and the gifts of the Spirit, however, we will be forced to conclude that we cannot use this explanation.) On the other hand, it is possible that God never intended that these gifts should cease, but rather it is *the church* that has rejected these gifts. The loss of these gifts could be due to the rise of an ungifted bureaucratic leadership who put out gifted people.[16] On this view, when people stopped seeking spiritual gifts (*in direct disobedience to God's commands*: 1 Cor. 12:31; 14:1, 39) and stopped making provision for their exercise within their churches, then they ceased to experience the gifts. Or their loss could be due to the judgment of God for the unbelief, apostasy, or legalism in the church. Any number of other reasons could also be given for the supposed absence of the gifts in church history.

Again, our decision must be based on clear and specific statements of Scripture regarding the nature and purpose of the miraculous gifts. Ultimately it is only Scripture, not historical research, that will settle this question.

Historical research is an imperfect science. Who really knows history that well? We only have a fraction of the literature from the period of the death of the last of the apostles up to the beginning of the Reformation. That is, for fourteen-hundred years we have very scanty historical sources on which to base our study. Is this sufficient evidence on which to base the conviction that the gifts of the Holy Spirit were lost to the church throughout its history?[17]

But were the gifts *really* lost? There is, in fact, ample evidence throughout church history for the use of the gifts in the church. After studying the historical documentation for the miraculous gifts of the Spirit, D. A. Carson, a highly respected New Testament scholar, concluded:

> There is enough evidence that some form of 'charismatic' gifts continued sporadically across the centuries of church history that it is futile to insist on doctrinaire grounds that every report is spurious or the fruit of demonic activity or psychological aberration.[18]

This evidence, however, has not always been handled in an impartial way. Often the reports of miracles have been discredited because it is alleged that the witnesses were gullible, or that they had incorrect theology.

Augustine, for example, began by believing that the miraculous gifts had been withdrawn from the church. Toward the end of his life, however, he wrote a series of retractions, and this is one of the statements he retracted. In *The City of God* (Book 22:8) he said that in less than two years he knew of over seventy recorded and verified instances of miracles in his city of Hippo. No less a figure than Augustine, writing in the fifth century, said that he could verify over seventy miracles in his city in a two-year period!

Warfield, who normally accepts Augustine as a reliable witness and who views him as having made a great contribution to the history of doctrine, will not accept Augustine's testimony here. One of the reasons that Warfield rejects Augustine's testimony is due to the fact that some of the healings Augustine reports were wrought through relics, specifically the bones of Stephen.[19] Apparently for Warfield this is a sufficient basis to demonstrate that Augustine is not a credible witness. Warfield never bothers to prove that these alleged healings through the bones of Stephen did not take place or could not have taken place. He never discusses the fact that the bones of Elisha actually raised a man from the dead (2 Kings 13:21) and the relevance of this text to the miracles cited by Augustine.

In fact, Warfield acknowledges that from the fourth century on there are numerous eyewitness reports of miracles and that these eyewitnesses were not obscure neurotics but were 'rather the outstanding scholars, theologians, preachers, organizers of the age.'[20] In this connection Warfield mentions Jerome, the leading biblical scholar of his day; Gregory of Nyssa; Athanasius; Chrysostom, the greatest preacher of the day; Ambrose, the greatest churchman of the day; as well as Augustine, whom Warfield credits as the greatest thinker of the day.[21] All of these leaders are dismissed by Warfield as unreliable witnesses to miracles. Warfield's biased treatment of the historical evidence has come under severe criticism.[22]

It might be well to point out here that strangeness is not a criterion for truth. Nor is it a criterion we would want to use in order to decide whether something is scriptural or unscriptural. There is much in Scripture that is exceedingly strange. The prophet Isaiah, for example, went naked and barefoot for three years as a sign against Egypt and Cush (Isa. 20:3). The prophet Hosea was commanded to marry a prostitute (Hos. 1:2). The dead bones of Elisha actually raised the dead (2 Kings 13:21). Peter's shadow healed the sick people on which it fell (Acts 5:15). Handkerchiefs and aprons that touched Paul's body healed the sick and drove out demons (Acts 19:12). And even stranger things than these can be found in Holy Scripture.

Suppose I were to tell you that I had a vision in which I saw the throne of God. In my vision there were four living creatures resembling a lion, a calf, a man, and an eagle, each of whom had six wings and were filled with eyes all around and within them. These creatures were saying 'Holy, holy, holy' as they flew around the throne of God day and night. Who would believe that this was a legitimate vision if it had not already been written in Revelation 4:6–8? I am not saying that we ought to believe every strange thing that is told to us. I am saying, however, that nothing should be discounted as untrue or unscriptural simply because it is strange.

Recent research is tending to view the reports of miraculous events throughout the church's history in a much more positive light.[23]

When I saw that I had falsely equated the apostles' ministry of signs and wonders with the healing gifts given to average Christians, my major theological objection to the contemporary ministry of miraculous gifts vanished. It was also helpful to understand that the healing ministry of Jesus and the apostles did not operate in some kind of automatic or mechanical sphere. It was a theological bias combined with a superficial reading of the New Testament that had led me to believe that they could heal at will. Now for the first time I was in a position to research with an open mind what the Scriptures said about healing and miracles.

I also began to read church history with an open mind, actually looking for evidence of the gifts of the Spirit. I found that there was much more historical evidence for the presence of the miraculous gifts throughout the history of the church than I had been led to believe.

I had two more major hurdles to cross, however, before I could study the Scriptures with a truly open mind on this issue. If believing in the gifts of the Spirit meant that I would share in the abuses of the charismatic movement, I wasn't sure that I wanted to believe in them. But quite apart from any of the abuses of the gifts, I had a revulsion to the revelatory gifts, especially the gift of tongues—they seemed so subjective to me. They also seemed to detract from the importance of the Bible and endanger its authority. Yet the teaching of Scripture was forcing me toward the gifts against my will.

6

Responding to Spiritual Abuses

Almost everyone has experienced or heard of abuses within the Pentecostal and charismatic movements and within other groups that believe in the gifts of the Spirit. Some of these abuses can be quite frightening. Before attending my first Vineyard meeting, I had only been to one meeting that could be called charismatic or Pentecostal. This took place during my junior year in college. A group of us, who were all working in a Christian ministry, decided to go hear a young Pentecostal evangelist who was holding a revival in a well-known Pentecostal church in our city. We were going to that service expressly to mock and to be entertained. We were not disappointed.

The young evangelist came out onto the stage dressed in the latest fashionable 'hippie' attire (the year was 1970). Instead of speaking from Scripture, he told the story of his personal conversion. Allegedly, he was converted while in jail on a drug charge. As he sat on the floor in a corner of his cell experiencing withdrawal symptoms, he saw the Lord Jesus and two angels floating over him. Jesus stopped to look down on the young man, but one of the angels grabbed the arm of Jesus and said, 'Come on Jesus; let's go. He ain't worth it; he's just trash.' Jesus told the angel to stop because he had mighty plans for this young man. Nothing the young evangelist said that evening had the ring of truth to it. Neither did his flamboyant style enhance his credibility, in our opinion.

The invitation given at the conclusion of his message was not for the salvation of sinners. Instead, an offer was extended to those who wanted to receive the baptism of the Holy Spirit and the gift of tongues. When the invitation was given, some of my friends went down to the front to get a closer look. They saw two men praying for a third man. The two men told the man to open his mouth and make sounds. The man did this, and immediately it was announced that he had received the gift of tongues.

Our experience that evening confirmed what we already knew: the gifts of the Holy Spirit were not being given, and all claims to those kinds of gifts today were just pretense on the part of gullible, deceived people. Or worse yet, they were deliberate deceptions.

Having been to one meeting where the gifts of the Spirit were abused or faked, I concluded that all meetings where the gifts of the Spirit were practiced were just like that one. It is not surprising that God did not let me see the genuine thing. When you go with a closed mind, it is rare for God to violate your prejudices. In those days I was not a sincere seeker. I should not have been surprised, therefore, if God chose not to throw his pearls to the swine.

It is undeniable that there are significant abuses within some groups that believe in and practice the gifts of the Spirit. I have witnessed emotionalism, exaggerations, elitism, prophetic words used in a controlling and manipulative way, and a lack of scriptural foundation in various meetings and movements. I would not say, however, that this is true of the majority of groups that practice the gifts of the Spirit.[1] And I find that the leaders I know personally among these movements are quick to correct these excesses and abuses.

The Significance of Abuses

What significance should we attach to these abuses? We should view them in the same light in which they are viewed in Scripture. Surprisingly, the Bible teaches that God works miracles among those who have spiritual abuses, doctrinal error, and even immorality.

Both the Old and the New Testament amply illustrate this point. Samson did not acquire his great strength by long, arduous workouts in a local gym. His strength was supernatural, for the Bible leaves no doubt that it was due to the empowering of the Holy Spirit (Judg. 14:6, 19; 15:14). On one occasion in the city of Gaza, Samson spent the night with a prostitute (Judg. 16:1). Surely we would expect that sexual immorality such as that would cause him to lose the power of the Holy Spirit. Yet when his enemies surrounded the city to capture him, God granted him the strength to uproot the gates of the city and carry them up to the top of a mountain in mockery of the Philistines (Judg. 16: 2–3).

The New Testament also has its examples. The church at Corinth was so rich in spiritual gifts that Paul was able to say that they did not lack *any* spiritual gift (1 Cor. 1:7). Yet they exhibited such a sectarian spirit that Paul called them 'worldly' (1 Cor. 3:1ff.). In addition, they had sexual immorality among them that was worse than the practices of pagans—and they tolerated that sexual immorality (1 Cor. 5:1–2). They were even guilty of getting drunk during the Lord's Supper! Some of the Corinthians embraced one of the worst doctrinal errors mentioned in the New Testament. They claimed that there was no resurrection from the dead (1 Cor. 15:12). Here was a church with significant moral abuses and doctrinal error, and yet it is one of the most richly gifted churches in the New Testament.

When Paul wrote to the churches of Galatia (probably in A.D. 49), doctrinal heresy had so gripped the churches that Paul could say to them, 'I am astonished that you are so quickly deserting the one who called you by the grace of Christ and are turning to a different gospel' (Gal. 1:6). The seriousness of their condition is revealed in another passage where Paul asked them, 'You foolish Galatians! Who has bewitched you? Before your very eyes Jesus Christ was clearly portrayed as crucified' (3:1).

The Galatian churches were on the verge of deserting the very gospel that had saved them, and yet at the very time Paul was writing his letter to the Galatians, God was performing miracles among them: 'Does God give you his Spirit and work miracles among you because you observe the law, or because you believe what you heard?' (Gal. 3:5). In the phrase, 'work miracles among you,' the verb *work* is in the present tense. This means that Paul claimed that miracles were happening among the Galatians at the same time he was writing his letter to them.

This brief survey leads us to three inescapable conclusions. First, the presence of abuses and even impurity in Christian groups where miracles occur does not prove that their miracles are not from God, any more than they did at Corinth. Second, the presence of doctrinal error in Christian groups where miracles occur does not prove that their miracles are invalid, any more than they did in the Galatian churches.[2] Third, miracles neither confirm nor support the *distinctive* doctrines or practices of individual churches or Christian groups. The miracles at Galatia did not support the heretical teaching there any more than the gift of miracles at Corinth supported their abuse of the Lord's Supper. According to Scripture, there is only one message that New Testament miracles support or confirm, and that is the gospel message concerning the person and work of Jesus Christ.

Much of the cessationist literature throughout this century has failed to grasp these three conclusions. Every time miraculous gifts appear in history, the cessationists look for abuses or doctrinal errors within the group where these gifts appear. When they find doctrinal errors or abuses, they immediately conclude that these gifts could not have been real.[3] They might as well conclude that the gifts at Corinth and in Galatia were not real either!

Noncharismatic Abuses Within the Church Today

People often use charismatic abuses to prove that the gifts of the Spirit are not given today. But that sword cuts both ways. There are abuses in all expressions of Christianity. It is just that we get used to our own abuses, and they don't seem as bad as those in the other groups. But are they?

While I was still a professor at Dallas Seminary, I was having lunch one day with a group of students and one of them mentioned John Wimber and Peter Wagner. Another replied, 'I have a serious problem with those two men.'

'Why?' I asked.

'Because they teach at Fuller Seminary.'

I asked him what was so bad about Fuller Seminary. He replied that as a faculty and a seminary board they would no longer unanimously affirm the doctrine of biblical inerrancy, and therefore, nobody who taught there could be trusted. As the discussion progressed, it was apparent that he felt quite strongly about this issue, even to the point of anger.

Later that day, the same student came into my office privately and confessed that he had been struggling with a fifteen-year addiction to pornography. He also told me that during the time he had been attending seminary he had visited prostitutes three times.

This young man was married, had children, and also was a pastor in a local church. What amazed me was that he did not consider the visits to the prostitutes as adultery. I was even more amazed to discover that he showed a far stronger reaction to Fuller Seminary's view of biblical inerrancy than he did to his own adultery. He felt more emotional intensity over the doctrine of inerrancy than over the fact that he had been in bondage to lust for fifteen years and had lived a lie before his family and church.

Later, when some men from a local charismatic church prayed for him (at his request) and asked God to break the power of lust over his life, he became extremely upset because one of the men prayed very softly in tongues. Again, he showed more concern over the fact that someone prayed in tongues than that he was an adulterer enslaved by lust.[4]

During the time I was trying to help that young man, I pondered his situation often. The most disturbing aspect was not that he had fallen into grievous sexual sin and was in the power of lust—I have seen that happen to Christians in every branch of the church today.[5] What disturbed me most about this young pastor was the obvious fact that he valued doctrine more highly than his moral life. This priority is not native to the regenerate heart. This priority was something his teachers had unwittingly instilled in him. He learned this emphasis from some of the religious authorities in his life who made doctrinal authority their highest value. This emphasis cannot be found in New Testament teaching.

In fact, this emphasis perverts New Testament doctrine because it views the mind as more important than the heart (that is, the affections) and claims that *believing* the right things is more important than *doing* the right things. This pastor made knowledge the supreme value in life. He had put his quest for purity of doctrine above his quest for purity in his own life.

I was now looking at the fruit of that kind of doctrine. A young pastor had lost the ability to weep over his sins, but he still had a passion to defend the authority of the Bible. This intellectual pursuit of doctrinal purity at the expense of our own personal holiness is an abuse as great as anything in the charismatic movement.

Let me give you another example. I know a man who is a seminary graduate. During the time that he was a seminary student and during the years after he graduated, he was a practicing homosexual. He was so skilled at leading a double life that none of his Christian friends, nor anyone in the church that he attended, ever suspected him. He was involved in some of the worst of the homosexual perversions.

His lifestyle went on for many years. Then he was suddenly stricken with a life-threatening condition and found himself strapped to a hospital gurney and wheeled into the operating room. The attending physician told him that in all likelihood he would not come out of the operating room alive.

When the man heard this, he cried out to God for mercy. He apologized to God for the double life he had been leading, for being unfaithful to God, and for deceiving his friends. He repented of his homosexuality and promised never to give into it again. He then asked God to heal him and to give him one more chance. How do you think God responded to a prayer like that, given those circumstances?

God spared his life. Not only that, but his recovery from the surgery and subsequent mending went much faster than any of his physicians would ever have predicted.

I would not call his speedy recovery a miracle, but a miracle did happen to him. When he came out of the surgery, all of the homosexual desire had left him. The cruel taskmaster he had served for so many years was nowhere to be found. He was free. The power of the blood of the cross had done a greater miracle than any physical healing I know of.

After leaving the hospital, this man decided to fulfill his vow to God. He thought the best place to start would be to go back to his church and make a full confession of his sin and deception. By now he had contracted AIDS, and he also wanted the elders of the church to anoint him with oil and pray for him in accordance with James 5:14–16.

You would think that the elders of the church would have

rejoiced to see this prodigal returning home. But that was not the case. First, some doubted that he was a believer. Second, they asked him to leave the church. Third, they refused to even pray for him and his healing, and as he dejectedly left the church, some would not shake his hand for fear of contracting AIDS.

I don't know about you, but if I had to choose between having the worst, crassest form of emotionalism in my church or living with the kind of coldhearted Pharisaism that this man experienced after his repentance, I would choose the emotionalism!

You may think these are isolated stories, but they are not. These kinds of incidents are not at all uncommon in that wing of the church which is anticharismatic and puts high value, perhaps the highest value, on the teaching of Bible doctrine. I lived in that wing of the church for over twenty years, and I have accumulated enough of these kinds of abuses to fill several books.

This particular branch of the church is just as guilty of abusing God's Word as anyone I have ever seen in the charismatic branch. They just do it in different ways. They don't believe in prophecy, so they can't use that as a means of controlling and manipulating people. But they do use God's Word and their interpretation of it to control and manipulate those in their churches.

J. I. Packer described this group when he wrote,

> In spite of their disdain for 'the traditions of men,' the insistence of many conservative Christians in demanding that adults accept traditions of faith and practice in the manner of children who are told to shut their eyes, open their mouths, and swallow whatever is tipped in is not a maturing thing; at best it leads to bigotry, at worst it leads to cultism.[6]

The part of the church that Packer was describing would undoubtedly mock the idea of papal infallibility. Yet they treat their own interpretive and expository tradition as infallible. And they further dishonor the Scripture by giving controversial passages the most ludicrous interpretation whenever those passages disagree with their own practices or interpretations.

When Fundamentalism Becomes Abusive

I do not want you to misunderstand the preceding examples. I am not criticizing my seminary. I owe Dallas Theological Seminary a debt I shall never be able to repay. My teachers passed on to me a love and holy respect for the Word of God that has been one of my most priceless treasures.

I was shown kindness, love, and affirmation by my teachers. I would not trade anything for my education or my years of employment by Dallas Seminary.

I am not criticizing my seminary nor other noncharismatic branches of the church. What I am criticizing is fundamentalism when it becomes abusive. I have already agreed that the abuses of the charismatic church are real and serious. I have not bothered to lavishly illustrate those abuses in this chapter. A recent rash of anticharismatic books has done this ad nauseam. What they have not done, however, is admit that their own abuses are just as serious. The kinds of abuses I have mentioned previously are the kinds of abuses that are not uncommon in fundamentalist churches or other churches whose highest value is doctrinal orthodoxy.

All churches have their own distinctive abuses. Some churches are more prone to emotionalism, while others are more prone to a cold legalistic self-righteous pharisaism. Both are seriously wrong. We are often blind to our own abuses because most abuses stem from a wrong emphasis or wrong application of a good thing. We do not abuse our weaknesses; we abuse our strengths. That is why our own abuses are so hard to see—they are a misuse of a strength, something that has blessed us and others.

Our Attitude Toward Spiritual Abuses

The purpose of this chapter is not to excuse charismatic or Pentecostal abuses or to condemn the abuses of some traditional churches. Rather, we need to cultivate a godly and scriptural attitude toward spiritual abuses—no matter where they occur.

There are two different attitudes we can take to spiritual abuses within the church. We can seek to control them by eliminating the thing that is being abused. We could, for example, eliminate the abuse of the gift of tongues by forbidding people to speak in tongues. We could also eliminate the abuse of various freedoms by prohibiting those freedoms. Even though the Scripture forbids this approach, it has been common since the beginning of church history and continues to this very day.

But how could a group that professes to believe in the Bible do this? It is simple; they rationalize away the particular biblical commandment in view. When Paul says not to forbid speaking in tongues (1 Cor. 14:39), some simply say that does not apply today.

The problem with that method, besides being dishonoring to Scripture, is that this kind of authoritarian control stifles spontaneity and drains away the very life of the church. It drives sin and abuse underground where it is much more difficult to deal with. I have seen much more wickedness and secret sin among authoritarian fundamentalist churches than anywhere else among the spectrum of Christian churches today.[7]

The better approach, in my opinion, is to view abuses and doctrinal errors as inevitable on this side of heaven. Instead of being shocked when we see them, we ought to graciously and patiently correct them. In some cases, we will find that what we thought was an abuse was not an abuse at all, but a step forward.

The ministers of George Whitefield's day (1714–1770), for example, viewed field preaching as dishonoring to the Gospel of

Jesus Christ. But eventually the church came around to seeing that those who opposed Whitefield were dishonoring the Gospel, and they accepted field preaching as a valid means of winning people to Christ.

We also need a healthy dose of humility. We need to recognize that our hearts are deceitful and desperately sick (Jer. 17:9). We need to realize that neither our interpretations nor practices are infallible. As J. I. Packer has said, we are 'victims and beneficiaries of our own traditions.'

It is *only* when we truly believe in our own capacity for being deceived that we can begin to see clearly. It is only when we appeal to God to reveal our faults that we will be delivered from the many blindnesses that beset us throughout our Christian lives. David confessed his relentless blindness when he prayed,

> Search me, O God, and know my heart;
>   test me and know my anxious thoughts.
> See if there is any offensive way in me,
>   And lead me in the way everlasting. (Ps. 139:23–24)

If 'the man after God's own heart,' who was even privileged to write a large portion of the Psalms, saw his need for God to reveal his faults and sins, how much more should we seek that revelatory ministry?

———————————————

It has been my observation that God does not normally violate the prejudices of religious pride. Many of the Pharisees went to their deaths absolutely convinced in the validity of their own traditions and prejudices. Their religious pride shut them off from the correction that God would so willingly have given them, for 'God opposes the proud but gives grace to the humble' (1 Pet. 5:5).

The tragedy is that many of their doctrines were biblical and true. Yet I would rather have some wrong doctrines and humility than to have perfect orthodoxy on every point and no humility. A person who has wrong doctrine and humility can be corrected. A person with mostly right doctrines and no humility will be resisted by the Lord he professes to serve.

7

Scared to Death by the Holy Ghost

On April 18, 1906, the *Los Angeles Times* reported a strange new revival that was occurring in the city. Under a headline that proclaimed 'Weird Babel of Tongues,' a reporter from the paper stated that

> meetings are held in a tumble-down shack on Azusa Street, near San Pedro Street, and the devotees of the weird doctrine practice the most fanatical rites, preach the wildest theories and work themselves into a state of mad excitement in their peculiar zeal. Colored people and a sprinkling of whites compose the congregation, and night is made hideous in the neighborhood by the howlings of the worshippers, who spend hours swaying forth and back in a nerve-racking attitude of prayer and supplication. They claim to have the 'gift of tongues' and to be able to comprehend the babel.[1]

That same day, the great San Francisco earthquake occurred, destroying much of that city. As the tremors from the earthquake were felt by those at Azusa Street, a 'spiritual earthquake' shook the meeting, which rose to a near hysteria level.[2]

Although the tremors from the San Francisco earthquake were felt up and down the California coast, the tremors from the spiritual earthquake spread throughout the country. The revival continued day and night for three years and gave birth to modern

Pentecostalism. Yet from the very beginning, the physical phenomena that occurred in the revival were ridiculed as a 'frenzy of
religious zeal,' and those who spoke in tongues were said to
'gurgle wordless talk.'

Unusual physical manifestations have been common throughout the history of the church, especially during times of revival.
Sometimes these manifestations have occurred in the most
unlikely settings.

During the Evangelical Revival of England in the late 1730s
and the early 1740s, John Wesley saw numerous 'outward signs'
occur during his preaching. On June 17, 1739, for example, while
Wesley was preaching in the fields and was 'earnestly inviting all
sinners to "enter into the holiest" by this "new and living way,"'

> many of those that heard began to call upon God with strong cries and
> tears. Some sunk down, and there remained no strength in them;
> others exceedingly trembled and quaked: Some were torn with a kind
> of convulsive motion in every part of their bodies, and that so vio-
> lently, that often four or five persons could not hold one of them.[3]

When his friend and fellow preacher, George Whitefield, first
heard about these signs, he objected strenuously. But on July 7,
1739, Wesley records in his journal:

> I had an opportunity to talk with him of those outward signs which
> had so often accompanied the inward work of God. I found his objec-
> tions were chiefly grounded on gross misrepresentations of matter of
> fact. But the next day he had an opportunity of informing himself bet-
> ter: For no sooner had he begun (in the application of his sermon) to
> invite all sinners to believe in Christ, than four persons sunk down
> close to him, almost in the same moment. One of them lay without
> either sense or motion. A second trembled exceedingly. The third had
> strong convulsions all over his body, but made no noise, unless by
> groans. The fourth, equally convulsed, called upon God, with strong
> cries and tears.

Wesley concludes his journal entry that day with the statement: 'From this time, I trust, we shall all suffer God to carry on his own work in the way that pleaseth Him.'[4]

During that same period, who would have thought that those kinds of 'signs' would have happened in a staid New England setting in what is now regarded as one of the greatest revivals in American history, the Great Awakening? Yet this is exactly what occurred regularly in the meetings of Jonathan Edwards, who is considered by many to be America's greatest theologian.

In describing one of the meetings in his church, Edwards writes the following:

> The affection was quickly propagated throughout the room; many of the young people and children . . . appeared to be overcome with the sense of the greatness and glory of divine things, and with admiration, love, joy and praise, and compassion to others that looked upon themselves as in a state of nature [unsaved]; and many others at the same time were overcome with distress about their sinful and miserable state and condition; *so that the whole room was full of nothing but outcries, faintings, and the like* (emphasis mine).[5]

During that fall, Edwards writes that

> it was a very frequent thing to see a house full of outcries, faintings, convulsions, and such like, both with distress and also with admiration and joy. . . . *It was pretty often so, that there were some that were so affected, and their bodies so overcome, that they could not go home, but were obliged to stay all night where they were* (emphasis mine).[6]

On another occasion Edwards describes the ministry of Mr. Buell, who

> continued here a fortnight or three weeks after I returned: there being still great appearances attending his labors; many in their religious affections being raised far beyond what they had ever been before; *and there were some instances of persons lying in a sort of trance, remaining*

perhaps for a whole twenty-four hours motionless, and with their senses locked up; but in the mean time under strong imaginations, as though they went to heaven and had had there a vision of glorious and delightful objects. But when the people were raised to this height, Satan took advantage and his interposition, in many instances, soon became very apparent: and a great deal of caution and pains were found to keep the people, many of them, from running wild (emphasis mine).[7]

These kinds of manifestations cause concern on two different fronts. As Edwards suggests in the last paragraph, even though the manifestations were legitimate reactions to a genuine work of the Spirit, they were capable of being perverted by Satan so that people could be led astray.

On another front, these kinds of manifestations caused a number of conservative Christian ministers to criticize Jonathan Edwards and his meetings as works of the flesh or of the devil. Some in Edwards' day were certain that these kinds of manifestations proved that the work in question was not from God.

Edward Gross is an example of one who today would take the side of Edwards' opponents and argue against Edwards' understanding of the physical manifestations. Gross cites Charles Hodge, who concluded

> that there is nothing in the Bible to lead us to regard these bodily affections as the legitimate effects of religious feeling. No such results followed the preaching of Christ or his apostles. We hear of no general outcries, faintings, convulsions, or ravings in the assemblies which they addressed.[8]

Contrary to Hodge's statement, there is much in the Bible to indicate that 'bodily affections' can be legitimate effects of the Holy Spirit. These physical manifestations occur in both the Old and New Testaments.

Physical Manifestations in Scripture

According to Scripture, the Holy Spirit's ministry will sometimes produce physical reactions in people. These reactions can vary from trembling, shaking, and trances, to even illness and physical collapse.

The divine works that produce these reactions may be divided into two categories. On the one hand, these responses are caused by spectacular and visible phenomena associated with the work of the Holy Spirit. The physical manifestations mentioned above can be caused by theophanies[9] (Ex. 19:16–25), angelic appearances (Matt. 28:4), the audible voice of God (Matt. 17:6–7), visions (Dan. 8:27; 10:1–11; Acts 10:10–23),[10] reactions to Jesus during his earthly ministry (John 18:6), and the appearance of the glorified Jesus (Acts 9:1–9). All of the phenomena just listed are more or less tangible and visible experiences.

The Scriptures also record physical manifestations to less visible works of God. People tremble in the presence of God when there is no other visible or tangible phenomena associated with his presence (no theophanies, angelic appearances, audible voice, and so on). Sometimes the psalmists trembled when they experienced the presence of God as the 'fear of the Lord.' The author of Psalm 119 writes, 'My flesh trembles in fear of you; I stand in awe of your laws' (v. 120).

It was not at all unusual for the people of the Lord to tremble in his presence. In fact, the Lord expected that response from his people. He said through the mouth of his prophet Jeremiah, '"Should you not fear me?" declares the LORD. "Should you not tremble in my presence?"' (Jer. 5:22).[11]

The important thing to notice is that the intangible presence of the Lord among those who fear him gives rise to the trembling (see also Isa. 66:2 and Ezra 9:4). Those who don't fear the Lord might not act in that fashion at all.

Weeping is another manifestation in response to the intangible presence of the Lord. When Ezra was reading the book of the law to the people, they began to weep spontaneously as they heard the words of the law (Neh. 8:9). Their weeping was not the result of hysteria or psychological manipulation, because the leaders of the meeting did not want the people to weep, and they attempted to restrain them (Neh. 8:9).

The ability to weep over the words of Scripture and over our failure to keep God's Word is something that ought to be cultivated and desired today. It is not a sign of weakness or emotional instability. Rather, it is a sign of sensitivity to God's Word and of our abhorrence of sin. It is also a sign of spiritual and emotional health. The inability to weep over these things, on the other hand, is a sign of a traumatized or hardened heart.

A trance can also be a response to the presence of the Lord. Paul, for example, fell into a trance during an ordinary experience of prayer. He explained his experience in the following way, 'When I returned to Jerusalem and was praying at the temple, I fell into a trance and saw the Lord speaking. "Quick!" he said to me. "Leave Jerusalem immediately, because they will not accept your testimony about me."' (Acts 22:17–18). The result of Paul's trance experience was not to give him any new revelation about the person or work of the Lord Jesus but rather to save his life and change the course of his ministry (see also Acts 22:19–21).

Sometimes believers may enter into a state that appears to be drunkenness in response to the presence of the Lord. This happened to Hannah during prayer (1 Sam. 1:12–17). And Saul, although the text does not use the term *drunk*, certainly appeared drunk when the Spirit came on him, and he stripped off all of his clothes and lay down for the whole day (1 Sam. 19:23–24).

On the day of Pentecost, some of the onlookers assumed that those who were filled with the Spirit were drunk. Their drunken appearance was not due to the fact that they were speaking in foreign languages. That in itself was a sign of intelligence, not drunkenness. Rather, their response to the Spirit evidently produced some characteristics that are normally associated with drunkenness.

Finally, there is another category of the work of the Spirit that frequently, though not always, produces a wide range of physical manifestations. I am referring to the casting out of demons, which may result in shrieks, convulsions, and unconsciousness, among other things (cf. Mark 1:23–28; 9:14–29).

All of these reactions make sense when we realize that a human being is more than just a mind and a will, and that God may touch our emotions and our bodies as well as our minds. At this point, however, I want to draw only one conclusion from the previous evidence—the Bible supports the fact that physical reactions to the work of the Spirit may occur in a wide variety of ways.

The Spirit Brings Order Out of Chaos

In Jonathan Edwards' day, some people failed to see the Great Awakening as a work of the Spirit of God because they said that God is a God of order, not of confusion (1 Cor. 14:33, 40). They felt that God could not be responsible for the physical manifestations in these meetings because they resulted in confusion. This charge is still being leveled at similar kinds of meetings today. Edward Gross again quotes Charles Hodge:

> The testimony of the Scriptures is not merely negative on this subject. Their authority is directly opposed to all such disorders. They direct that all things should be done decently and in order. They teach us that God is not the author of confusion, but of peace, in all the churches of the Saints (1 Cor. 14:33, 40). These passages have particular reference to the manner of conducting public worship. They forbid everything that is inconsistent with order, solemnity, and devout

attention. It is evident that loud outcries and convulsions are inconsistent with these things, and therefore ought to be discouraged. They cannot come from God, for he is not the author of confusion.[12]

The reply Edwards gave to the charges of his critics applies to modern-day critics as well:

> But if God is pleased to convince the consciences of persons, so that they cannot avoid great outward manifestations, even to interrupting and breaking off those public means they were attending, I do not think this is confusion or an unhappy interruption, any more than if a company should meet on the field to pray for rain, and should be broken off from their exercise by a plentiful shower.
>
> Would to God that all the public assemblies in the land were broken off from their public exercises with such confusion as this the next Sabbath day! We need not be sorry for breaking the order of means, by obtaining the end to which that order is directed. He who is going to fetch a treasure need not be sorry that he is stopped by meeting the treasure in the midst of his journey.[13]

In other words, Edwards is saying that God may use chaotic means to bring order. Watching a person writhing on the floor while he is being delivered of a demon may not appear very orderly to an audience. But if the person is truly delivered from that demon, the result will bring God's order into that person's life.

It would be a great mistake, then, to use Paul's admonition that all things be done decently and in order to such a degree that we actually quench the fire of the Spirit.

Tests that Reveal a Genuine Work of God

Sometimes what we interpret as spiritual abuses are not abuses at all but a genuine work of the Holy Spirit. But how can we discern what is genuine from what is not?

The criticisms that Jonathan Edwards received during the Great Awakening prompted him to write his classic essay, 'The Distinguishing Marks of a Work of the Spirit of God.' In that essay, Edwards sets forth the criteria for determining what is a genuine work of the Holy Spirit. His first problem was to determine the significance of the bodily manifestations that were occurring during his meetings. He writes that

> a work is not to be judged of by any affects on the bodies of men; such as tears, tremblings, groans, loud outcries, agonies of bodies, or the failing of bodily strength. The influence persons are under is not to be judged of one way or other by such affects on the body; and the reason is because the Scripture nowhere gives us any such rule.[14]

In other words, the manifestations themselves prove nothing. The chief reason they prove nothing is that Scripture does not give us any universal rule with which to judge these manifestations. The Scriptures certainly allow that these manifestations may be legitimate reactions to a genuine work of God. But the Bible does not teach they are always genuine. In some cases the physical manifestations may not be due to the work of the Spirit at all but simply to some aspect of human nature or even demonic causes. It is also true that the Holy Spirit can do a powerful work where there are no manifestations present. People can be healed or saved without groanings, tremblings, or other observable physical phenomena. It is even possible for demons to be cast out without any of these accompanying phenomena.

The first and foremost test of any ministry, work, or teaching is whether it agrees with the teachings of Holy Scripture. However, we must be sure in these cases that the Scriptures are the standard and not our own particular interpretation of Scripture.

At one time it was common among certain fundamentalist groups to claim that women acted immodestly and violated Paul's instruction in 1 Timothy 2:9 if they used cosmetics. Today hardly anyone would agree with that interpretation of 1 Timothy 2:9. Women who wore makeup in the first part of the twentieth century did not disobey Scripture but rather a fundamentalist interpretation of Scripture. Before we pronounce a practice un-scriptural, we ought to be quite sure that it really does violate the clear, unambiguous teaching of Scripture.

Edwards concluded that when the Scriptures do not speak directly to a particular issue, the only test for determining a gen-uine work of God is *whether that work manifests the fruit of the Holy Spirit.*[15] This is precisely the test that Jesus gave us to discern between true and false prophetic ministry:

> By their fruit you will recognize them. Do people pick grapes from thornbushes, or figs from thistles? Likewise every good tree bears good fruit, but a bad tree bears bad fruit. A good tree cannot bear bad fruit, and a bad tree cannot bear good fruit. Every tree that does not bear good fruit is cut down and thrown into the fire. Thus, by their fruit you will recognize them. (Matt. 7:16–20)

Testing the fruit of a work is absolutely essential in cases where the Scriptures are silent. This test also applies in cases where people espouse correct doctrine but the fruit of their lives and ministry shows that they are not submitting to that doctrine. They may be attempting a conscious deception, or they may them-selves be deceived. In either case the fruit of their ministry will give them away.

Again, we are not to evaluate something by how bizarre or strange it may seem to us. Strangeness is not a scriptural rule to determine whether an action or ministry is from God.

Suppose we were to see a man who was an alcoholic, a wife-beater and a God-hater, shrieking at the top of his voice and then falling down motionless for twenty-four hours during a religious meeting. What if that man arose never again to drink or to hit his wife but rather began to love her as Christ loved the church and to love God and his Word? As bizarre as th at might seem to us, we would have to conclude that the Holy Spirit had been at work in his life. Neither the devil nor the flesh produces love for God, love for one's family, or freedom from addictions. Just as these kinds of things happened during the great revivals of the past, so they are happening today where people refuse to quench the fire of the Spirit.

Responding to Physical Manifestations Today

When God is pleased to give physical manifestations today, we should accept them from his hand, but we should not make the mistake of glorifying them. When we assign the manifestations great prominence and spend a good deal of time talking about them, we will invariably lead people into false beliefs and a wrong emphasis. After all, it is not the manifestation that is of ultimate significance but rather the work of the Spirit. The manifestation is merely a reaction to the Spirit's work. We want to honor the work of the Spirit in convicting, forgiving, saving, healing, and delivering—not the physical reaction to his work.

If we attach great significance to the manifestations, people will equate the manifestations with the work of the Spirit and even view them as a badge of spirituality. When that happens, insecure people often imitate these manifestations to draw attention to themselves and to appear 'spiritual.'

An equally significant mistake would be to try to suppress the manifestations. Imagine a person who is under such intense conviction by the Holy Spirit for his sins that he has an acute sense of the torments of hell and is trembling as a result of that conviction. Now imagine the immense folly of approaching a person like that and telling him to snap out of it! If we attempt to suppress a real physical manifestation of the Holy Spirit's work, we are in danger of putting out the fire of the Spirit.

Nor should we fear genuine physical manifestations. I frequently encounter Christians who have no difficulty at all in believing that demons can speak in an audible voice, prompt thoughts, produce physical sensations and other bodily effects, but they don't believe God can or would do these things today. Anytime they see one of these physical manifestations, therefore, they automatically assume that it is a work of the devil.

All fear of the devil is *irrational* fear. No Christian should ever fear Satan or any demon. The only person a Christian is taught to fear in the New Testament is God himself. If God is the cause of these manifestations, he will use them for good. If the devil is the cause of a particular manifestation, it can be stopped through the power of the blood of Christ. In either case we have no scriptural basis for fearing the physical manifestations.

Finally, we should never be disappointed when God does not give physical manifestations to accompany a genuine work of the Spirit, nor should we ever try to produce them through suggestion or any other natural means. God does not need the manifestations in order to accomplish his purposes. If we attempt to manufacture these responses, we can pollute a pure work of the Spirit and bring it to an end.

I want to offer one last bit of advice on this point. It used to bother me when I saw people 'faking' physical manifestations in meetings. That happened in Edwards' day, and it happens today. In fact, it will happen anywhere there are genuine physical manifestations in response to a powerful work by the Holy Spirit. The genuine will always be counterfeited. Sometimes the counterfeit is easy to spot, and sometimes it is not so easy. My experience with these false manifestations has led me to believe that they are not nearly as serious as I first imagined.

The kind of people who are led to *voluntarily* shake their hands or tremble at the beginning of the worship service are not normally 'dangerous' people. They are most frequently insecure and lonely believers. Throughout the week hardly anyone pays attention to them. Often the only time anyone shows them love or affection is in a meeting at church, when someone walks over to them to lay a hand on them and pray for them. They often use trembling or shaking or some other physical sign as a means of attracting attention to themselves and receiving ministry from other people in the body of Christ. I have paid close attention to this phenomena over the last few years, and I have found it to cause very little serious difficulty to anyone. Hardly anyone is fooled by it, and the only people who are really put off by it are visitors who are observing the service with little or no understanding of these matters. If the visitors are sincere and have not come just to criticize, they could always ask someone who understands the dynamics of these 'false responses' and receive an adequate explanation for what is troubling them.

In the few cases where a person's behavior is truly bizarre and exhibitionist, pastoral leaders should approach that person and gently but firmly stop that behavior. I have found that when we talk about the scriptural significance of the physical manifestations and discuss them openly there is very little abuse in this area.

8

Were Miracles Meant to Be Temporary?

N o one ever just picked up the Bible, started reading, and then came to the conclusion that God was not doing signs and wonders anymore and that the gifts of the Holy Spirit had passed away. The doctrine of cessationism did not originate from a careful study of the Scriptures. The doctrine of cessationism originated in *experience*.

The failure to see miracles in one's own experience and to locate them in past history required an explanation. How do you explain an absence of miracles in your experience when the New Testament is filled with miracles? There are essentially three possibilities. First, there is something wrong with your experience. Second, God has withdrawn miracles because he only intended them to serve temporary purposes. Third, the answer is locked in divine mystery, like the mystery of election or predestination. The first answer would lead you to expect the miraculous when your experience was corrected. The second answer wouldn't lead you to expect the miraculous at all. The third answer leaves the question open.

As far as I know, no one has ever really attempted to argue for answer three. Since the days of the Reformation, many Protestant theologians have argued for answer two, that the gifts were only temporary in nature. The Reformers had two major reasons for formulating and systematizing theological arguments against contemporary miracles. First, their enemies, the Catholics, appealed to Catholic miracles in support of Catholic doctrine. In effect they said, 'We have miracles that show God approves of our doctrine. Furthermore, we have a long history of miracles stretching back to New Testament times. What miracles can you point to that show that God approves of your doctrine?' This attack led the Reformers both to deny the validity of Catholic miracles, past and present, and to formulate theological arguments against contemporary miracles.[1]

But I believe that was not the major reason that the Reformers attempted to use the Scriptures to argue against contemporary miracles. I believe the major reason was their lack of experience of the miraculous. Had they witnessed noteworthy miracles, they would never have attempted to argue that miracles were meant to be temporary.

Thus the Reformers were confronted with a choice: was their lack of experience of the miraculous due to a defect in their experience or to a divinely planned obsolescence of miracles? They chose to believe the latter. They now had the monumental task before them of explaining why God would be so liberal in giving miracles to the first-century church and so stingy with miracles in the centuries that followed. The trick was to prove that miracles were meant only to serve temporary purposes in the first century. But how could they prove that?

They essentially had three ways of proving this. The first, and by far the best, was specific biblical statements that God intended miracles to be temporary. The second was theological deduction. This way of arguing is not as strong as specific statements of the Bible, but it is a valid way of proving doctrines. The third line of proof was experience. They could draw conclusions from their own experience or from the experience of others in past history.

Thus they could examine the preceding 1,300 years of church history to see if there was firm evidence of the gifts of the Spirit among Christians in the preceding centuries.

The argument from experience is, without a doubt, the weakest of the three kinds of arguments. When we examine past history, we often cannot be sure of the facts or the interpretation of those facts. Moreover, when we look at our own experience we may know the facts but not the *reason* for the facts. We may know, for example, that we are depressed but not know why we are depressed. Did we do something to bring on the depression? Is it a result of circumstances beyond our control? Thus, even when we can accurately ascertain the facts, we may not understand the reason for those facts.

The Reformers left no doubt which of three kinds of arguments they valued above all the others. *Sola Scriptura* ('only the Scripture') was one of the great battle cries of the Reformation. Yet here they faced not only a formidable obstacle but an insurmountable obstacle, for they could not produce one specific text of Scripture that taught that miracles or the spiritual gifts were confined to the New Testament period. Nor has anyone else since then been able to do that.[2]

Having been deprived of the most powerful weapon in their arsenal, specific statements of Scripture, the Reformers were forced to appeal to theological deductions. But how were they ever going to deduce that miracles were intended to be temporary from a book that begins with miracles, persists in miracles, and ends with miracles?

The Primary Cessationist Argument

Here is how they did it. The Reformers argued that the primary purpose of New Testament miracles was to authenticate the apostles as trustworthy authors of Holy Scripture. How would this argument prove that miracles were temporary? Because after the apostles had written the New Testament, *miracles would have fulfilled their purpose and would no longer be necessary*, for now the church would possess forever the miraculously attested written Word of God.[3] This remains the primary argument among modern cessationists.

It would be useless for cessationists to prove that the primary purpose of miracles was to authenticate Jesus. If that were true, then there would be no explanation for why the apostles did miracles. If the primary purpose of miracles was to authenticate the Lord Jesus as the Son of God, why did the apostles have to do miracles? Why couldn't they just talk about the miracles that Jesus did, as many preachers do today?

Nor can cessationists say that the major purpose of the miraculous was to authenticate the *message* about Jesus. If that were true, they would have no explanation for why miracles were not still needed to authenticate the message about Jesus. In other words, if the first-century generation of new converts needed miraculous authentication of the gospel message, why wouldn't the succeeding generations of potential converts need that same miraculous authentication of the message?

The only defensible position is to maintain that miracles authenticated the apostles. If someone asks why only the apostles needed authentication for their witness to be credible and not the succeeding generations of witnesses, the cessationists have an answer ready at hand. The apostles were not just any witnesses. They were unique in that they were the writers of Holy Scripture. Therefore, more would be required to give them credibility than any other witnesses in history. So the purpose of miracles was not simply to authenticate the apostles as reliable witnesses to Jesus. Miracles showed them to be trustworthy teachers of doctrine and ultimately authenticated them as the divinely accredited human authors of Scripture. In practical terms this means that the real purpose of miracles was to authenticate or confirm the Scriptures. Once they had written the Scriptures, miracles would no longer be necessary, for now the church would possess the written Word of God.

In order to make their case, cessationists have to prove two things. First, they have to show that miracles authenticated the apostles. Second, they have to demonstrate that this was the *primary* purpose of miracles. If it could be shown that miracles did not authenticate the apostles or that there were other equally important purposes behind miracles or the miraculous gifts of the Spirit, then their whole case collapses.

Like most people in my theological circles, I had accepted the cessationists' explanation of the purpose of miracles, especially as it received its formulation in Benjamin Breckenridge Warfield's *Counterfeit Miracles*. Like other fundamentalists, I was sure that I believed this because it was what the Scriptures taught.

When I look back on that period of my life, I know that I did not believe this because the Scriptures taught it. I believed it because I hadn't seen any miracles, and I needed a biblical justification for my lack of experience. That twenty-minute phone call with Dr. White led me to examine the cessationists' argument with a much more open mind. This time I found the argument to have about as much strength as a sparrow in a hurricane. What I thought was my strongest argument against the contemporary ministry of miraculous gifts turned out to be my 'strongest weakness.'

After my first conversation with Dr. White, I was determined to look up every reference to healing and miracles in the New Testament to see exactly what it said about the purpose of miracles. I had never done that before! What I found convinced me that healing and miracles were *not* meant to be temporary.

A Closer Look at Miracles

The first thing I noticed was that there are very few direct statements in the New Testament regarding the purposes of miracles.
I never found a statement to the effect that 'God gave miracles in
order to . . .' I discovered that the purpose of miracles is sometimes indicated by 'function' words accompanying the miracles
themselves. Mark, for example, says that miracles 'confirm'
(Mark 16:20). John says that they 'testify' (John 5:36). Peter says
that Jesus was 'accredited' by miracles (Acts 2:22). At other times
the purpose of a miracle must often be inferred from the context
or from the results of the miracle.

One clear purpose of miracles was to authenticate the charac-
ter of Jesus and his relationship with his heavenly Father. In this
regard, miracles demonstrate the following: God is with Jesus
(John 3:2); Jesus is from God (John 3:2; 9:32–33); God has sent
Jesus (John 5:36); Jesus has authority on earth to forgive sins
(Mark 2:10–11; Matt. 9:6–7; Luke 5:24–25); Jesus is approved by
God (Acts 2:22); the Father is in Jesus and Jesus is in the Father
(John 10:37–38; 14:11); in Jesus the kingdom of God has come
(Matt. 12:28; Luke 11:20); and Jesus is the Messiah (Matt.
11:1–6; Luke 7:18–23) and the Son of God (Matt. 14:25–33).

A second purpose of miracles was to authenticate the message
about Jesus. This was the major function of the miracles as far as
the ministry of the apostles was concerned. Mark says that the
Lord 'confirmed his word [that the apostles preached] by the
signs that accompanied it' (Mark 16:20).[4] When Luke was
describing the ministry of Paul and Barnabas at Iconium, he said
that the Lord 'confirmed the message of his grace by enabling
them to do miraculous signs and wonders' (Acts 14:3). Notice that
in both of these texts the Lord does not confirm the apostles
themselves but rather 'his word' or 'the message' that the apostles were preaching. Signs and wonders do not testify to the

apostles but to the message of salvation preached by the apostles. So the two principal things that are authenticated by miracles are the Lord Jesus and the message about the Lord Jesus.

When I looked up all of these references, I was astounded to discover that not one reference ever said that miracles bore witness[5] to the apostles, confirmed[6] the apostles, or attested to the apostles. In short, miracles do *not* authenticate the apostles! And if we think about the theology of the New Testament, this makes perfect sense. With the coming of Jesus Christ, God wants all attention directed to his Son. The primary task of the Holy Spirit is to exalt Jesus Christ. God is not interested in bearing witness to his servants but rather to his Son and the message about his Son.

The Argument from 2 Corinthians 12:12

Sometimes people appeal to 2 Corinthians 12:12 as a text that seems to say that signs and wonders authenticate the apostles. The translation of the NIV does give that impression: 'The things that mark an apostle—signs, wonders and miracles—were done among you with great perseverance.' This translation, however, is inaccurate. A literal translation is, 'The signs of an apostle were performed among you in all endurance with signs and wonders and miracles.'

In this passage Paul uses 'sign' (semeion) in two different ways. The first use of 'sign' in the phrase 'signs of an apostle' cannot refer to miracles, for then Paul would be saying that 'the miracles of an apostle were done among you with signs and wonders and miracles.' What would be the point of such a statement? Paul does not say that 'the signs of an apostle' *are* miracles, but rather that 'the signs of an apostle' are *accompanied by* signs, wonders, and miracles.[7] If Paul had meant that the signs of his apostleship were signs and wonders and miracles, then he would have used a different construction in the Greek language.[8]

What then were the signs of Paul's apostleship? In contrast to the false apostles (2 Cor. 11:13–15), Paul appeals to his suffering as a vindication of his apostleship (2 Cor. 11:16–33, cf. Gal. 6:17; 1 Cor. 4:9–13; 2 Cor. 6:3–10).[9] Hughes suggests that Paul's blameless life was a sign of his apostleship.[10] Plummer suggests that the effectiveness of Paul's preaching, that is, the many conversions among those to whom Paul preached, was also a sign of his apostleship.[11] In addition to these signs, Martin adds the call of God (1 Cor. 1:1; 2 Cor. 1:1).[12] According to Martin, since miracles can be counterfeited by false apostles,

> Paul is insisting in 12:12a that such signs are not the primary criterion for deciding whether or not a person is an apostle. Instead, he is suggesting that the true signs of apostleship—his life and ministry—are the signs that matter the most. . . . To say that 'signs and wonders and mighty works' are the primary signs of apostleship goes against Paul's teachings of chaps. 11–13 (as well as chaps. 1–9).[13]

I agree with Martin's conclusion that 'the works of Paul (in 12:12b) are the workings of, and not the proof for, his authentic apostleship.'[14]

When I really began to ponder the idea that the miracles were given to authenticate the apostles and their ministry, I saw that it was not only unscriptural but illogical. If the primary purpose of signs and wonders and miracles was to confirm the apostles, then why did Stephen and Philip do signs and wonders? If someone says that it was because the apostles laid hands on Stephen and Philip, that doesn't really answer the question. If the primary purpose of miracles was to authenticate the apostles, then why did any one else have a ministry of signs and wonders or miracles? Why did God give gifts of healing and miracles to the church? (1 Cor. 12:7–10; Gal. 3:5). I have never read or heard of a sufficient answer to that question.

There is yet another serious problem with this whole argument.

Let's review a point made earlier: If Jesus' miracles were sufficient to authenticate him as the Son of God and to authenticate his message, why did the apostles have to do miracles? The standard reply is that the apostles had to do miracles to show that they were trustworthy witnesses to Jesus Christ and trustworthy teachers of doctrine. But why couldn't they just preach about the miracles as much of the church does today? Can't we be regarded as trustworthy witnesses today without doing miracles? If we can, then why did the apostles need miracles? The Reformers replied that the apostles were more than just witnesses, they were inspired writers of inerrant Scripture. Miracles were necessary to confirm their writings as Scripture. This is the assumption lying at the bottom of the whole argument, but is it a biblical assumption? Were miracles necessary to confirm the Scriptures?

Does the Authority of Scripture Rest on Miracles?

None of the writers of Scripture ever appealed to miracles to support their claims that they were writing Scripture. They certainly knew that they were writing Scripture. For instance, Paul wrote, 'If anybody thinks he is a prophet or spiritually gifted, let him acknowledge that what I am writing to you is the Lord's command' (1 Cor. 14:37, cf. 1 Thess. 4:15). However, Paul did not appeal to the miracles in his ministry to support the fact that he was writing Scripture. Nor did Peter, when he referred to Paul's writings as Scripture (2 Pet. 3:16).

No text of Scripture says that the authority of Scripture rests on miracles! In reality, it is just the opposite. Scripture tests miracles, but miracles are not a test for Scripture. Moses made this plain long ago. He warned the people that if a prophet or a dreamer of dreams gave them a sign or a wonder, and it came to pass, they were to *ignore* that miracle if it contradicted what had already been revealed to them (Deut. 13:1–5). If the primary function of miracles was to confirm Scripture, how would anyone judge the miracles of false prophets (Matt. 7:15–23), false christs and their prophets (Matt. 24:24), or the Antichrist (2 Thess. 2:9)?

This theory is also inconsistent with the actual character of the canon of Scripture. We have authors of Scripture who were not apostles and who never did any recorded miracles! These include Mark, Luke, and Jude (the brother of the Lord who wrote the letter of Jude). The book of Hebrews is even anonymous! All of these writers were non-apostles, and none of them have recorded miracles. Do these books have less authority than Paul's letters? If the authority of Scripture rests on miracles done by its authors, then these writings would of necessity have less authority.

If those who hold this theory respond that Luke was a friend or a partner with Paul in ministry, and that is why his writing is to be viewed as inspired, then they would have to abandon the idea that miracles were needed to confirm Scripture. They would have to add a new criterion for canonicity: friendship or partnership with the apostles. This criterion for canonicity also lacks any direct scriptural support. If they argue that Peter commissioned Mark to write the gospel of Mark, they are now relying on tradition rather than Scripture itself. That puts them in the awkward place of having tradition establish the authority of Scripture rather than Scripture being our ultimate authority.

In any case, we have five works that constitute a very large portion of Scripture—the Gospel of Mark, the Gospel of Luke, the book of Acts, the letter of Jude, and the book of Hebrews—that cannot be explained by the theory that miracles were necessary to authenticate the Bible.

Orthodox theology has long held that the authority of Scripture does not rest on miracles. The authority of Scripture rests on its Author.[15] Although there may be a number of factors that help to convince us of the authority of Scripture, we are ultimately persuaded of its authority by the inward testimony of the Holy Spirit.[16]

Were Miracles Needed to Launch the Church?

Some people teach that miracles were necessary for the gospel message to gain a hearing in the first century. They see the miracles and healings of Jesus and the apostles as a sort of rocket booster to get the church 'launched' and to get the gospel message an audience. Later, after the church was established and the gospel message had a place among other world religions, then the rocket booster could be jettisoned without any great loss to the church.

Thomas Edgar expresses this view when he writes,

The beginning Church was in a different situation from that of the Church after the first century. By the end of the first century the Church and Christianity were established in the major centers of the known world . . . The initial stages of Christianity, however, had no background from the human perspective. The message was unusual and astounding. A man executed in a very small country was presented as the Son of God, who came to die for all men; to those who trusted in Him, God would surely by grace forgive their sins. Few people outside Israel had ever heard of Jesus. He died before the Church was established. He was executed after a brief career. Such facts at least show the difficulty faced by the early evangelists. Who could accept such a message?

However, the miraculous sign gifts put this whole message in a different perspective, since the miracles were evidence that the message was from God. The situation since the first century has never been the same. Missionaries going to jungle areas are referring to an individual with a reputation in the world, to a recognized religion and religious Figure, as far as the world is concerned. These missionaries come from groups of believers in countries where this religion is prevalent. It may be considered helpful by many to have miraculous confirmation of this gospel today. This may or may not be true, since full and well-testified confirmation has already been given by Christ and the apostles and is still ignored by those who live in countries where it is well known. There can be little doubt, however, that the need for confirmation at the beginning was greater than the need for this today.[17]

In other words, the infant church needed miracles to help it grow up, but the mature church no longer needs them. This argument has a contradiction in it which Edgar does not attempt to resolve. If the church in the first century needed miracles for its growth and extension, why would it not need them in the twentieth century? If miracles were beneficial to the church then, why not now? Long ago Warfield charged that this explanation was unscriptural.[18] Indeed, during his whole discussion Edgar does not cite one verse of Scripture to support his theory. Warfield also pointed out that this line of reasoning was illogical and ridiculed it as 'helpless.'[19]

Edgar's explanation is also false because it substitutes worldly recognition for God's power. Edgar maintains that after Christianity 'had become a *recognized* group with some *reputation*' (emphasis mine), it no longer needed the power of miracles. Who would want to trade the miraculous power of God for worldly reputation? Warfield answered a slightly different form of this theory when he wrote, 'When the protection of the strongest power on earth was secured [i.e., the Roman empire] the idea seemed to be the power of God was no longer needed.'[20] Where in the Scriptures can anyone find support for such an idea?

Finally, there is something else in this argument that is troubling to me. I have already stated that one of the legitimate functions of the miracles of the Lord and the apostles was to authenticate or testify to Jesus and the message about him. But were miracles ever *necessary* in order for people to believe in the gospel? Edgar writes as though they were, at least in the beginning of the church. Why? According to Edgar the historical obscurity and novelty of the gospel message seemed to have required miracles to prove it. He asks, 'Who could accept such a message?' This is dangerously close to demeaning the inherent power of the gospel message. Surely the gospel which 'is the power of God for salvation' was sufficient apart from miracles. Surely God did not *have to do* miracles in order to achieve his ends.

The greatest miracle in the world is that God loves us and his Son died for us. His love for us is, and forever will remain, an inexplicable mystery. The most amazing supernatural event ever to occur was the incarnation and then the death of the eternal Son in the place of sinful humanity, followed by his bodily resurrection. Surely the greatest wonder is that by faith alone in Jesus Christ we receive the gift of eternal life. Surely the greatest power any human will ever know is the power of the cross of Jesus Christ. Through the cross we not only have forgiveness but also access into God's glorious presence.

The power of Christ's death is so great that no Christian has to live under any moral bondage. No Christian has to be at the mercy of lust, anger, sin, fear, death, or Satan. Surely this good news is the greatest news that has ever been given. Surely this message is greater than any miracles accompanying it. Surely the gospel is capable of capturing the hearts of people without requiring any accompanying miracles!

When I was seventeen years old and committed to rebellion, my heart was completely captured by Jesus when I heard a friend tell me about the inexplicable grace of the gospel. I knew nothing of the rest of the New Testament, nothing of the other miracles, and yet that night, December 18, 1965, at 2:00 A.M., by faith alone in the Lord Jesus Christ I became a new creation. That is exactly what the apostle Paul said the gospel message would do. He wrote:

I am not ashamed of the gospel, because it is the power of God for the salvation of everyone who believes: first for the Jew, then for the Gentile. For in the gospel a righteousness from God is revealed, a righteousness that is by faith from first to last, just as it is written: 'The righteous will live by faith' (Rom. 1:16–17).

Paul had supreme confidence in the great and glorious gospel of Jesus Christ. He did not put his confidence in miracles, in human ability, or even in human godliness. This message is the most glorious message ever heard by human ears. It is the only answer to the human dilemma.

Edgar says, 'Who could accept such a message?' For one, Lydia and her family had no trouble at all accepting this message as they heard Paul preach it without any accompanying miracles (Acts 16:14–15). In the first century the Holy Spirit was perfectly capable of producing conviction and belief without miracles (John 16:8). John the Baptist's ministry also brought conviction and repentance, but John did no miracles (John 10:41). Even the world religions and cults have been born and are flourishing without the power of miracles. Do we seriously want to claim anything less for the power of the gospel of Jesus Christ?

I believe that miracles do have an authenticating function, and later I will argue that they can open wide doors for preaching the gospel and even bring people to repentance. However, the simple preaching of the gospel could do all of these things without miracles at *any* time in history and can still do them today. When miracles are given by God to authenticate gospel preaching, it is done on the basis of grace, not out of a divine necessity to make up for a deficiency in the gospel message. Miracles are a gracious gift from God which may serve *many* functions, but we should never isolate one function and view it as the ultimate and necessary purpose of miracles unless we have clear biblical evidence for doing so.

Using the Gospels and Acts to Support Miracles Today

It has been said that we cannot use the Gospels and Acts as evidence that God heals or works miracles today because they are 'transition' books. Acts gives us the record of the transition from the Old Testament era to the New Testament era. Acts shows the church in its infancy, its immaturity. Therefore, we cannot determine what is supposed to be normal in church life based on the book of Acts. All we can determine is what was normal in the immaturity of the church. Above all, we cannot draw doctrine from the book of Acts—or so the argument goes. Doctrine for the church is to be drawn from the epistles of Paul.

If this argument were valid, it would actually mean that the Gospels and Acts would tell us nothing about Jesus' attitude toward healing and miracles today. It would only reflect his attitude at the beginning of the church's birth. This argument is false for a number of reasons.

First, theologians have always used the Gospels and Acts for doctrine. For example, since Calvin's day Reformed theologians have been delighted to use John 6:44 and Acts 13:48 to prove the doctrine of unconditional election. Likewise, dispensationalists appeal to the Gospels and to Acts to support their dispensationalism. John 1:17 is used by dispensationalists to prove there is a clear distinction between the dispensations of law and grace. Professors of missions and evangelists regularly use the Gospels and Acts to teach doctrines of missions and evangelism. The Gospels and Acts are major sources for our doctrine of Christology. They are primary sources for the study of how the New Testament uses the Old Testament. The book of Acts is also crucial in determining what we believe about church government (cf. Acts 20:17ff.). It is simply not true that we cannot use the Gospels and Acts for doctrine. Everyone does it.

What this argument really means is that we may not use the

Gospels and Acts to determine doctrine about supernatural events in the life of the church today. In other words, people who use this argument are actually employing an antisupernatural hermeneutic when they read the book of Acts.

Let me explain what I mean by this and then illustrate it.

Hermeneutics is the science of interpretation. It deals with the rules of interpretation, that is, how we ought to interpret the Scriptures (or any written text, for that matter). An antisupernatural hermeneutic is a system of interpretation that eliminates the supernatural elements of the Bible. German liberal theologians such as Bultmann did this by 'demythologizing' the New Testament miracles. They claimed the miracles did not occur at all; they were stories invented to give expression to myths that had been current in the ancient Near East. Conservative writers who would never dream of treating the Scriptures in this cavalier manner have another way of employing an antisupernatural hermeneutic. They have a system of reading the Bible which says that all the miracles occurred back then, but they are not meant for today.

For example, when one of my students would tell me he wanted to become a missionary and plant churches because he was inspired to do this as he read Paul's story in the book of Acts, I would give him my blessing. I had no problem believing that God would use Paul's story in Acts to inspire a student to become a missionary and plant churches. I thought this was a valid use of Scripture. But if that same student were to tell me that after reading the book of Acts he wanted God to use him in a healing ministry, I would have immediately corrected him. I would have told him that this was a false use of the Scripture. In other words, I employed a system of interpretation that said, 'You are free to copy the nonmiraculous elements in the Gospels and Acts, but you are not free to copy the miraculous elements.'

I was reading the Gospels and Acts through the lens of an

antisupernatural hermeneutic. Every time I came upon a miraculous story, these lenses agreed that the story happened, but they filtered out any present-day miraculous application of that passage.

How does one justify this antisupernatural hermeneutic? Where in the Scriptures are we told to read the Bible like this? Where in the Scriptures are we given a hermeneutic that says you may copy the things that are nonmiraculous, but you cannot copy or expect the miraculous events for today?

This argument is false for a second reason. In the ancient world, especially in the ancient Near Eastern world of which the Bible is a part, the most common way to communicate theology was to tell a story. Stories were written to communicate theological doctrine. Sometimes modern writers treat the Gospels and Acts as if they were nothing more than 'newspaper' accounts of what happened. They are definitely more than this; they are themselves theologies. When Luke wrote his Gospel and the book of Acts, he selected all of his material very carefully to teach definite theological truths to his audience.[21]

This is still common today in the East. I just returned from a large conference in Singapore, and one of the pastors there told me that it was very common for one of the Chinese Christian fathers in his church to answer his child's theological question with a story. When we think about how much both the Old and New Testament consist of narrative literature, we are forced to conclude that God also liked this method of teaching theology.

In my copy of the King James New Testament, the Gospels and Acts take up 205 pages, the Pauline Epistles 87 pages, other epistles 34 pages, and Revelation 22 pages. The Gospels and Acts make up 59 percent of the New Testament. All of the Epistles together make up 35 percent. If the argument were true that we cannot use the Gospels and Acts as sources of doctrine, that would mean we would have to discard virtually 59 percent of the

New Testament as doctrinally worthless. That would give us only 35 percent of the New Testament from which to determine our doctrines!

Of course, nobody really believes this. They only mean you cannot use the Gospels and Acts to determine the relevance of miracles for the church's present ministry, and this is a completely arbitrary decision. It is not based on the teaching of the Bible but rather on a personal prejudice.

A third reason that this argument is false is because it contradicts Scripture. The apostle Paul said that 'All Scripture is given by inspiration of God, and is profitable for doctrine[!], for reproof, for correction, for instruction in righteousness' (2 Tim. 3:16 KJV). Paul said *all Scripture*—not just the Epistles but the Gospels and Acts—is profitable for teaching.

The argument contradicts Scripture in another way. At least six times in Paul's writings he either commands Christians to follow his example as he follows Christ's example, or he approves of those who follow his example (1 Cor. 4:16–17; 11:1; Phil. 3:17; 4:9; 1 Thess. 1:6; 2 Thess. 3:9). Paul did not make a distinction between those elements in his life that were miraculous and those that are not viewed as miraculous. Paul copied Christ. Christ had miraculous elements in his life, and so did Paul. Are we only to imitate those nonmiraculous elements in the lives of Jesus and Paul? Are they simply to be examples for moral living but not for miraculous ministry? Paul makes no such distinction when he exhorts us to imitate him.

We must remember that the only inspired record we have, or ever will have of church history is the book of Acts! This is the only period of church history where we can be absolutely sure that our record is one hundred percent accurate. It is the only period of church history where we can be absolutely certain of God's opinion of the church's life and ministry.

The book of Acts is the *best* source that we have to demonstrate what normal church life is supposed to look like when the Holy Spirit is present and working in the church. Here we find a church that has passion for God, is willing to sacrifice—even to the point of martyrdom—and is a miracle-working church. Why would we think that God wants the church to be something different today? Would anyone seriously rather have the church in Calvin's day or the church in twentieth-century America as the model of normal church life?

Remember a point mentioned earlier: If you take a new convert, who prior to his conversion knew nothing about the history of Christianity or the New Testament, and you lock him in a room with a Bible for a week, he will come out believing that he is a member of a body that is passionately in love with the Lord Jesus Christ and a body that consistently experiences miracles and works miracles. It would take a clever theologian with no experience of the miraculous to convince this young convert differently.

———————————————

Whatever purposes we assign to the miracles of the New Testament period, we cannot say that God did them out of *necessity* to make up for deficiencies surrounding the initial preaching of the gospel. The healings and miracles were entirely gracious on God's part. The gospel could have and would have been believed apart from any miracles. Nor can we say that God did miracles to authenticate the apostles or to prove the authority of Scripture.

Yet the entire New Testament—including the Gospels and Acts—reveals that God did do miracles, he did heal people, and he had important purposes for these activities. We will explore these purposes more fully in the next two chapters.

9

Why Does God Heal?

Over eighteen years ago we found out on a Friday afternoon that my wife was pregnant with the little baby who would become our firstborn son. We had a great celebration on Friday night with our family, but on Saturday morning Leesa had to be rushed to the doctor because her body was threatening to miscarry the child. The doctor, who was also a good friend, said, 'I have to be honest with you. I know how much you want this child, but most likely this pregnancy is going to end in a miscarriage. I will give you the appropriate medicine, and I will send you home to rest, but I don't think any of this is going to help. I don't want you to get your hopes up.'

We sat on the couch in our little apartment later that day and just cried. We went through all the emotions associated with such a tragedy. But in the midst of my sorrow I thought, 'Wait a minute. I don't take one man's opinion in theology; why should I take one man's opinion in medicine?'

I had another friend who was a medical doctor and who lived in another state. He had written a textbook on gynecology. I called my friend and said, 'We have just come from the doctor, and he says Leesa may have a miscarriage. I want your opinion.'

'What are her symptoms,' my friend asked.

I then listed her symptoms.

'She has been diagnosed correctly. There is an eighty percent chance that even if this child were born he would be so physically deformed or mentally deficient that you would spend much of the rest of your life and money trying to care for him. Most likely Leesa is going to have a miscarriage, and ultimately that may prove to be a blessing from the Lord. You are both young, and you will be able to have other children. If you weren't Christians, I would just tell you this is nature's way of eliminating something that is not strong enough to survive. But since you are Christians, I am telling you that I think God is sparing you a great deal of suffering and expense by allowing this baby to be miscarried.'

Eighteen years ago I took comfort in those words and resigned myself to losing the child. Today, with what I know of God's nature, purposes, and power, I would never take comfort in words like that, nor would I resign myself to losing a child. But in those days I was a different person with a smaller theology and a lot more restrictions on God.

I hung up the phone and walked back in the room to Leesa. I wanted her to draw comfort from these same words. She was still sitting on the couch crying. Her face was red and swollen, her nose was running, and her eyes were almost swollen shut. I said, 'Leesa, it's going to be O.K. I just talked to another doctor.' Then I related to her everything our friend had just told me over the phone. But it was as though Leesa didn't hear a word I said.

I thought that she was too upset to listen. So I moved closer to her and repeated more loudly everything I had just told her. She still refused to acknowledge me. At that point I started to get angry, because she simply wasn't listening to reason.

But her anger interrupted mine. Even though her eyes were almost swollen shut, anger flashed out of them like lightning. She said, 'I don't care what you say. There is no way I can believe that losing this little baby would be a blessing. I love this baby with all my heart. The worst thing in the world that could happen to me

would be to lose this child. I don't care how defective this child is
or how this child is born. I will spend the rest of my life caring for
this baby if God will just let me have him.'

I was dumbfounded. I also had the feeling that I was standing
on holy ground. I decided that it would be better not to say anything else, even though I could not enter into or even understand
my wife's feelings for this little baby.

How could she feel this way about that unborn child? She had
only known she was pregnant for a little over twenty-four hours.
In the space of that twenty-four hours, all this child had done for
her was to make her sick and to threaten her life. And now she
says that for her the worst thing in the world would be to lose the
child? Where did she get that kind of love? Where did that kind
of compassion come from? As I sat there stunned, pondering
these questions, the word *raham* exploded in my brain like a bullet from an angelic sniper.

The major way to express God's compassion in the Old Testament was to use the Hebrew word *raham*, 'womb.'[1] Why in the
world did the Hebrews pick the word 'womb' to express God's
compassion? Most likely it came from a Hebrew husband's
observing the intense feelings his pregnant wife had for the
unborn infant inside her womb. He knew she had feelings and a
love for that child that he could not yet experience.

In my spirit I looked up to heaven and said, 'God, this is not just
how my wife feels about her unborn child, this is how you feel
about us, isn't it?'

You see, we are just like that infant in the womb. We are
morally helpless and totally dependent on God for our very lives.
The child that Leesa was carrying had caused her pain and threatened her life. We, too, have caused God pain. Not only have we
threatened the life of his Son but we actually took his Son's life.
Yet our heavenly Father can still be touched by our pain. He hates
the loss of even one of his 'little ones' (Matt. 18:6). Because God

is compassionate, he has an intense longing for his people and desires to help them in all of their difficulties.

When some people try to tell me that God no longer heals, or that he only heals rarely, I want to ask them, 'Where has the Lord's compassion gone? Does Jesus Christ no longer walk among our churches? Does he no longer notice our pain? Does he no longer care for the families who have loved ones in mental hospitals, or whose babies are born with twisted bodies?' I don't think his compassion has changed at all. I think he is just as willing as he was in the first century to touch both our spirits and our bodies. I think it is the church that has changed, not God.

In this chapter we will explore not only God's compassion but also some of the other reasons why he healed in the past and continues to heal today.

God Heals Out of Compassion and Mercy

The healing ministry of Jesus was motivated by compassion. A typical incident is recorded in Matthew 14:13–14:

> When Jesus heard what had happened, he withdrew by boat privately to a solitary place. Hearing of this, the crowds followed him on foot from the towns. When Jesus landed and saw a large crowd, he had compassion on them and healed their sick.

Compassion motivated Jesus to heal lepers (Mark 1:41–42), the demonized youth (Mark 9:22), the blind (Matt. 20:34), and even to raise the dead (Luke 7:11–17). In Matthew the feeding of the four thousand is motivated not by a desire on Jesus' part to demonstrate that he is the bread of life, but rather by his compassion for the multitude (Matt. 15:32). Likewise, Jesus healed the blind (Matt. 9:27–31; 20:29–34), the demonized (Matt. 15:22–28; 17:14–21) and the lepers (Luke 17:13–14) in response to their cries for mercy. Even the healing of the most severely demon-possessed person in the New Testament is attributed ultimately to God's mercy (Mark 5:19).

The sheer number of the texts just mentioned demonstrates that God's compassion and mercy were major factors in the healings of the New Testament.[2] As Jesus walked the dusty roads of Palestine, he was touched by the pains and the sicknesses of people all around him. He did not shrink back in disgust from those whose bodies were filled with leprosy. He actually put his hands on their infected bodies and healed them. He could be moved in his spirit as he watched a funeral procession where they were carrying out a widow's only son. When they brought the lame and the blind and the maimed to him, he was not aloof from their pain. He did not give them theological platitudes; he *healed* them.

Understanding Christ's compassion for the sick and hurting has great practical ramifications. I frequently meet people who are enthusiastic about praying for the sick. They devote a significant amount of their time each week to praying for hurting people. But some of them see very little healing taking place. After talking with them for a while, it is not difficult to see why they have so little success. Often their primary motivation in praying for the sick is to see something exciting, something supernatural, or to prove to their theological opponents that God does heal after all.

These are not New Testament motivations for healing. God is not in the business of gratifying our desires for excitement nor in helping some of his children win arguments over others. He is in the compassion business. To the degree that you can enter into his compassion for the sick and for the hurting, you can be a vessel through whom the healing power of Jesus can flow. If you really want to be used in a healing ministry, ask your heavenly Father to let you feel his compassion for the hurting.

To argue that Jesus has withdrawn his healing ministry from the church today is to argue that he has also withdrawn his compassion from the church. But if we believe in a compassionate

Savior, we ought to have confidence in his desire to heal in the church today.

God Heals to Glorify Himself and His Son

Sometimes the stated purpose for healing is to bring glory to God. That was one of the primary purposes in raising Lazarus from the dead. Jesus told the disciples, 'This sickness will not end in death. No, it is for God's glory so that God's Son may be glorified through it' (John 11:4). And then he said to Martha, 'Did I not tell you that if you believed, you would see the glory of God?' (John 11:40). Of course, this miracle also demonstrated that Jesus is the resurrection and life, but the *stated* purpose is that God might be glorified. Actually, these two purposes are not in contradiction. When Jesus raised Lazarus from the dead, he demonstrated that he was the resurrection and the life, and this demonstration brought great glory to God and to the Son of God.

The same purpose is also seen in apostolic healings. Peter explained the healing of the lame man at the temple gate called Beautiful in the following way:

> When Peter saw this [the people's wonder and amazement over the miracle that had just taken place], he said to them: 'Men of Israel, why does this surprise you? Why do you stare at us as if by our own power or godliness we had made this man walk? The God of Abraham, Isaac and Jacob, the God of our fathers, *has glorified his servant Jesus*. You handed him over to be killed, and you disowned him before Pilate, though he had decided to let him go. (Acts 3:12–13, emphasis mine)

This healing achieved its intended effect, for Luke later says that 'they were all glorifying God for what had happened' (Acts 4:21 NASB).

This was a normal response among people who observed the miraculous ministry of Jesus. They frequently responded by praising and glorifying the God of Israel. For example, Matthew tells us,

And great multitudes came to Him, bringing with them those who were lame, crippled, blind, dumb, and many others, and they laid them down at His feet; and He healed them, so that the multitude marveled as they saw the dumb speaking, the crippled restored, and the lame walking, and the blind seeing; *and they glorified the God of Israel.* (Matt. 15:30–31 NASB, emphasis mine)

This is a major theme in Luke's gospel. The people glorified God when they saw Jesus heal the paralytic lowered through the roof (Luke 5:24–26), when Jesus raised the widow of Nain's son from the dead (Luke 7:16), when he healed the woman bent over double by a spirit (Luke 13:13, 17) and when he healed the blind man (Luke 18:42–43). Luke brings this theme to a fitting conclusion at the triumphal entry of the Lord Jesus when he writes, 'When he came near the place where the road goes down the Mount of Olives, the whole crowd of disciples began joyfully to praise God in loud voices for all the miracles they had seen' (Luke 19:37).

Jesus actually expected people who received the healing power of God to glorify him. After healing the ten lepers and seeing that only one returned to give thanks, Jesus said, 'Were there not ten cleansed? But the nine—where are they? Was no one found who turned back to give glory to God, except this foreigner?' (Luke 17:17–18 NASB).

The nature miracles of the Lord Jesus also served to glorify God. When he turned water into wine, John says that this 'revealed his glory' (John 2:11).[3] All of these texts demonstrate that miracles were given not only to authenticate Jesus and his message but also to bring glory to God the Father and God the Son.

Like God's compassion, this purpose is not rooted in some temporary historical circumstance. God has always been concerned to bring glory to himself and to his Son. Healing today serves the same function. I have observed on many occasions that when

God heals someone, whether publicly or privately, in a hospital room or at home, people respond by glorifying and praising God.

This theme of glorifying the Lord through healings and miracles was prominent in the ministry of William Duma. This man was a famous black South African preacher who was used in many notable miracles and healings until his death in 1977. Duma's reputation was so great that white people visited his church seeking to be healed by Jesus Christ. This was in a time and place when it was not acceptable for whites to visit black churches.

Duma was a very holy man who went on an annual twenty-one-day fast in complete solitude to gain direction for the coming year from the Lord for his ministry. Yet he would not credit his holiness as the secret of his healing ministry. The title of his biography, *Take Your Glory, Lord*, reveals the real secret. When he laid his hands on the sick to pray for them, his dominant thought was that the Lord would be glorified. The Lord honored that desire with many notable miracles, including raising a young girl from the dead.[4]

This brings me to one of the most common hindrances to healing in the church today. I see many people who want to have a healing ministry in their church. Often they tell me that when they lay their hands on sick people to pray for them, they are worried about how foolish they will look if God doesn't heal the sick person. This is especially true when people first begin to pray for the sick.

Worrying about how we look when we pray for the sick is not a very effective way of getting our prayers answered. That is because God is not primarily concerned about how we look. He allowed his Son to appear foolish to the world when he died on the cross (1 Cor. 1:18–25). He also allowed his apostles to be made spectacles before the whole universe (1 Cor. 4:9–13). Why would we think that God is concerned about our reputation when he let the apostles appear as 'fools for Christ' (1 Cor. 4:10). He isn't going to heal someone to keep us from looking foolish. He will, however, heal someone to bring glory to his Son. The Scriptures demonstrate this, and so does the experience of men and women who have been used to heal in miraculous ways.

I went through this fear when I first began to pray for the sick. I wondered what my colleagues at seminary might think of me. I also wondered what my friends in the church would think of me. For many years I had taught them that God rarely, if ever, healed through supernatural means in our time. What would they think of me if I began to pray for the sick, and people did not get healed?

In those early days the Lord 'made a deal' with me. It was as though he said, 'If you won't take the credit when someone gets healed, then you won't have to take the blame when they don't get healed.' In other words, if we will be careful to give the Lord glory for every healing, every miracle, and every answer to prayer, then he is willing to take all the blame for those who don't get healed.

Actually, one of the clues that some present-day healing ministries are in significant trouble is the celebrity status given to and accepted by those who have been used in significant healings. Frequently, naive and misguided Christians show great deference to those who have been used in a healing ministry—or those who have a *reputation* for having a healing ministry. Sometimes ministers and evangelists encourage this practice by telling great stories in which they themselves are the center of attention rather than the Lord Jesus. This giving and receiving of glory among themselves can bring harm or even destruction to those involved in this process (see the Lord's rebuke to the Pharisees in John 5:44).

I believe that some people who advertise great healing ministries are frauds. I believe that others, at the beginning of their ministry, were used in a significant way by the Lord for healing and miracles. But along the way they allowed themselves to become deceived, and now they are promoting themselves more than the Son of God. That kind of promotion may get large crowds and bring in significant amounts of money, but it does not please the Lord. Eventually those who promote themselves will lose their ministries and their intimacy with the Lord.

If you want to be used by the Lord in a significant way when you pray for the sick, cultivate a desire to see the Son of God glorified. Wanting only the Son's glory is the most effective way I know to keep ourselves from being deceived and led into error.

God Heals in Response to Faith

A woman who had a hemorrhage for twelve years sneaked up behind Jesus, touched the edge of his cloak, and then was instantly healed of her hemorrhage. Jesus, having felt power leave his body, turned to find the woman. When he found her, he said to her, 'Take heart, daughter, your faith has healed you' (Matt. 9:22). It was the faith of a Canaanite woman that moved Jesus to heal her demonized daughter. He said to her, 'Woman, you have great faith! Your request is granted' (Matt. 15:28). What motivated the Lord Jesus to heal the paralytic who was lowered through the roof at Capernaum? The Scripture says that 'when Jesus saw their faith,' (Matt. 9:2), he healed the paralytic.[5]

This same principle of God's healing in response to faith is found in the ministry of the apostles. Luke records that

> in Lystra there sat a man crippled in his feet, who was lame from birth and had never walked. He listened to Paul as he was speaking. Paul looked directly at him, saw that he had faith to be healed and called out, 'Stand up on your feet!' At that, the man jumped up and began to walk. (Acts 14:8–10)

The New Testament clearly teaches that God responds to faith for healing.

Three healing stories in the ministry of Jesus are of particular significance for the Lord's healing ministry today. The first story describes two blind men who came to Jesus requesting healing. Jesus asked them, 'Do you believe that I am able to do this?' (Matt. 9:28). Jesus' question not only underscores the importance of faith for healing but also tells us something about the nature of faith. Faith in God for healing means believing that he has the ability to heal. Although I have encountered some Christians who say they do not think God can heal them today, the vast majority of Christians claim that he can. They say that God can do anything. That is what they say with their mouths and with their minds, but with their hearts they are saying something quite different.

Once I was sitting around the table having a discussion with a group of professional theologians. The subject turned to healing, and the men began to make jokes. They started to enumerate the things they would not ask God to heal. Some said they wouldn't ask God to heal blindness or deafness. Others said they wouldn't ask God to heal a deformity or to cause an amputated limb to grow out. When they got through listing all the things that they wouldn't ask God to heal, there wasn't much left to pray for except colds and headaches. Before the discussion was over, all the professors in that group had virtually denied the possibility of any New Testament miracles occurring today.

Now each man would have said that God *could* heal a blind eye or raise the dead. With their mouth they would even affirm that God *does heal* today. But the fact that they would not pray for any of these things meant that on a *practical level* they were actually denying God's ability to do these things today. They were giving intellectual assent to the *proposition* that God can heal, but in their hearts they had no real confidence in the *Person* of God to heal anything really 'difficult.' You see, the question is not *can* God heal, but *does* God heal. You will never ask God for anything you do not believe he does today.

In the second story a leper came to Jesus and said to him, 'Lord, *if you are willing*, you can make me clean' (Matt. 8:2, emphasis mine). That man certainly believed in Jesus' ability to heal a terminal disease. He freely acknowledged, 'You can make me clean.' But he also understood something else about faith. He did not assume that he would automatically be healed simply because he believed in Jesus' ability to heal. He said, Lord, 'if you are willing.' The faith that God requires for healing is not a *psychological certainty* that he is going to heal us or those we pray for. It is faith in his ability to heal and in his good will to heal. It is confidence that God loves his children and regularly heals them.

There is a doctrine of healing today in some parts of the church that borders on presumption. It assumes that it is God's will to heal all sickness in this life. According to this teaching, all we have to do is confess and claim our healing, and God is *obligated* to heal. The leper did not take that approach. He knew that Jesus could heal him. But he also added, 'Lord, if you are willing, you can make me clean.' Jesus honored his faith by saying, 'I am willing. Be clean!' (Matt. 8:3). The leper did not assume that Jesus *had* to heal in response to his faith.[6]

I once heard a report of a woman who had been healed after she confessed 184 times that, 'I am healed.' The man giving the report said, 'What if she had stopped on the 183d time?' Now I am not denying that the healing took place. I am not denying that God healed that woman after she had confessed 184 times that she was healed. God doesn't demand that we have perfect theology or practice in order for him to act in our lives. I do believe, however, that this kind of teaching can be destructive. It puts the burden on the person who wants to be healed, rather than putting confidence in God's goodness and his ability. It forces a person to 'whip up' a psychological certainty for healing, a certainty that God may not be giving at all. And it adds a condition for healing—the condition of psychological certainty—that God does not require.

I know that there are occasions when God does give a psycho-logical certainty for a healing. There have been a number of instances in my life over the last few years when I have prayed for someone's healing, and I had no doubt at all that God was going to heal.

About two years ago a young mother in our church, Karen Hersom, called me. She was so upset and crying so hard that I could barely understand her. Karen was six months pregnant and had been to her physician. Her sonogram had shown that she had a baby girl and that one of the little baby's kidneys had shriveled and stopped growing. The doctor had told Karen that the kidney had 'died' and would not function. The doctor assured her, how-ever, that the other kidney was normal and that her baby would be able to function quite well with one kidney. That news, how-ever, did not comfort Karen at all and she was worried sick about her baby.

While she was telling me these facts over the phone, a divine peace settled on me, and I found myself saying to her, 'Don't worry, Karen. We will pray for you, and God will heal your baby.'

'Do you really think so?' she said.

'Yes,' I said. 'Just come in and everything will be O.K.'

When I hung up the phone, I began to realize what I had just said. I had done something that I rarely ever do when praying for the sick. I had promised Karen healing.

When Karen came into my office the next day, my friend Steve Zarit and I prayed for her. There were actually some physical manifestations of God's power on Karen as we prayed. Approxi-mately ten days later she went to the same doctor, had a second sonogram, and both of the baby's kidneys were exactly the same size, both now healthy and normal. The baby was born three months later in perfect health.

Before then, and since then, I have prayed for babies who were miscarried and other newborn babies who died. I cannot produce a psychological certainty for healing in individual cases. When I do have it, it is a gift from God that can only be received, not manufactured. However, if you do not really believe in God's ability and willingness to heal, you will probably never experience that kind of faith for healing.

The third story, which describes the demonized epileptic boy in the ninth chapter of Mark, teaches another important principle about faith for healing. The father had brought his tormented son to the disciples, but they could not drive out the demon (v. 18). If the father had any faith at the beginning, the disciples' failure had certainly caused that faith to wane if not entirely disappear. The father said to Jesus, 'But if you can do anything, take pity on us and help us' (v. 22). Jesus replied that *everything is possible* for him who believes' (v. 23, emphasis mine). This is a principle that Jesus consistently taught (see Matthew 21:21–22). Jesus does not put any limitation on what we may ask God to do. Why should we limit God?

The seminary professors I mentioned a moment ago would not ask God to heal blind eyes or amputated limbs, but they would pray for God to heal headaches, guide a physician's hands in surgery, and help the medicine do its job. Why limit God to healing headaches or guiding a physician's hands? Church leaders are effectively limiting God's ability to heal when they refuse to teach about healing and do not encourage prayer for the sick.

Perhaps you have never seen the Lord heal a blind eye or an amputated limb, but why let your experience put limits on God? You believe that he can act supernaturally in other ways. Why not believe that he can heal a person's body supernaturally?

During the time when I was a student and teacher in seminary, it was common to hear students give testimonies regarding how God had supernaturally supplied their needs. It was not uncommon for a student to say that he needed $139.12 to pay his electric bill, and without telling anyone about it, a check for

$139.12 arrived in the mail just in time for him to pay his bill. I have heard numerous stories like that. The majority of Christians have no difficulty at all in believing that God acts supernaturally in financial situations like that. Why is it so difficult to believe that he could straighten a spine, or regulate someone's body chemistry so that their diabetes leaves?

Does God have a more difficult time straightening a crooked spine than meeting your financial needs? Of course not. It's just that we often pray about our financial needs with faith, and we do not pray about our physical needs with faith. If God healed in response to faith in the New Testament, then why wouldn't he heal today in response to faith? Where there is a lack of healings today, I do not believe the problem lies with God's ability or willingness, but rather with the church's ability to believe God for healing.

Remember these three characteristics of faith:

1. Faith in Jesus' ability to heal is also faith that he *does* heal.
2. Faith in Jesus' desire to heal is not to be equated with psychological certainty. He will heal when we don't have psychological certainty.
3. Faith does not put restrictions on God's ability to act on behalf of his children, for 'everything is possible for him who believes.'

God Heals in Response to His Own Promise

There is yet another irrefutable reason for believing that healing ought to be a primary ministry of the church today. In James 5:14–16, God commissioned the whole church to heal:

> Is any one of you sick? He should call the elders of the church to pray over him and anoint him with oil in the name of the Lord. And the prayer offered in faith will make the sick person well; the Lord will

raise him up. If he has sinned, he will be forgiven. Therefore confess your sins to each other and pray for each other so that you may be healed. The prayer of a righteous man is powerful and effective.

Now ask yourself, why would God command the church to pray for the sick and promise the church healing if they prayed, unless God intended healing to be a normative part of church life? Many churches who believe in the infallibility of their Bibles hardly know that James 5:14–16 is in their Bibles. I taught seminary classes for ten years before I ever encouraged students to apply James 5:14–16. Those who discipled me never told me it was the church's responsibility to anoint the sick and pray for them.

Church members will never ask their elders for healing prayer unless they are taught to do so, and they will never have confidence in God to heal unless they are taught that God does heal and the reasons why he heals. As soon as we began to teach and practice James 5:14–16 with a little anticipation, God began to heal in our church. Ruth Gay, the lady I mentioned in chapter 2 (pp. 31–32) who was healed of an aneurysm, was one of the first for whom we prayed.

Note that it is not only the elders who pray for the sick. In verse 16 James commands all Christians to 'pray for each other so that you may be healed.' If the whole church were to take God's command seriously, we would see a great deal more healing than we see presently.

In this chapter we have seen that God's healing ministry is rooted in his eternal desire to glorify himself and his Son, his deep compassion for those who are suffering, and his constant willingness to respond to those who have faith. He also heals in response to his own command and promise to the church. These four reasons alone ought to convince us that God's purposes for healing are rooted in his unchanging nature, not in temporary historical circumstances.

Yet the Scriptures give other reasons why God heals. Although these are discussed at length in appendix A, I will mention them briefly here. He heals to lead people to repentance and open doors for the gospel. He heals to remove hindrances to ministry and service. He heals to teach us about himself and his kingdom. He heals to demonstrate the presence of his kingdom. He heals simply because people ask him. And he heals for sovereign purposes known only to himself.

None of these reasons is based on the changing historical circumstances of the first-century church. They are rooted in the character and eternal purposes of God. If the Lord healed in the first century because he was motivated by his compassion and mercy for the hurting, why would we think he has withdrawn that compassion after the death of the apostles? Why would we think he no longer feels compassion when he sees lepers or those dying from AIDS? Why would we think he is now content to demonstrate that compassion only by giving grace to endure the suffering rather than grace to heal the condition? If Jesus and the apostles healed in the first century to bring glory to God, why would we think God has discarded a major New Testament instrument for bringing glory to himself and his Son?

In fact, every one of the biblical purposes for healing is still valid today. To the degree that any individual or church will align themselves with these purposes when they pray for the sick or minister to the hurting, they will see healings take place in their ministry.

10

Why God Gives Miraculous Gifts

In the fall of 1987 I was helping to lead a weekly Bible study. On this particular Wednesday night there were perhaps one hundred people in attendance. At the conclusion of the meeting, we gave people in the group an opportunity to share publicly anything they thought the Lord might have revealed to them that would be edifying for those present. A young woman named Karen Fortson (now Mrs. Tom Davis) was sitting on the front row. She stood up immediately and very gently said, 'The Lord has shown me that a young man is attending this meeting for the first time tonight, and he is in bondage to pornography. The Lord wants to help him and not embarrass him. He should see one of the leaders afterwards so that they can pray for him.' Karen told me after the meeting that she was so certain the Lord had spoken to her that she was actually afraid to turn around. She thought the Lord would show her who this young man was, and she didn't want to know!

When the meeting was over, the young man came up to me trembling and sweating with an ashen face. He said, 'I am the one the young lady was talking about.' He had been in bondage to pornography since his early teens. Although he was now a seminary student with a wife and children, he was still in bondage to pornography—in fact, it was stronger than ever. But before the evening was over, he was making a full confession to me and another pastor, and we were praying for him.

In 1 Corinthians 14:24–25 Paul describes what happened in our Bible study that evening:

> But if an unbeliever or someone who does not understand comes in while everybody is prophesying, he will be convinced by all that he is a sinner and will be judged by all, and the secrets of his heart will be laid bare. So he will fall down and worship God, exclaiming, 'God is really among you!'

That seminary student did not believe the gifts of the Spirit were given today, and he had some hostility to the gift of tongues. He certainly qualified as 'someone who does not understand.' He had never been to our weekly Bible study before. In fact, he had come that night to evaluate it. But God had decided to evaluate him!

Stories such as this are not at all uncommon. Yet in spite of reports that God is using miraculous gifts in the church today, many people argue that these gifts ceased with the deaths of the apostles. This issue must be settled by specific statements of Scripture, not by vague theological deductions or simple assertions. 1 Corinthians 12–14 offers six reasons why miraculous gifts will continue in the church until the Lord returns. The most important of these reasons is the stated purpose of the gifts.

God Gave Spiritual Gifts to Strengthen the Church

Paul leaves no doubt regarding the purpose of all the spiritual gifts. Each gift is given to strengthen and build up the church. In 1 Corinthians 12:7 Paul writes, 'Now to each one the manifestation of the Spirit is given *for the common good*' (emphasis mine). What kinds of gifts does Paul have in mind when he makes this statement? In the next four verses he goes on to say:

To one there is given through the Spirit the message of wisdom, to another the message of knowledge by means of the same Spirit, to another faith by the same Spirit, to another gifts of healing by that one Spirit, to another miraculous powers, to another prophecy, to another distinguishing between spirits, to another speaking in different kinds of tongues, and to still another the interpretation of tongues. All these are the work of one and the same Spirit, and he gives them to each one, just as he determines.

Paul reaffirms the purpose of spiritual gifts in 1 Corinthians 14:26. Notice again the specific gifts he mentions. 'What then shall we say, brothers? When you come together, everyone has a hymn, or a word of instruction, a revelation, a tongue or an interpretation. All of these must be done *for the strengthening of the church*' (emphasis mine).[1]

Because God gave spiritual gifts to strengthen the church, healing, miracles, tongues, and prophecy were not confined to the apostles or just a few people in the first century. They were widely distributed across the church. To review a point made earlier: prophecy is found in the church at Rome (Rom. 12:6), in the church at Corinth (1 Cor. 12:10), in the church at Ephesus (Eph. 4:11), in the church at Thessalonica (1 Thess. 5:20) and in the church at Antioch (Acts 13:1). The New Testament also names a number of individuals who were not apostles, but who either were called prophets or exercised revelatory gifts. There were the prophet Agabus (Acts 11:28; 21:10–11), the prophets Judas and Silas (Acts 15:32), Philip's four virgin daughters who were prophetesses (Acts 21:9), and Ananias (Acts 9:10–19). The gift of miracles was in operation in Corinth (1 Cor. 12:10) and in the churches of Galatia (Gal. 3:5). The gift of tongues is found at Jerusalem (Acts 2:1–13), at Cae sarea among the Gentile converts (Acts 10:44–48), at Ephesus (Acts 19:1–7); at Samaria (Acts 8:14–25), and at Corinth (1 Cor. 12–14).[2]

The value of spiritual gifts in strengthening the church is

particularly true of the gift of prophecy. Paul maintains that 'everyone who prophesies speaks to men for their strengthening, encouragement and comfort' (1 Cor. 14:3). Again, he writes that 'he who prophesies edifies the church' (1 Cor. 14:4).

Since edification is the primary purpose of spiritual gifts, how can anyone conclude that they have been taken away from the church? If they built up the church in the first century, why wouldn't they built up the church in the twentieth century? The Bible's own statements about the purpose of spiritual gifts force us to conclude that they were meant to continue until the Lord returns. Only then will there no longer be any need for spiritual gifts.

God Commands Us to Eagerly Desire Spiritual Gifts

Since spiritual gifts build up the body of Christ, it is not surprising that Paul commands the Corinthians three times to 'eagerly desire' or 'strive after' spiritual gifts (1 Cor. 12:31; 14:1, 39). He did not tell them simply to accept or to tolerate the gifts but to be 'zealous' about them.[3]

Paul did not want the Corinthians, or any other New Testament Christians, to have a passive attitude toward spiritual gifts. That is all the more significant considering the situation at Corinth, where the misuse of spiritual gifts had caused serious problems. The church at Corinth had gone 'gift crazy.' Paul's solution to that controversy, however, was not to abandon the gifts or to be passive about their use but to strive after them and use them in accordance with the rules he lays down in chapters 12–14.

Much of the church is presently disobeying God's command to strive after spiritual gifts. Part of the church is not only passive about the gifts but actually hostile toward them. They persecute those who pursue the gifts and discourage others from pursuing them. This is sheer disobedience to the written Word of God.

The majority of those who believe the miraculous spiritual gifts have ceased claim they ceased either with the completion of the New Testament or with the death of the last apostle. The last New Testament book to be written was Revelation, which most New Testament scholars date around A.D. 95, although some have dated it as early as A.D. 69. Most likely, the last apostle to die was John, who would have died sometime shortly after A.D. 95. Paul wrote 1 Corinthians around A.D. 55. That means Paul's command to pursue spiritual gifts, especially the gift of prophecy, only had value for approximately forty years in the church. With the death of the last apostle and the completion of the book of Revelation, 1 Corinthians 12:31, 14:1, and 14:39 have been set aside on this view. It is impossible for me to believe that Paul would have commanded Christians to seek something that would only be valid for forty years after the command was given. I know of no analogy for that kind of interpretation anywhere else in the New Testament.

Why did Paul command Christians to eagerly desire miraculous spiritual gifts? Because they were valuable in building up the church. They were valuable then, and they are valuable now.

God Commands Us Not to Forbid Speaking in Tongues

The gift of tongues is easily the most controversial of all the gifts in the church today. That was also true in the church at Corinth in the first century. There are many reasons for this, but chief among them is the attitude of some people who have received the gift of tongues. They assume that the gift of tongues is the greatest of all the gifts, and they believe they are more spiritual than other Christians because they have the gift of tongues.

One of the reasons God wants us to regard others as more important than ourselves (Phil. 2:3) is that when we begin to view ourselves as spiritually superior, we always cause strife in the church. The strife associated with the misuse of tongues has led a number of pastors to say to me that even if the gift of tongues is being given today, they don't want it in their church.

I can identify with their feelings. For a long time after I had begun to believe that the gifts of the Spirit were given today, I still had an emotional reaction to the gift of tongues. I didn't care anything about it, and I certainly didn't want it. In light of the problems the misuse of this gift can cause, that is a natural reaction. However, it is not the reaction the apostle Paul had nor wanted in the church.

Because the gift of tongues was so controversial and potentially explosive, you would have thought that Paul might have told the Corinthians, 'No longer speak in tongues.' In reality, he said just the opposite 'Do not forbid speaking in tongues' (1 Cor. 14:39). Whether we like it or not, the holy inerrant Word of God commands us not to forbid speaking in tongues. If tongues were simply a temporary gift that would be withdrawn in thirty-five to forty years, Paul's command would make no sense at all. Why endure something so controversial for the next forty years? Why not just forbid its use altogether?

Once, in a conversation with a seminary professor, I challenged the rule at his academic institution that would not admit students into the school who spoke in tongues. I reminded him that Paul said, 'Do not forbid speaking in tongues.' He replied, 'That is not the Word of God for today.' When I challenged him to prove that biblically, he could not do so. Yet he was confident that 1 Corinthians 14:39 was no longer a part of the Word of God for today.

What would conservative theologians say today if I were to apply that same procedure to other of Paul's texts? Suppose I said that Paul's command that 'everything should be done in a fitting and orderly way' (1 Cor. 14:40) is not the Word of God for today. I can't prove that biblically, but I am sure it was just part of Paul's cultural environment. Or perhaps it was just a unique problem they had in the church at Corinth. Or what if I said Paul's instruction, 'To the married I give this command (not I, but the Lord): A wife must not separate from her husband' (1 Cor. 7:10), is not part of God's Word for today. I can't prove it with specific texts of Scripture, but I have some theological and historical reasons why I don't think it applies today. If I wrote either one of those things in an article, or even said them in a conference somewhere, I can guarantee you that within a matter of months a number of articles and tapes would be distributed throughout the church to demonstrate that I had become a theological liberal who no longer valued God's Word.

Yet orthodox theologians and Bible teachers have done this very thing with 1 Corinthians 14:39. They have set aside a part of the Word of God as void! And they have done so without specific biblical proof. If I were going to set aside a part of the New Testament as no longer valid for today, I could not do that on the basis of theological deductions or later historical experience. I would have to have a specific text in the New Testament that told me a particular command has now been nullified.

The Apostle Paul Valued the Gift of Tongues

Even when I was convinced that the gifts of the Spirit were not for today, there were two passages in 1 Corinthians 14 that I hated to think about. I could not understand why the apostle had included them. The first was his statement, 'I would like every one of you to speak in tongues' (1 Cor. 14:5). How could he mean that? It was just as disturbing to know that he also said, 'But I would rather have you prophesy.'

I did not believe Paul meant all Christians should speak in tongues. For example, he viewed his celibacy as a spiritual gift and wished all Christians could be celibate (1 Cor. 7:7 uses *charisma* in reference to Paul's celibacy). But he certainly was not saying that all Christians are *supposed* to be celibate. He simply placed a high value on his celibacy. My problem was that he seemed to place the gift of tongues on the same high level that he did his own celibacy! What was so great about the gift of tongues that would lead Paul to wish everyone had that gift?

The second statement that caused me concern was his declaration, 'I thank God that I speak in tongues more than all of you' (1 Cor. 14:18). Paul likely means three things by this expression. First, he spent more time speaking in tongues than anyone in Corinth. Second, his gift of tongues was greater in its intensity than anyone else's gift at Corinth.[4] Third, Paul is very likely referring to his devotional prayer life, because he qualified verse 18 by saying, 'But in the church I would rather speak five intelligible words to instruct others than ten thousand words in a tongue' (1 Cor. 14:19).

How could this man who was burdened with so much responsibility spend more time than anyone else speaking in tongues? He could only do so if he found the gift of tongues immensely valuable in cultivating his spiritual life and intimacy with God. Indeed, this is precisely what Paul claimed for the gift of tongues when he said, 'He who speaks in a tongue edifies himself' (1 Cor. 14:4).[5] That is why he wished all Christians had that gift. Does that sound like the attitude of someone who thought tongues were of temporary value to the church? And I must remind you that we have more than just Paul's attitude in view here, for Paul is writing under the inspiration of the Holy Spirit. He is giving us not just his opinion but God's opinion of the gift of tongues.

I could not find one other example in Paul's writings where he placed such a high value on something that was supposedly limited to the first century. I have to confess that it also troubled me that Paul valued something that repulsed me.

Spiritual Gifts Are Necessary for the Health of Christ's Body

In 1 Corinthians 12:4–11, Paul emphasizes that there are different kinds of gifts given to the body, but they are all given by the Holy Spirit. Then in verses 12–27 Paul compares the variety of gifts within the church to a physical body. His point is that all of the gifts are necessary for the health of the church, just as all the various parts of the body are necessary for the health of the body. He says, for example, 'If the whole body were an eye, where would the sense of hearing be? If the whole body were an ear, where would the sense of smell be?' (v. 17). And again he writes, 'The eye cannot say to the hand, "I don't need you!" And the head cannot say to the feet, "I don't need you!"' (v. 21). He concludes this section by saying, 'If one part suffers, every part suffers with it' (v. 26).

Paul uses the body metaphor to argue that *all* the spiritual gifts are necessary for the body of Christ to remain healthy.[6] When people argue that the miraculous gifts of verses 8–10 ceased with the death of the apostles, they obliterate Paul's analogy of the human body. They also say just the opposite of Paul, 'All parts of the body are *not* necessary.' Who would have ever gotten that out of Paul's specific statements in 1 Corinthians 12–14?

Spiritual Gifts Will Not Cease Until Christ Returns

Paul told the Corinthians, 'You do not lack any spiritual gift [*charisma*] as you eagerly wait for our Lord Jesus Christ to be revealed' (1 Cor. 1:7). Here Paul connects spiritual gifts with the return of the Lord Jesus. That seems to suggest that the Corinthians, and indeed all Christians, will find these gifts valuable until Christ returns. In 1 Corinthians 13:8–12, however, Paul goes beyond mere suggestion and plainly states that the gifts of the Spirit will not be taken away until Jesus returns. Paul writes,

> Love never fails. But where there are prophecies, they will cease; where there are tongues, they will be stilled; where there is knowledge, it will pass away. For we know in part and we prophesy in part, but when perfection comes, the imperfect disappears. When I was a child, I talked like a child, I thought like a child, I reasoned like a child. When I became a man, I put childish ways behind me. Now we see but a poor reflection as in a mirror; then we shall see face to face. Now I know in part; then I shall know fully, even as I am fully known.

Paul admits that there will be a time when prophecies, tongues, and knowledge will cease. In fact, there will be a time when *all* the spiritual gifts will cease—at the return of the Lord Jesus Christ. Three phrases in 1 Corinthians 13:8–12 lead us to that conclusion. Paul says that spiritual gifts will pass away (1) 'When perfection comes,' (2) when 'we shall see face to face,' and (3) when 'I shall know fully, even as I am fully known' (vv. 10, 12). Let's look briefly at the meaning of each phrase.

Some have attempted to say that the word 'perfection' (v. 10) refers to the maturity of the church. If the full maturity of the church were in view, this would be an acceptable interpretation. The word translated 'perfection' can refer to maturity, and verse 11 does have an analogy involving maturity. Spiritual gifts have been given to bring the church to full and complete maturity, and when that has been accomplished, the gifts will no longer be necessary. But Scripture clearly teaches that full maturity or 'perfection' will not be reached until Christ's return (see 1 John 3:2–3 and Eph. 5:27).

If some lesser form of maturity is meant, however, this interpretation faces insurmountable difficulties. For one thing, it cannot satisfy the needs of verse 12. Who in the church today would say that they see Jesus Christ face to face? Or who would claim that they know as fully as they are known by God? In fact, who would even suggest that the church has reached a maturity beyond that of the first-century church?

Others attempt to argue that 'perfection' refers to the completed canon of Scripture. When the last book of the Bible was written, the church had its complete Bible and no longer needed the miraculous spiritual gifts. This view also has decisive arguments against it. First, nowhere in the immediate context does Paul talk about Scripture or the collection of the books that became Scripture. Second, we cannot say today that because we have the Scriptures, we see Christ face to face, nor can we say that we know fully even as we are fully known. Also, if this view were correct, we would have to say that 'Paul saw but a poor reflection as in a mirror, but we see face to face; Paul knew in part but we know fully, even as we are fully known.' Even though we have the completed Bible today, would anyone seriously want to argue that our knowledge and experience of God are superior to the apostle Paul's?[7]

The expression 'face to face' (v. 12) also points to the return of Christ. In the Old Testament this meant to see God personally. For example, Jacob saw God face to face as he wrestled with the angel of the Lord (Gen. 32:30). After the angel of the Lord had visited Gideon in the wine press, Gideon exclaimed, 'I have seen the angel of the LORD face to face' (Judg. 6:22). Exodus 33:11 says that 'The LORD would speak to Moses face to face, as a man speaks with his friend.'[8] When Paul uses this expression, therefore, he is referring to the time when we shall see Jesus face to face. That time can only refer to his return, when every eye will see him (Rev. 1:7).

Finally, the statement, 'Then I shall know fully, even as I am fully known' (v. 12) can only refer to the Lord's return.[9] Paul is not saying that when the Lord returns, believers will be omniscient like the Lord. Rather, we will know accurately without any misinformation or misconceptions. Presently our heart is deceitful and sick (Jer. 17:9). But when the Lord returns, he will remove every trace of sin from our heart, so that then we shall know as fully as we are known.

Why does God continue to give miraculous gifts to the church? As we have seen in this chapter, 1 Corinthians 12–14 gives us six reasons that apply just as much today as they did in the first century:

1. God gives miraculous gifts to strengthen the body of Christ.
2. God commands us to eagerly desire the miraculous spiritual gifts, especially prophecy.
3. God commands us not to forbid speaking in tongues, even when the gift of tongues is being significantly misused.
4. Paul's high esteem for the gift of tongues indicates that the gift has significant value in cultivating intimacy with the Lord.
5. Paul's analogy that the church is like a physical body indicates that all the spiritual gifts are necessary for the health of the body of Christ.
6. Scripture specifically states that the miraculous gifts of the Spirit will not cease until the return of the Lord.

In light of these six specific statements about the miraculous gifts of the Spirit, it is virtually impossible to argue that either Paul or the Scriptures foresaw the passing away of the gifts before the return of the Lord.

11

Why God Doesn't Heal

On January 15, 1990, Duane Miller, the pastor of the First Baptist Church at Brenham, Texas, lost his voice at the conclusion of the Sunday morning service and couldn't preach Sunday evening. His physician told him to take a six-month leave of absence. When he failed to recover, the doctors told him the myelin sheath to his vocal cords had been damaged and that he would not get his voice back. He tried voice therapy, but that didn't help, and so he had to resign his pastorate in the fall of 1990. Early in 1992 he began to teach a Sunday school class at First Baptist Church in Houston. He was able to do this by using a special microphone, but even with the special microphone his throat was so sore that he could hardly eat or drink for two days after teaching.

On Sunday morning, January 17, 1993, he had just finished reading Psalm 103:3 to his Sunday school class: 'Who forgives all your sins and heals all your diseases.' He stopped to comment on that verse, saying that there are two extreme views regarding healing. Listen to Duane's own words:

> I had said that on the one side there is the group that believes God always heals miraculously and on the other is the group that says it never happens. But what you have to realize is that puts God in a box, I said, and He won't be put in a box.

I told them that what you have to do with divine healing is just stand back and say, 'I know God does that from time to time and I can't tell you why. I don't understand why some are healed and some aren't and leave it there and say that is in the Lord's wisdom; so be it.'

I had just finished saying that and started to read the next line of the Psalm: *'He redeems my life from the pit . . .'*

AND MY VOICE changed. I heard the first word and felt in my throat that what I had been feeling was gone. There was none of the feeling there that I had had for three years.

I would love to tell you I knew exactly what it was . . . and that I expected God to do it and wasn't surprised. But it would be a lie. It scared me to death.

I stopped, startled, and then said two or three words, thinking, 'Am I hearing what I think I hear?'

I said to them that I didn't understand what was going on, but that God was doing something.

I tried to get back to the lesson, but I couldn't and nobody cared. People began to applaud. Everybody was weeping. There were about 200 in the class and there were no dry eyes. Somebody began to sing the doxology. Someone else said we had witnessed the power of God. We just thanked the Lord for what He had done and walked out of the church.[1]

Almost three years to the day after Duane Miller lost his voice, the Lord gave it back to him again. The Lord didn't explain to Duane why he lost his voice or why the Lord decided to give it back to him.

In the last two chapters I have tried to explain some of the reasons why God heals and gives miraculous gifts today. Yet there are occasions when no reason can be found for a miraculous display of God's power or for the withholding of that power. Sometimes God heals without giving any reason. The introduction to the story of the paralytic who was lowered through the roof in Capernaum simply states that 'the power of the Lord was present for him to heal the sick' (Luke 5:17).[2]

On the other hand, God may refuse to heal or deliver without any explanation. For instance, in Acts 12 both James and Peter were put in prison by Herod. God allowed James to be killed, but supernaturally delivered Peter. The Scriptures do not explain why God did that. Neither divine nor human reasons are given to resolve this mystery. James' death and Peter's deliverance simply served God's sovereign purposes. In our attempts to understand why God heals and why he doesn't heal, we must always keep in mind that his ways are not our ways (Isa. 55:8). Yet the Bible does give some very definite reasons why God's miraculous power may be withheld in various situations.

Apostasy

Anything that drives away the presence of God will also cause him to withdraw his miraculous power.[3] When the people of God commit apostasy[4] and turn from God to pursue other things in his place, he withdraws his beneficial presence from his people. That may happen to an individual, to a group, or even to a whole nation.

Some of the psalms were written during periods of apostasy in Israel's history. Psalm 74 is one of these psalms and was probably written during the time of the exile, when the Babylonians over-ran Israel and deported many of the Israelites.[5] In verse one the psalmist laments that God has rejected his people, and in the following verses he describes the devastation Israel's enemies have brought on the nation because it is no longer protected by God's power. Then he changes the nature of his lament in verses nine to eleven:

> We are given no miraculous signs; no prophets are left, and none of us knows how long this will be. How long will the enemy mock you, O God? Will the foe revile your name forever? Why do you hold back your hand, your right hand? Take it from the folds of your garment and destroy them!

The absence of miraculous signs and prophetic ministry was not a normal situation in Israel, according to the psalmist. It was evidence of severe divine judgment on the land. The apostasy of the Israelites caused God to withdraw his miraculous power from the whole nation.

Psalm 77 is similar, but it probably was written at another time in Israel's history. In the middle of the psalm the author describes God's judgment because of apostasy, and then the psalmist offers his response to God's judgment:

> Will the Lord reject forever? Will he never show his favor again? Has his unfailing love vanished forever? Has his promise failed for all time? Has God forgotten to be merciful? Has he in anger withheld his compassion? Then I thought, 'To this will I appeal: the years of the right hand of the Most High.' I will remember the deeds of the LORD; yes, I will remember your miracles of long ago. I will meditate on all your works and consider all your mighty deeds. Your ways, O God, are holy. What God is so great as our God? You are the God who performs miracles; you display your power among the peoples. (Ps. 77:7–14)

According to the psalmist, God was so angry with his people that it seemed he might reject them forever.[6] Their apostasy kept them from experiencing his favor, unfailing love, and compassion. One concrete evidence that God was not showing compassion to his people was the lack of his power and miracles in the nation. The psalmist refers to miracles as something that happened 'long ago' (v. 11). The psalmist is not content, however, to live under that kind of judgment.

He asks God to give fresh displays of his power (v. 11). (The 'right hand' of God is used in Scripture as a designation of his power.) Even though he was not currently experiencing God's power, he does not refer to God as 'the God who performed miracles,' but rather uses the present tense 'the God who *performs* miracles' (v. 14, emphasis mine). In other words, the psalmist clearly realizes that the absence of miracles during his time was due to the people's apostasy, not to a change in God's attitude toward miracles.

Perhaps the best illustration of the effect of apostasy is found in the book of Judges. The book of Judges is written in a cyclical pattern. The cycle has four phases. First, the people commit apostasy. Second, God gives them over to foreign oppressors. Third, the people repent and cry out for mercy. And fourth, God raises up a judge who delivers them from the foreign oppressors.

During the time of their apostasy, they experience the absence of God's presence and, therefore, of his miraculous power. However, when the people repent and cry out to God, he sends them a deliverer like Samson, through whom the power of God flows, and the people are rescued from their enemies. The book of Judges illustrates that one of the surest ways to lose God's presence, and therefore his miraculous power, is through apostasy.

In the Old Testament, apostasy most frequently took the form of idolatry. Although idol worship is still a problem in those parts of the world where religions like Buddhism and Hinduism have significant influence, that form of apostasy is expressed differently in more Westernized cultures. The apostle Paul called greed idolatry (Col. 3:5). This form of idolatry is very much alive in the Western church. In fact, some parts of the church in America use greed as a major motivation for giving to the Lord's work. Some preachers talk like Jesus was wealthy and wore designer jeans, and that he wants all of us to be wealthy. According to them, the more we give, the more we will get. This 'baptism of greed' is actually a form of idolatry and, if persisted in, will drive the Lord's presence away and cause the church to lose his power.

We may commit apostasy in other ways. If a Christian gives himself over to immorality, he commits moral apostasy. John said that, 'If we claim to have fellowship with him yet walk in the darkness, we lie and do not live by the truth' (1 John 1:6). God will not have fellowship with us if we walk in the darkness and, therefore, we will lose both his presence and his power.

Finally, it is possible to commit doctrinal apostasy. It seems that this is what Hymaneus and Alexander did, causing Paul to hand them over to Satan that they might be taught not to blaspheme (1 Tim. 1:20). Liberal churches that deny the deity of Jesus, his substitutionary atonement, his virgin birth, his bodily resurrection, his bodily return, heaven, hell, justification by faith alone, the authority of the Scriptures, and so on, cannot have the power of God displayed in their midst. You will most likely never see divine healings or miracles among individuals or churches like this.

The power of God may remain on an individual or on a group for a time after they have embarked on a course of apostasy. Even the woman Jezebel at Thyatira was given time by God to repent of her immorality before God judged her (Rev. 2:21–23). That is due to the kindness of God, a kindness that Paul said was meant to lead God's rebellious children to repentance (Rom. 2:4). Even the divine patience can be exhausted, however, and when it is, his presence and power leaves and judgment begins.[7]

Legalism and Lukewarm Faith

Isaiah recorded one of the most tragic judgments ever brought on the nation of Israel:

> The Lord has brought over you a deep sleep: He has sealed your eyes (the prophets); he has covered your heads (the seers).[8]

The divine stupor that God sent to Israel kept them from understanding why they were being judged and therefore kept them from repenting so that their judgment might end. He even blinded the eyes of the most spiritually sensitive people in Israel, the prophets and seers who were supposed to act as watchmen for Israel. Isaiah said that even if his vision of the nation's judgment were written down and handed to them, their blindness was so complete they would not be able to read it (Isa. 29:11–12). What caused the Lord to remove the ministry of his revelatory Spirit from his people? Just after he recorded this judgment Isaiah wrote,

> The Lord says: 'These people come near to me with their mouth and honor me with their lips, but their hearts are far from me. Their worship of me is made up only of rules taught by men.' (Isa. 29:13)

The legalism of the Israelites drove out the presence of God. They kept an outward form of religion, but they let their hearts wander far from God. Legalism always blinds its adherents to spiritual reality. Legalism drives out the revelatory ministry of the Holy Spirit. Think about that for a minute. How many legalists have you known? How many legalists have ever confessed to you that they were legalistic? I have never heard a person caught in the midst of legalism confess that he or she was legalistic. I have heard many people caught in the midst of immorality confess their immorality, but I have never heard a legalist confess legalism. There is something so blinding about that sin.

The worst thing about legalism is that it drives away the presence of God. At the beginning of his ministry, Isaiah had a vision of the Lord complaining about the multitude of sacrifices brought to him in a legalistic way (1:11). He heard the Lord exclaim, 'Stop bringing meaningless offerings!' (1:13). The Lord said that he would not look on the Israelites when they prayed, nor would he listen to their prayers (1:15). Not even their fasting could get the Lord's attention (58:3). Legalism simply cuts us off from the presence of the Lord.

There is a good reason for this. Legalism is more than simply following man-made rules or keeping a correct external behavior while letting our heart wander away from God. These are both forms of legalism, but the essence of legalism is far worse than either of these. The essence of legalism is trusting in the religious activity rather than trusting in God. It is putting our confidence in a practice rather than in a Person. And without fail this will lead us to love the practice more than the Person.

The goal of all of life is to love God with all of our heart, soul, strength, and mind. Legalism is a direct challenge to the greatest of all the commandments because it shifts our attention and confidence away from the person of God to religious activities. God did not tolerate it among ancient Israel. Jesus would not tolerate it among the scribes and Pharisees. And he will not tolerate it among his people today. Legalism is prevalent in the church today, just as it was in first-century Judaism during Jesus' ministry. The scribes and Pharisees never knew the power of God, nor will the legalists among the church today.

The sister to legalism is a lukewarm complacent faith. The pre-eminent example of this in the New Testament is the church at Laodicea. It was one of the wealthiest churches in Asia, but Jesus said that it was lukewarm (Rev. 3:16). The definitive characteristic of a lukewarm church is an attitude that says, 'I am rich; I have acquired wealth and do not need a thing' (Rev. 3:17). When we come to the point where we have lost our hunger for God and are satisfied with our present spiritual condition, then we have become lukewarm. We are always to be thankful for everything we have in God, but never content with our present spiritual condition. We are always to want more of God, more of his presence, and more of the character of Christ formed in us (Gal. 4:19). When we stop wanting more, we enter into a complacent state and become what Jesus calls lukewarm. If we stay lukewarm, he says, 'I will spit you out of my mouth' (Rev. 3:16, NASB). Whatever else 'spit you out' means, it surely includes the loss of his beneficial presence and his power.

Whereas apostasy is the loss of purity, legalism and lukewarm faith result in the loss of intimacy with God and unity with one another. Intimacy with God is absolutely essential for ministry.

Remember that Jesus only did what he saw his Father doing (John 5:19). The miraculous ministry of Jesus was absolutely dependent on his intimacy with his Father. Likewise, the ministry of the apostles was absolutely dependent on their intimacy with Jesus, for without him they could do nothing (John 15:5). Therefore, the loss of intimacy means the loss of power for ministry.

The loss of intimacy with God invariably leads to the loss of unity among believers. Unity rests on the foundation of hearing God's voice and following his present priorities for our lives. Jesus prayed for the unity of believers so that the world would know that the Father sent Jesus and loves the church (John 17:23). Without unity the church will never have credibility in the world or have power to fulfill its ministry.

Apostasy, legalism, and lukewarm faith are serious problems in the church today. These things significantly hinder God's miraculous ministry among contemporary believers. However, I believe that there is another factor that is a greater hindrance than all three of these put together. I am referring to the present unbelief that is rampant in the church.

Unbelief

When Jesus visited his own hometown, Nazareth, he was greeted with unbelief and even disdain. What effect did that have on his miraculous ministry? Mark said that, 'He could not do any miracles there, except lay hands on a few sick people and heal them. And he was amazed at their lack of faith' (Mark 6:5–6). Some people have a difficult time with the phrase 'could not.' The Son of God is omnipotent. How can it be said of an omnipotent being that 'he could not do any miracles there'? Yet there are some things a perfect, omnipotent being cannot do. For example, he cannot lie (Heb. 6:18). He cannot have fellowship with darkness (1 Cor. 6:14; 1 John 1:6). Is Mark 6:5 in this same category?

Matthew wrote about the same incident, but he did not say that Jesus *could not* do miracles in Nazareth. He said, 'And he *did not* do many miracles there because of their lack of faith' (Matt. 13:58, emphasis mine). I think Matthew helps us understand what Mark meant. I do not think we are supposed to interpret Mark's 'could not' in an absolute sense. There are occasions in which Jesus did miracles where there seemed to be no faith at all.[9] I think what Matthew and Mark are telling us is that, in general, Jesus will not work miracles in an atmosphere of unbelief. James states this principle in another way. He told his readers that, 'You do not have, because you do not ask God' (James 4:2). In other words, you will not ask God for something you do not believe he will give you.

Remember the story I told earlier about sitting around a table with a group of theologians who were laughing as they were listing all the illnesses for which they would not pray (p. 126)? While they were laughing and listing the things they wouldn't pray for, I couldn't help but think of James 4:2. When one man said that he wouldn't pray for blind eyes to be healed, James 4:2 came to my mind and I thought, *Guess what you will never see healed!* These men will never ask for miraculous healings, and probably they will never see miraculous healings. 'You do not have because you do not ask God.'

If you haven't seen any truly miraculous healings, ask yourself how often you pray for these things. I am not talking about the kind of ritualistic prayers where an absentee sick person's name is mentioned in a list with others in a Sunday service so that we can ask God to guide the doctors hands, comfort the family, and let them know that all things work together for good. These kinds of prayers are frequently offered as a pastoral courtesy with no real expectation or anticipation that God will do a miracle. When I ask you how often you pray for miraculous healings, I am asking how often do you go into a hospital room and pray for the sick and suffering to be miraculously healed? How often do you lay your hands on the sick in your church and pray for them? Most of the people I talk with who have never seen a miracle are people, by and large, who never take the trouble to go and lay their hands on sick people in believing prayer. Conversely, I have yet to find anyone who regularly lays hands on the sick in believing prayer who doesn't see at least some miraculous healing.

The surprising thing to me today is not how little God heals among the conservative evangelical church, but that he heals at all. So much of the church is so filled with unbelief that I am truly amazed that anyone ever gets healed.

Most of the conservative seminaries I am acquainted with are not teaching their students about God's willingness to heal. Many are actually teaching that God does not heal in any significant way, and some are actually teaching that the desire for miracles is evil.[10] The graduates of these seminaries are becoming the pastors of the church in America. They are teaching the church just what they learned in seminary. Is it surprising, therefore, that a significant part of the church today experiences very little of the miraculous power of God?

Although I am no longer a seminary professor, I am still invited to give lectures in seminary classrooms and other academic settings. In my travels I meet many seminary professors and church leaders. I am finding that fewer of these leaders are willing to take the position that the gifts of the Spirit passed away with the apostles. In fact, I frequently hear leaders say, 'I am open to the gifts of the Spirit and to God doing healing miracles.' Often people say this as though they think there is something noble about being 'open.' However, being open doesn't count very much with God. A person who is simply open is still a person who does not yet believe.

If a non-Christian died while he was open to the possibility that Jesus may have died on the cross for his sins, that person would still go to hell. It is not being open that gets blessing from God, it is believing and pursuing what he promised. Jesus never said, 'Blessed are the open.'

Would you give your money to a stock broker who said that he was open to making a profit with your life savings? Being open simply doesn't count for very much. I am sure in most cases it is better than being hostile, but a state of openness is not going to cause us to advance in spiritual things. Paul did not tell us to be open to the spiritual gifts; he told us to pursue them diligently (1 Cor. 12:31; 14:1, 39). In the first century, people pursued Jesus and the apostles for healing and for miracles. They took their sick to them, expecting both diseases and demons to leave. I do not believe the church today will see widespread healing and miracles until it once again hungers for these things.

The Redemptive Value of Suffering

Most of the time when the New Testament speaks of suffering it is not referring to enduring physical illness but rather to enduring persecution for righteousness sake. Nevertheless, I am still convinced that sometimes there is a divinely intended blessing in some physical sicknesses. In these cases God does not heal a condition or grant the miracle for which we are praying but instead gives us the grace to endure the unpleasant condition.

No one really knows what Paul's 'thorn in the flesh' was. It may have been an illness, or then again it may have been some type of persecution that he was receiving. Whatever it was, God chose not to remove it. Paul says,

> Three times I pleaded with the Lord to take it away from me. But he said to me, 'My grace is sufficient for you, for my power is made perfect in weakness.' Therefore I will boast all the more gladly about my weaknesses, so that Christ's power may rest on me. That is why, for Christ's sake, I delight in weaknesses, in insults, in hardships, in

persecutions, in difficulties. For when I am weak, then I am strong. (2 Cor. 12:8–10)

Paul found redeeming grace when he endured unrelieved suffering for Christ's sake.

Peter expresses the 'refining' value of suffering in a different way. He wrote,

> In this you greatly rejoice, even though now for a little while, if necessary, you have been distressed by various trials, that the proof of your faith, being more precious than gold which is perishable, even though tested by fire, may be found to result in praise and glory and honor at the revelation of Jesus Christ. (1 Pet. 1:6–7, NASB)

Peter says four things that ought to give us great comfort whenever God does not answer our prayers to remove suffering. First, he tells us that suffering is for 'now.' Sometimes when we go through a period of suffering, we are tempted to think that it is going to last forever, but Peter encourages us to think of it as just for 'now.' Second, he says the duration is 'for a little while.' In the light of eternity all suffering will amount to no more than just a breath or a vapor. Third, Peter says that the suffering comes to us only 'if necessary.' Finally, the outcome of all of our suffering is compared to a refining process, 'tested by fire,' in which our character is improved. This results in praise and glory and honor being given to the Lord Jesus Christ. When we endure unmitigated suffering without letting it diminish our love or confidence in the Lord Jesus Christ, this conforms us even more to his image and brings great glory to him. So if you have confidence in God to heal, and you ask him to heal but he does not, it may well be that he is going to let you bring glory to his Son through your suffering. If this is his intention, he will also give you the grace to endure the affliction.

I need to warn you about something. You would make a horrible mistake if you assumed that redemptive suffering is the same thing as God's judgment for our sin or discipline of our sin. When Peter used the phrase 'if necessary,' he was not referring to judgment. God may allow suffering to come to us for a variety of reasons other than judgment for our sin. Job was considered by God the most righteous and blameless man on earth, yet God allowed Job to suffer horribly. Certainly this suffering had a refining effect on Job's character, but under no circumstances will the Bible allow us to view Job's suffering as God's judgment on him. I find all too often that many of God's children mistakenly assume that their afflictions are evidence of God's judgment on them.

I do believe that God can send catastrophic judgments into our life for our sin (cf. 1 Cor. 5:1–5). However, I think that he only does this for significant acts of rebellion on our part. If you are not in rebellion against your Lord, and yet you are suffering, do not let the Devil torment you with condemning thoughts of judgment.

My own practice is to pray for my experiences of suffering to be healed or relieved unless the Lord specifically tells me that he does not intend to remove the suffering. In that case I want to trust him as the loving heavenly Father he is and endure the suffering he has allowed to come my way with love and confidence in my heart. I try to reject all of the condemning thoughts that 'the accuser of our brothers' (Rev. 12:10) is so quick to heap on me, otherwise the refining effect that God intends the suffering to have on me may be greatly reduced.

Sovereign Timing and Sovereign Mysteries

I mentioned at the beginning of this chapter that there are times when God chooses not to give any reason at all for why he heals or why he does not heal. When Jesus was at the Pool of Bethesda, he only healed one paralytic (John 5:1–15), even though there were sick people lying all around the pool. We are never told why it was the Father's will only to heal that one person and to allow all the other sick people to continue suffering.

I once went to pray for a little baby who had been born without a brain. Only a small portion of the brain stem had developed. This baby was born to a Christian family who had already lost two sons to tragic deaths. When I was asked to go into the intensive care unit and pray for the little child, I thought I experienced faith rising in my heart. I remembered a famous medically documented healing of a baby boy born in Vancouver, British Columbia, with almost an identical condition. The boy's father, Paddy Duclow, had described the healing to me which mystified the doctors in Vancouver and made his son a medical phenomenon in that city. I was thinking of this healing when I went into the intensive care unit to pray for the little baby.

I was amazed when I saw the baby boy. He was beautiful! He looked so healthy and normal. The family's pastors and I prayed for the child, and even though we had no sense of God's special divine presence, we thought there was a good chance that the little boy would be healed. Instead, the next day the little boy died. When I returned home to my own city, I found that the Lord had healed a woman of a venereal disease in our church, a woman who had not been particularly repentant. I felt anger rising within me. I asked God why he would heal a woman who did not deserve healing and let an innocent little baby die.

It was as though the Lord said to me, 'So who *does* deserve healing? Are you going to be the one who decides how to dispense my mercy?' That rebuke was enough for me. God didn't explain to me why the baby died and why he healed the woman, but he did remind me that he truly is sovereign and he does not have to explain himself to anyone.

I am sure that other factors influence miracles or the lack of miracles. I am sure that there are ebbs and flows in outpourings of miraculous healing, just as there are in revival history. In every age people are always being saved and always being healed, but there are times of sovereign outpourings of grace when these things happen in abundance. The church has not experienced constant revival, but rather has come in and out of revival over the last two thousand years. Some parts of the church have never experienced revival. For example, with the exception of the aboriginal people, the Australians have never experienced a revival. We would, of course, be wrong to conclude from this that God is not giving revivals any longer. It simply illustrates that there are ebbs and flows in the history of revival.

Besides the ebbs and flows in God's divine timing and the redemptive value of suffering, I am sure that there are other biblical factors that influence the frequency of miracles. But surely the main human factors that inhibit the outpouring of God's miraculous power are those mentioned in this chapter: apostasy in all of its various forms, legalism and lukewarm faith, and unbelief.

By the way, any church—charismatic, Pentecostal, Third Wave, noncharismatic, or anticharismatic—can be guilty of the three negative reasons that I have given to partially explain why God may not heal (that is, apostasy, legalism and lukewarm faith, and unbelief). Even a church with a strong theoretical belief in divine healing can actually be filled with unbelief when it comes to the practical business of praying for its sick members. In fact, based on my personal experience, I would have to say that this latter phenomenon is not all that uncommon.

I do not believe that these negative factors will ever be overcome simply by resisting them. The antidote for these sins is the pursuit of a Person. The Lord gave Solomon a promise that is still valid for today:

If my people, who are called by my name, will humble themselves and pray and seek my face and turn from their wicked ways, then I will hear from heaven and will forgive their sin and will heal their land. (2 Chron. 7:14)

If the church would follow that counsel, I believe God would give us anything we ask for (assuming, of course, that our request is consistent with Scripture). I believe he would give us revival, miracles, divine revelation and, above all, an intimacy with him that few of us have ever experienced. One of the great tasks of church leaders of our generation is to get the church to believe this promise. We need to cast our unbelief aside and pursue the unlimited Lord of the Scriptures.

SEEKING THE GIFTS AND
THE GIVER

12

Pursuing the Gifts With Diligence

Leesa and I have a very dear friend who is afflicted with severe headaches. So far no physician has been able to come up with a cause or a cure for these headaches. Sometimes the headaches are debilitating, and sometimes they stop just short of being debilitating. Our friend is a wonderful wife and mother, and she loves God with all of her heart. She spends the early morning hours of every day meditating on the Bible and laboring in prayer for the advancement of God's kingdom. She told us the other day that those first few hours of the morning were her primary reason for living. She is convinced that God has put her on the earth to labor in prayer for God's glory to be revealed. She has been as faithful in prayer as anyone I have ever known.

We have prayed for the Lord to heal our friend of these headaches, but so far they have actually gotten worse. Recently a physician prescribed a drug that has been successful in taking away the pain. The problem is that she has to take the drug before she goes to sleep, and it leaves her groggy until about mid-morning. Now our friend is caught in this dilemma: if she takes the drug she cannot concentrate well enough to pray or meditate in the morning, but if she does not take the drug she has to endure severe headaches. Her prayer time is so important to her that she frequently forgoes the medication and endures the pain of the headaches in order to continue her morning intercession.

I am frequently asked by healthy people why I believe healing is so important. Ask our friend suffering from the headaches why healing is important. She will tell you that the physical pain can be excruciating, but she will also tell you that the way the pain interrupts her prayer life is just as frustrating, if not more so. Sure, God has given her the grace to endure both the pain and the frustration, and she will continue to endure if she has to. But she would prefer to have grace for healing.

Sick people have no difficulty in telling you why healing is important. In fact, everyone really believes in the importance of healing. We have hospitals and a medical profession because people believe in the importance of healing. In the Western world the medical community has gotten so proficient at healing that people do not think they need God for healing anymore. Divine healing does not seem very important until we reach the point where physicians and modern medicine cannot help us. Anyone who has a chronic condition that cannot be cured or significantly alleviated through modern medical means will soon have a different perspective on the importance of divine healing.

I have stood beside a hospital bed and watched a cute little boy dying of AIDS. The doctor and the hospital had done all they could. They had told the parents it was hopeless. The family's church had told them it was hopeless and had even preached against divine healing. Yet the little boy's parents hoped that their church was wrong. The anguish on their faces spoke volumes about the importance of divine healing.

You do not have to have AIDS to realize that divine healing is important. None of our illnesses or pains are too insignificant to bring to the Lord. He actually commands us to 'cast all your anxiety on him because he cares for you' (1 Pet. 5:7). It is legitimate to bring anything to him that causes us anxiety. It may be an illness or a chronic condition that the medical community cannot heal, or it may be an illness for which we cannot afford treatment. Whatever it is, we have the divine permission to bring it to him first of all.

Healing is so important to our heavenly Father that he has commanded the elders of the church to pray for the sick as part of their normal shepherding ministry (James 5:14–16). Our Father is concerned about the whole person. He is concerned about our body and our emotions, not just our minds and our wills. There is a Gnostic mentality in much of the church today that teaches that God is not really concerned about our bodies. The apostle John did not share the Gnostic mentality of his day. He showed God's concern for the body, when under the inspiration of the Holy Spirit, he wrote to Gaius, 'Dear friend, I pray that you may enjoy good health and that all may go well with you, even as your soul is getting along well' (3 John 2).

Healing is not the only spiritual gift that is important. The Lord commands us to eagerly desire the gifts, especially prophecy (1 Cor. 12:31; 14:1, 39). The gifts were given to us as tools to edify the body (1 Cor. 12:7). We can never get too knowledgeable in the Word or too mature for spiritual gifts. I don't know anyone who has reached the level of maturity or knowledge that the apostle Paul had reached. Yet Paul never felt that he outgrew his need for the gifts.

Each of the miraculous gifts, as well as the other spiritual gifts that are not normally classified as miraculous, have valuable contributions to make to Christ's body. But these contributions will never be made, and the growth that could have come to the body will be lost, unless the leadership of the church learns how to cultivate these gifts within the body.

How to Cultivate the Gifts of the Spirit

Some people have a difficult time understanding how you can cultivate or develop a gift that is supernaturally empowered.[1] This difficulty stems from viewing the miraculous gifts as magical or mechanical. A teacher can grow in the gift of teaching, and an evangelist can grow in the gift of evangelism. Why is it difficult to believe that someone can grow in the gift of healing or prophecy?

The truth is that we can grow in every spiritual exercise and every spiritual gift. There are a number of important things we can do to cultivate the gifts of the Spirit in our own lives and in our church.

First, you must be convinced that the Bible teaches the gifts are for today and that they are important; otherwise you won't have faith to exercise them or to pray for them. Likewise, you must be confident that the gifts are given to all Christians (1 Pet. 4:10) rather than just a few specially deserving people. Once I came to these two conclusions, I was in a place to begin to cultivate the gifts in my own life.

As soon as I was convinced that the Scriptures taught the gifts of the Spirit are for today, I began to pursue them diligently. The most important thing I have done in pursuing the gifts has been to pray very specifically for the gifts I felt the Lord wanted to give me. Even though the Holy Spirit distributes the gifts to each one just as he wills (1 Cor. 12:11), Paul still encouraged the Corinthians to pray for gifts. If you have the gift of tongues, for example, Paul says that you should pray for the gift of interpretation (1 Cor. 14:13). Don't be passive. Don't say, 'God can give me any gift he wants to.' God could also make you a great Bible scholar if he wanted to, but I don't know any great Bible scholars who got that way without diligently pursuing the knowledge of the Bible. Nor do I know any great evangelists who got that way without diligently pursuing evangelism.

Remember, 'You do not have, because you do not ask God' (James 4:2). I pray every single day specifically for the gifts of the Spirit that I want to be operative in my life. For example, healing is one of the gifts that I want to regularly experience in my ministry. I pray every day for the Lord to give me authority and power in this gift. I mention specifically the kinds of diseases and conditions that I want to see him heal when I pray for people.

Probably the second most valuable thing I have done in my pursuit of spiritual gifts is that I have attempted to use them on a regular basis. More often than not this involves some risk, and specifically the risk of looking foolish. Almost as soon as I began to ask God to give me a healing ministry, I began to pray for sick people. Most of the sick people I prayed for at first did not get healed. When I first began to give words of knowledge in public, I also had some embarrassing moments. But there is no other way to grow in anything apart from constant practice and risking. The only good athlete you will ever see is a bad one who didn't give up. The only good disciple you will ever see is a bad one who didn't give up. When the disciples first started out with Jesus, they were incredibly dull and not particularly promising. However, the eleven who didn't give up became the leaders of the church. Think of the spiritual gifts in terms of the parable of the talents (Matt. 25:14–30). If we don't risk, our gift will not grow, and if our gift does not grow, the Lord will not be pleased with us.

A third thing I have found helpful is, of course, to study the gifts. The Scriptures have a great deal to say about spiritual gifts, as well as numerous examples of supernatural ministry. The Bible offers us many helpful principles concerning the miraculous ministry. I have read and continue to read a number of books dealing with the ministry of the gifts of the Spirit, as well as biographies of Christians who were used powerfully in supernatural ministries.

Another thing that has been extremely helpful to me in my

pursuit of spiritual gifts is having friendships with people who are more advanced in the gifts than I am. The Scriptures say that 'as iron sharpens iron, so one man sharpens another' (Prov. 27:17). I will forever be indebted to friends like John Wimber and Paul Cain who have 'sharpened' me in the area of spiritual gifts. Friendships are a far more serious matter than most people realize. We are going to be like our friends (Prov. 13:20). That is why it is so important to cultivate friendships with people you admire and want to be like.

It is also helpful to have a nonthreatening atmosphere when you begin to practice the gifts of the Spirit. If your church does not believe in the gift of tongues, the Sunday morning worship service is not the place for you to begin practicing that gift. One of the most helpful, nonthreatening places to begin to learn about the gifts of the Spirit is in small, informal home groups of ten to twenty people. The small size makes it possible to get to know one another relatively well and to feel a degree of security. It is much easier to attempt to give a prophetic word in front of twenty people who know you and love you than in front of five hundred people on Sunday morning who may not know you at all. In an informal setting like a home group, it is easier to talk about the ministry that was attempted that evening and analyze it than in a much larger and more formal setting.

I have also found conferences on spiritual gifts to be helpful. In the ideal conference there will be a number of speakers on different subjects who have had a wide range of experience in the miraculous gifts of the Spirit. There will be healing and revelatory power in that conference so that the participants can see firsthand how these gifts work. The ideal conference of this nature is one whose purpose is to train the participants in the gifts of the Spirit. In these kinds of conferences you have the opportunity to actually exercise the gifts of the Spirit, as opposed to just watching a gifted individual use his gift.

We want to pursue spiritual gifts for the right reasons. Years ago, while I was jogging along a river bank, I was praying for the Lord to release greater healing gifts in my ministry. As I was praying very specifically, a voice erupted inside my mind and said, 'What do you want these gifts for?' I recognized that voice immediately as the voice of the Lord, and it offended me. Among other things, my pursuit of the gifts of the Spirit had cost me dear friendships. I was pursuing the gifts of the Spirit for God. Why would he ask me a question like that? I slowly realized, however, that an omniscient Being does not ask questions for information. The question had been for my sake, not to fill up gaps in God's personal knowledge of my psychology. As I began to ponder that question slowly and painfully, impure motives in my request began to emerge. I realized that there was still a great deal of carnality in my desire for the gifts of the Spirit.

One of the greatest mercies that God can give to his children is to show them their sin. You cannot repent of sin that you cannot see. When the divine light exposes our darkness, we can repent, confess, and receive his forgiveness (1 John 1:9). Without the revelatory ministry of the Holy Spirit, we cannot understand the motives of our heart (Jer. 17:9–10). All of this is extremely important in our pursuit of spiritual gifts, because our motives are a significant factor in the release of power in our lives.

Remember what moved Jesus to heal and to do miracles. He did miracles to prove that he was the Son of God, to show the truth of the gospel, to bring glory to God, to display compassion for the hurting, to open doors for evangelism, and so on. When we share his motives, he can trust us with his power. As I pray for the release of spiritual gifts in my life, therefore, I also pray for the heart and the affections of the Lord Jesus to be released in my life.

Finally, as you are learning about spiritual gifts, be patient. Don't despise the day of small beginnings. Be thankful for everything you are learning and for every answer to prayer the Lord gives you. Be thankful even for the frustration you feel when things seem to be going too slowly. If you will persist in your pursuit of the Lord and his gifts, more will be given to you than you ever dreamed to ask.

People who want more of God and more of the gifts of the Spirit almost always feel that things are moving too slowly. They almost always fear that they are going to miss out. But if you really desire more of God and more of his gifts, it is a sign that the mercy of God is resting upon you. These desires were put into your heart by your heavenly Father, and he has not drawn you this far to abandon you or leave you unfulfilled. The holy frustration you feel right now is meant to drive you on. He wants you to be thankful for what you have, but he never wants you to be content with your present level of divine intimacy. Like the apostle Paul, he wants you to press on 'to know Christ and the power of his resurrection and the fellowship of sharing in his sufferings, becoming like him in his death' (Phil. 3:10).

Put Your Confidence in Christ

If you really want to experience the supernatural ministry of the Holy Spirit, perhaps the most important thing I can tell you is to put your confidence in Christ's power, wisdom, and goodness, not in your own godliness or traditions. The power for miracles does not come out of our godliness, rather it was bought with the blood of God's Son. After Jesus had healed all of the sick people in Capernaum, Matthew said, 'This was to fulfill what was spoken through the prophet Isaiah: He took up our infirmities and carried our diseases' (Matt. 8:17). Matthew quoted from Isaiah 53, that great chapter in the Old Testament which describes Jesus' substitutionary death on the cross in the place of sinners. Matthew is teaching us that the power for healing can only be found in one place, in the cross of Christ.

Don't ever try to talk God into healing someone because that sick person deserves it. No one is healed because they deserve it. We are only healed because of the goodness of the Son of God expressed in his sacrifice for us. Never make the mistake of thinking that when you pray for someone it is your godliness or the power of your personal holiness that will bring healing for that person. Remember that after Peter was used to heal the lame man who sat at the temple gate, he said to an astonished crowd of onlookers, 'Men of Israel, why does this surprise you? Why do you stare at us as if by our own power or godliness we had made this man walk? The God of Abraham, Isaac and Jacob, the God of our fathers, has glorified his servant Jesus' (Acts 3:12–13). Put your confidence in Christ rather than in your own goodness or the goodness of those for whom you pray.

Never rely on formulas or traditions. The seven sons of Sceva, a Jewish chief priest, thought they had discovered the right formula for casting out demons. One day they said to a demon possessed man, 'In the name of Jesus, whom Paul preaches, I command you to come out' (Acts 19:13). They got the right name, 'Jesus.' They even had the right Jesus, the one 'whom Paul preaches.' And finally, they had the right command, 'Come out.' According to the formula, they had everything right, but the demon did not come out. Instead he overpowered all seven men and sent them running for their lives naked and bleeding! They had the right formula, but they did not have the right relationship. Divine power does not travel in *words* but in *a personal relationship* (John 5:19; 15:5). We cannot simply go around saying the right words and shouting the right commands and expect results. Jesus had to be led by his Father, and so do we.

I have to remind myself of this principle all the time. Sometimes the Lord will lead me to pray a certain way or do a certain thing, and it proves to be effective for someone's healing or for casting out a demon. My tendency is to want to turn that successful prayer into a formula. I think that if it worked before, it will work again. It is so easy to put our confidence in formulas or in our traditional ways of doing things. It feels so much more secure than trying to listen to our heavenly Father for moment-by-moment instructions. Yet the one who had the most super-natural ministry of all said, 'The Son . . . can do only what he sees his Father doing' (John 5:19). Jesus must be our model, not our formulas or our traditions.

There is another way that tradition can work against us. A friend of mine, Dr. Ralph Neighbour, Jr., wrote a book with one of the best titles I have ever heard—*The Seven Last Words of the Church: 'We've Never Done It That Way Before.'* What Dr. Neighbour was saying was that our enslavement to tradition can cause us to miss out on the present leading of the Holy Spirit. If God was really serious when he said, 'My thoughts are not your thoughts, neither are your ways my ways' (Isa. 55:8), then we will miss God's leading by constantly relying on our reasoning, our inter-pretations, and our traditions.

So much of the church is afraid to try anything new or differ-ent from their traditions. They are afraid of being deceived. They are afraid of the New Age infiltration. In fact, they are afraid of *anything* that does not agree almost perfectly with the way they have been doing things for the last fifty years. Too much of the church has more confidence in Satan's ability to deceive us than in Jesus Christ's ability to lead us.

Don't get me wrong—I do think that various occult and New Age movements constitute a serious threat to the church. But there is a far greater threat to the life and power of the church than the New Age. Legalism, pharisaism, and enslavement to tradition are far greater threats within the church than anything that could attack us from without. This blind traditionalism sucks the very life out of the church and persecutes any new work the Holy Spirit wants to establish among us.

It is absolutely imperative, therefore, that *we put our confidence in the Lord's ability to lead us, not in Satan's ability to deceive us.* And we must put our confidence in the power of the blood of Christ, not in our godliness or our traditions.

Identifying Your Gifts

Identifying our spiritual gifts is not nearly as difficult as some would imagine. There are several keys to discovering gifts. The most obvious and practical clue is your degree of success in various attempts at ministry. The areas in which you are most successful are likely to be those areas in which you are gifted. If you repeatedly fail in your attempts at teaching but have success in your attempts at evangelism, that may indicate that you have an evangelistic gift rather than a teaching gift. Normally, you will have to minister in various areas before you can determine which gifts you have.

I also find that our desires frequently indicate the gifts that we have or the gifts the Lord wants to give us. When I began to desire to be used in a healing ministry, I had no evidence in my previous ministry that the Lord had gifted me in that way. As I began to pray for the Lord to use me to heal and then began to pray for people to be healed, I discovered that this was one of the gifts the Lord wanted to give to me. Remember, you must not be passive in regard to your spiritual gifts. Do not say, 'The Lord can give me any gift he wants, so I will just wait for him.' That is, of course, theologically correct, but it often becomes an excuse for passivity. Remember, Paul told us to eagerly desire spiritual gifts (1 Cor. 12:31; 14:1, 39). He also told us that we could pray for spiritual gifts (1 Cor. 14:13). Turn your desires into prayers, and soon you will know the gifts the Lord wants to give you.

The counsel of others can also be important. It is always possible for us to deceive ourselves about our gifts. I have a friend who has an amazing gift of evangelism. Yet he is ignoring that gift of evangelism and trying to become a teacher. I don't think he has the gift of teaching, nor do others who know him well. In situations like these the counsel of others, especially trusted friends, can save us a lot of frustration and wasted effort.

Finally, gifts can be given through the laying on of hands with prophetic utterance. In the New Testament the apostles could do this, as Paul did for Timothy (2 Tim. 1:6). But apostles were not the only ones who could impart spiritual gifts. Paul exhorts Timothy, 'Do not neglect your gift, which was given you through a prophetic message when the body of elders laid their hands on you' (1 Tim. 4:14). Timothy had received a spiritual gift through the laying on of Paul's hands and through the laying on of the elders hands.

I have seen that happen a number of times over the past few years. After John Wimber prayed for me several years ago, I noticed an immediate increase, both in words of knowledge and healings, whenever I prayed for people. I have seen this happen on numerous occasions when Paul Cain has prayed for people to receive various spiritual gifts. I do not think this is automatic. It must be done under the leadership of the Holy Spirit or nothing will happen.

We can identify our spiritual gifts, therefore, in at least four ways: through our success or lack of success as we attempt to minister with various gifts, through our desires, through the counsel of others, and through prophetic impartation of spiritual gifts.

When You Find Yourself in Transition

Virtually every week I meet people or receive calls from people who find themselves in transition. They have been part of a church or a religious tradition that has rejected the contemporary use of the miraculous gifts, but for various reasons they now find themselves believing in these gifts and wanting to pursue them. Frequently this transition is accompanied by a great deal of conflict—churches are split, lifelong friendships are torn apart, marriages are strained, abusive accusations are hurled back and forth, and so on. I have been on both sides of this issue, and I know that much of this conflict is not necessary or inevitable.

Let's take the worst-case scenario. You are part of a group that does not believe in the miraculous gifts of the Spirit and is even hostile to those who believe in such gifts. Now all of a sudden you find yourself being drawn to the gifts of the Spirit, and you become convinced that they are for today. What do you do? The first thing that most people do is to assume that since God is changing them, he is also changing their church or their group. That may or may not be true, but you are clearly not entitled to that assumption. This is especially crucial if you are the pastor of a church that has been hostile to those who practice the gifts of the Spirit. The first thing you must ask the Lord to show you is whether he is changing you alone or both you and your church. Don't naively assume that because he is changing you, he is also going to change your church.

Don't misunderstand me. I believe that ultimately the Lord wants to change the whole church. I believe that in my lifetime the majority of the church is going to believe in and practice the gifts of the Spirit. All of the current statistical evidence from church growth studies indicates that the church is moving swiftly and inevitably to the miraculous gifts of the Holy Spirit. The church is returning to its first-century heritage. I am completely convinced that until the whole church embraces the gifts of the Spirit, we are losing a significant measure of our effectiveness.

However, God has his own timetable for all of us. He did not call the apostle Paul when he called the apostle John. God the Father is going to answer his Son's high-priestly prayer that the

church may 'be brought to complete unity to let the world know
that you sent me and have loved them even as you loved me'
(John 17:23). One day the church will be unified over the issue
of the miraculous gifts of the Spirit. That issue was settled when
the Lord Jesus Christ uttered his high-priestly prayer. The timing
of that unity has already been fixed in heaven, but you and I do
not know how this is going to work out on an individual basis.
Therefore, we must give everyone freedom to hear the Lord's
voice for themselves on this issue. Never assume that your change
automatically entails the change of those to whom you minister
or with whom you fellowship.

If you are the pastor of a church that does not want to pursue
the gifts of the Spirit, and yet the Lord is leading you to pursue the
gifts of the Spirit, most likely you will have to resign your pastorate. It is absolutely critical in this situation that you hear from
the Lord. If he tells you he is going to change your church, then
you should stay at your church and let him lead you in those
changes. But at this point it is much more important for you to let
the Lord change you than to change your church. If he is not
changing your church, and you do in fact resign, he has already
prepared another place for you. However, he may not take you to
that place right away.

One of my classmates from seminary very successfully pas-
tored a church for over ten years. Under his ministry the church
grew significantly. When he became convinced that the gifts of
the Spirit were for today, he knew that the Lord was not changing his church at that time. He resigned and has been in secular
employment for the last two years. He and his wife joined another
church that believes in and practices the gifts of the Spirit. Occasionally he teaches and preaches in that church, as well as preaching in other churches. It has been very difficult for my friend and
his wife to have been out of professional ministry for these last
two years. However, now it looks as though God is about to lead

them back in to the full-time ministry. Looking back on this time, they both tell me that they are very grateful for the two years they have had in which to learn so much about the gifts of the Spirit without the pressure of leading a church. God has many different ways of bringing us all to the same goal.

Sometimes, when you have spent a long time rejecting the gifts of the Spirit and come to believe in them, you almost feel as if you are being born again. You feel as if you have a whole new Bible. By that latter statement I mean that the Gospels and Acts come alive for you in a way that they never have before. Things that you had relegated to the first century now become a possibility for today's church. This is a wonderful awakening, but like other awakenings your enthusiasm can do a lot of harm, as well as a lot of good. Let me give you some advice about things not to do during this time.

If your pastor and the leadership of your church do not view your change in a positive light, resist the attempt to label them. Resist the attempt to pressure them. Instead, pray for your pastor and the leadership of your church. Pray for God to richly bless their ministries and for them to hear accurately the voice of the Holy Spirit. Don't assume that hearing the Holy Spirit means that they will follow in your steps. It may be that God has them on a different timetable than you.

Your pastor already has enough criticism and negative pressure without you adding to it. I have been a pastor for much of my adult life, and I know how difficult it is. A few people actually believe that you can do no wrong and will blindly follow you any-where. But most of the time somebody is mad at you because you are going too far, and somebody else is mad at you because you are not going far enough. Remember how much mercy God has shown you, and show a little of that mercy to your pastor and leadership.

Above all, never join a group in your church that is against your pastor and the leadership. It would be much better for you to leave your church and your friends than to rebel against the authority structure God has placed over you. If the Lord wants to change that authority structure, he is perfectly capable of doing so without your assisting other people in an unholy coup.

During your transition time, even if you do not join an unholy coup, it is likely that some of your friends will misunderstand you, will think that you are taking on a holier-than-thou attitude, and will accuse you of participating in secret meetings for the 'spiritual elite' in the church. Some may even say that you are a tool of Satan who has been raised up to cause strife in the church. When unkind things are said about you, it is natural to become defensive. When unkind things are said about you because you are pursuing something you think is right, it is natural for you to take on a self-righteous martyr's complex. The tendency is to think that you and the others with you are the only ones really interested in truth and the only ones ready to sacrifice for what they believe. Those on the other side of the fence can see this attitude immediately, and it only intensifies the conflict.

Solomon had some great advice about responding to unkind things people say about you. He said, 'Do not pay attention to every word people say, or you may hear your servant cursing you—for you know in your heart that many times you yourself have cursed others' (Eccl. 7:21–22). The truth is that we have all said negative things about our friends when we have disagreed with them, and the truth is that most of the time we really didn't mean it.

I have been through one of these conflicts that I am describing. I said unkind things about others and to others, and I had unkind things said about me. Yet when it actually came time to part, and I had to look my dear friends and colaborers in the eyes, we embraced each other and cried. We didn't mean the unkind things we had said. We really didn't. How I wish I had followed the advice I am giving you now. The cause of Christ will never be advanced by Christians attacking one another.

One of the most eloquent admonitions I have ever encountered along these lines is in Bishop Burnet's preface to the classic work *The Life of God in the Soul of Man,* written by Henry Scougal in the latter part of the seventeenth century. Here is what Burnet wrote:

> There is scarce a more unaccountable thing to be imagined, than to see a company of men professing a religion, one great and main precept whereof is mutual love, forbearance, gentleness of spirit, and compassion to all sorts of persons, and agreeing in all the essential parts of its doctrine, and differing only in some less material and more disputable things, yet maintaining those differences with zeal so disproportioned to the value of them, and prosecuting all that disagree from them with all possible violence; or if they want means to use outward force, with all bitterness of spirit. They must needs astonish every impartial beholder, and raise great prejudices against such persons' religion, as made up of contradictions; professing love, but breaking out in all the acts of hatred.[2]

Somewhere someone has to stop this. Someone has to stop returning insult for insult, unkindness for unkindness. Why not make up your mind that no matter what is said about you, you are not going to reply in kind. And never forget that immediately after Paul told his readers to 'eagerly desire the greater gifts,' he wrote, 'If I . . . have not love, I gain nothing' (1 Cor. 13:3).

13

A Passion for God

One of the most pleasant tasks that I had as a seminary professor was to teach the book of Psalms. I love meditating on the Hebrew text of the Psalms and trying to unravel the meaning of intricate figures of speech. As much as I love the Psalms, however, there were two things that consistently 'bothered' me whenever I meditated on the Psalms in those days. I felt uneasy about the psalmists' intense pursuit of God. Let me give you a few examples of the kind of intensity that troubled me.

> As the deer pants for streams of water,
>   so my soul pants for you, O God.
> My soul thirsts for God, for the living God.
>   When can I go and meet witph God? (42:1–2)

> O God, you are my God,
>   earnestly I seek you;
> my soul thirsts for you,
>   my body longs for you,
> in a dry and weary land
>   where there is no water. (63:1)

> One thing I ask of the LORD,
>   this is what I seek:

that I may dwell in the house of the LORD
  all the days of my life,
to gaze upon the beauty of the LORD
  and to seek him in his temple. (27:4)

My eyes stay open through the watches of the night,
  that I may meditate on your promises. (119:148)

When C. S. Lewis attempted to describe this phenomenon in the Psalms, he refused to call it 'the love of God' because he thought that would be misleading. Instead he referred to the psalmists' intensity as an 'appetite for God.'[1] Lewis felt that some people might think the expression 'appetite for God' was too harsh. Personally, I think it is too tame for what we encounter in the Psalms. I would rather use the expression, *hunger for God*, or *passion for God*. The writers of the Psalms had a longing for God's presence that was overwhelming—and that bothered me.

It bothered me because I began my Christian life with at least some of that longing. When I was seventeen years old, as a new convert, I remember staying up late at night after everyone else in my house had gone to bed, so that I could talk with God and have no interruptions or distractions. I can remember running to the mailbox to receive my latest packet of Navigator verses to memorize and then staying up till 3:00 or 4:00 in the morning, meditating on those verses and memorizing every one of them.

No one made me do these things. I did them because I hungered after God. But by the time I had become a seminary professor and was teaching these things in the Psalms, I was no longer staying up late at night to memorize the Bible. I could not say with the psalmist that 'my eyes stay open through the watches of the night, that I may meditate on your promises' (Ps. 119:148). I am not saying that I never experienced God's presence during those later years. I did have some tender moments with the Lord, but I could not say with the psalmists that my soul consistently 'thirsted' for God. I felt a twinge of guilt every time I read or taught one of those passages like the ones previously quoted.

The second thing that bothered me in the Psalms was the emotion of the psalmists. They exhibited not only an intense joy in the Lord but also called others to the same joy as though it was supposed to be normative for every believer. It is one thing for the psalmist to say something like, 'Let Israel rejoice in their Maker; let the people of Zion be glad in their King' (Ps. 149:2). I could have rationalized that one away. But the psalmist does not stop there; he goes on to explain what he means by 'rejoice in their Maker.' In the next verse he exhorts the people to 'praise his name with dancing and make music to him with tambourine and harp' (Ps. 149:3).

Dancing?

Yes, the psalmist said we are to praise God with dancing. The psalmist's joy was so great that it took his whole body, not just his voice, to give it adequate expression.

This was not an uncommon way to express intense joy in the Lord. Miriam, David, and Jephthah's daughter were so overcome with joy in the Lord that they all danced before him.[2] I am not trying to make an argument for dancing in our church services today; instead I am illustrating the point that the joy of the Lord was so great in these saints that they could not keep from dancing.

Joy was just one of the emotions I encountered again and again in the Psalms. The psalmists could also express an almost limitless grief or sadness over their sin or over the absence of God's presence. Listen again to the author of Psalm 42:

> My soul thirsts for God, for the living God.
>   When can I go and meet with God?
> My tears have been my food day and night,
>   while men say to me all day long,
>   'Where is your God?' (42:2–3)

Anyone who has read the Psalms at all knows that the psalmists are capable of great emotional extremes. And I did not like this characteristic of the Psalms. I did not mind emotion being displayed in a football game or some other athletic contest, but it seemed out of place in religious settings.

In commenting on the absence of emotion in the worship of his denomination, C. S. Lewis said, 'We have a terrible concern about good taste.'[3] I felt that emotion in religion was in poor taste. I disliked and distrusted emotion. Weak people were emotional; strong people were not.

To this day I have a vivid picture in my mind of one of my boys crying when he was seven years old. He was crying not because he had injured himself, but because his feelings were hurt. As I looked at him crying, I felt a mild revulsion. I interpreted those tears as weakness, and I did not like seeing that in my own son.

I loved to say that I lived by the Word of God, not by my feelings. I had preached so many sermons on this theme that I had come to regard feelings and the Word of God as mutual enemies.

The thing that so troubled me about the Psalms was that they did not share my view of emotions. The psalmists seemed to give full vent to their feelings. They were unashamed in their passionate hunger for God, in the intense joy they felt in his presence, and in the tears they shed over their sin or his absence. It bothered me that my experience did not match theirs, and I could not find a satisfying method to rationalize away their experience. Was their experience supposed to be normative? Why was mine so different?

Although I am no psychologist, I think I understand why I came to distrust and dislike emotions so much. My aversion to feelings came through a combination of a childhood trauma and a theological system that I adopted a few years after my conversion.

When I was a young boy, I admired my father more than any other man—more than any hero in the movies or on television. I viewed him as incredibly intelligent. He seemed to have an answer for every question that I ever asked him. I also viewed him as physically powerful. He had fought in World War II, and even after he had been wounded by exploding shrapnel that had been driven deep into his back, he kept on fighting for two days. To my young mind he was a man's man in every way.

It happened not long after my twelfth birthday, while we were all away from the house.

My dad walked into the kitchen, poured some whiskey into some coffee, and used the mixture to wash down some barbiturates. He scribbled out a one-page note, and then he walked into the living room where he put a sad piano piece called 'Last Date' on the record player. He adjusted the phonograph so that it played the record again and again. He listened to that record play through several times before he took one of the family guns and put an end to his depression and confusion.

My dad left behind a thirty-four-year-old widow with an eleventh-grade education and four young children to care for. I was the oldest at twelve; my sister was the youngest at three. Somewhere out of that trauma I made up my mind that I was going to be strong, and that I would never let myself be hurt like that again.

My mother's father died that same year from a heart attack. Suddenly I was the man of the family, and I took on a stoic resolve that left no room for emotions.

Five years later I was wonderfully and thoroughly converted at the age of seventeen. I think I could have made peace with my emotions, and even embraced them, if it had not been for the theological system I found myself adopting a few years later.

Rationalizing Our Lack of Passion

I have already confessed that there was a gulf between my experience of God and the psalmists' experience of God. If I were totally honest, I would have to admit that my experience was not only different from that of the psalmists but also different from that of every great hero in the Bible. They all seemed to exhibit a *continuing* passion for God that I had lost.

I had to do one of two things. I had to somehow get that passion back, or I had to find a good excuse for not having passion any more. I adopted a theological system that gave me an excuse for not having passion for God.

Here's the system in a nutshell. Feelings are deceptive and are not to be trusted. In fact, all things subjective are to be distrusted. The Bible is objective, and therefore it alone can be trusted. The Bible tells us that the greatest commandment is to love God and our neighbor as ourselves (Matt. 22:36–40). This love is not primarily a feeling. Instead, love is actually obedience to the commands of God. After all, Jesus said this explicitly in John 14:15, 21, and 23:

> If you love me, you will obey what I command.
>
> Whoever has my commands and obeys them, he is the one who loves me.
>
> If anyone loves me, he will obey my teaching.

I took all this to mean that feelings are not important as long as we are obeying the Lord. Right feelings should follow right actions, but even if they don't, the most important thing is obeying the commands of God. Since the Bible is the objective record of God's commands, it should be a simple matter to tell whether we are obeying the commands of God and, therefore, loving God.

This was the system that I had adopted and preached for years. This system kept me in bondage to an anemic version of Christianity and offered a convenient way to rationalize my lack of hunger for God.

Let me illustrate why this is a defective version not only of New Testament Christianity but also of love.

Over the years I have had a number of men, both from my seminary classes and from my churches, confess to me their attraction to pornography. A number of these men had successfully resisted the temptation to defile themselves with either pornographic books or movies. Yet they were troubled because in their hearts they found that they still wanted to look at pornography. There was an unwanted affection or emotional attachment to pornography in their hearts. I used to tell them not to worry about this as long as they were not looking at pornography. After all, right feelings are supposed to follow right actions, so their feeling would change soon enough. Yet sometimes their feelings did not change. Sometimes they went on for years.

According to my system, these feelings really were not important as long as the men were obeying. However, look at it from their wives' perspective. Were their wives satisfied that their husbands were longing to look at other women's bodies? Even though some of these husbands had not given in to the sin of pornography, their wives felt betrayed and hurt by the fact that their husbands were desiring it.

Every husband and wife knows that this is a defective form of Christianity. Is this the best that God has for us; to resist sin with the discipline of our wills, but to be in bondage to sin in our hearts?

On other occasions I have counseled with couples where the husband was a kind and faithful provider for his wife, but he had lost his passion for her. He no longer felt about her the way he did when they were courting and in the early years of their marriage. He had been doing the right things, but the feelings were no longer there. What wife would be satisfied with that kind of love?

I had embraced a form of Christianity that radically separated obedience and feelings. Obedience without emotion is nothing more than discipline or will power. It is not love. You cannot take the passion out of love and still have love. True love manifests itself not only in acts but also in feelings. Affection and passion are indispensable aspects of love for God.

The goal of the Christian life is not simply external obedience to the written commands of God. The goal of the Christian life is to obey God *from the heart* (Rom. 6:17; Eph. 6:6). No one can obey God from the heart unless the commands of God are written on his heart. This is the great difference between the Old Testament saint and the New Testament believer. Because we have access to the ministry of the Holy Spirit, he writes the commands of God on our hearts (Jer. 31:33; Heb. 10:16). We do not have to be content with external obedience. We can hate what God hates and love what God loves.

I was defending a system that actually justified lukewarm feelings toward God and his children. Yet Jesus said to the Laodiceans, 'So, because you are lukewarm—neither hot nor cold—I am about to spit you out of my mouth' (Rev. 3:16).

In 1746 Jonathan Edwards published a book, *The Religious Affections*, in which he argued that 'true religion must consist very much in the affections.'[4] Edwards saw that one of the chief works of Satan was

> to propagate and establish a persuasion that all affections and sensible emotions of the mind, in things of religion, are nothing at all to be regarded, but are rather to be avoided and carefully guarded against, as things of a pernicious tendency. This he knows is the way to bring all religion to a mere lifeless formality, and effectually shut out the power of godliness, and everything which is spiritual and to have all true Christianity turned out of doors.[5]

Edwards went on to say,

> As there is no true religion where there is nothing else but affection, so there is no true religion where there is no religious affection. . . . If the great things of religion are rightly understood, they will affect the heart. . . . This manner of slighting all religious affections is the way

exceedingly to harden the hearts of men, and to encourage them in their stupidity and senselessness, and to keep them in a state of spiritual death as long as they live and bring them at last to death eternal.[6]

Edwards took great pains to prove from the Scriptures that true Christianity is a religion of the emotions as well as the will. He showed that the Scriptures place a great deal of value on 'fear, hope, love, hatred, desire, joy, sorrow, gratitude, compassion, and zeal.'[7] We cannot love God or obey God without these sanctified emotions.

Getting Seduced

The irony is that almost everyone begins the Christian life with a passionate love and longing for Jesus. Along the way many of us lose that passion, but it does not have to stay lost—unless our theology says it is *normal* to live the Christian life without passion for Jesus.

When I was converted at seventeen, I had no religious or church background of any kind. Immediately, I fell in love with the Lord Jesus. I began to devour his Word. I talked to him constantly. I witnessed to every one of my non-Christian friends, again and again. I was so overzealous that I lost all but two of my friends. This loss did not affect me that much because I was so in love with Jesus that nothing else really mattered to me. Eventually I lost my first love and adopted a theology that justified that loss. It wasn't my theology, however, that caused me to lose my first love. It was something else.

After about a year, the original passion I had for the Lord Jesus began to fade somewhat. I could not point to the day or hour when it happened, nor could I give you a reason for it, but something was definitely different. The passion that I originally had for Jesus had subtly but surely been transferred to my denomination.

I loved my denomination. In our church we talked a lot about our denomination and how proud we were of it. It became difficult for me to understand why all true Christians would not want to be a part of my denomination. I also remember thinking that my church was perhaps the best church in the whole denomination.

I do not think that I ever loved my denomination too much, nor my church too much. The problem was that I loved Jesus too little in comparison with my church. Deception like this occurs so slowly and is so subtle that it is almost impossible to see while you are trapped by it. Eventually I repented of putting my church ahead of Jesus, and that original passion for him began to return.

I was seduced again in my quest to cultivate love for the Lord Jesus. It happened this way.

In the process of getting theologically trained and becoming a seminary professor, I developed an intense passion for studying God's Word. I found myself loving the Bible more than I loved the Author of the Bible. I was caught in this trap for more years than I like to remember.

Without realizing it, I began to think of the essence of the Christian life as Bible study or Bible knowledge. C. S. Lewis referred to my error this way, 'One is sometimes (not often) glad not to be a great theologian; one might so easily mistake it for being a good Christian.'[8] This is an easy trap to fall into when you live in an academic community whose major purpose is to teach the Scriptures and to train others to teach the Scriptures.

It took me too long to learn that knowing the Bible is not the same thing as knowing God, loving the Bible is not the same thing as loving God, and reading the Bible is not the same thing as hearing God. The Pharisees knew the Bible, loved the Bible, and read the Bible, but they did not know, love, or hear God.

One day Jesus said to them,

And the Father who sent me has himself testified concerning me. *You have never heard his voice* nor seen his form, nor does his word dwell in you, for you do not believe the one he sent. You diligently study the Scriptures because you think that by them you possess eternal life. These are the Scriptures that testify about me, yet you refuse to come to me to have life. (John 5:37–40, emphasis mine)

These men spent hours every day studying the Scriptures, and yet the Son of God said that they had never heard his Father's voice at any time. It is possible to read the Bible every day of our lives and never hear the voice of God!

The irony of all this was that I had given many sermons on the importance of doing what the Bible says, not just knowing what it says. Yet the majority of my efforts and time were given to understanding the Bible and orthodox theology rather than pursuing the Son of God and becoming like him. I had no idea of the depth of the deception that had gripped me.

Here are some obvious signs in the lives of those who put the Bible ahead of Jesus. They talk more about the Bible than they do about Jesus. Having right doctrine is more important to them than having a right life. This means that the ultimate test for admission into their groups is what you believe, not how you act. Their leaders can be harsh and authoritarian. Sins of pride, arrogance, and religious cruelty are often excused or overlooked. Preaching the Word is more important to them than modeling the Word.

I hate to admit this, but all those characteristics were true of my life when I put the Bible above the Lord Jesus. The problem was not that I loved the Bible too much, but that I loved Jesus too little in comparison with the Bible.

Some people get seduced by making *external* moral behavior and duty the essence of the Christian life. Those who do this will end up with the same kind of self-righteousness that characterized the Pharisees. Consider what Jesus said to those guilty of this sin:

Woe to you, teachers of the law and Pharisees, you hypocrites! You give a tenth of your spices—mint, dill and cummin. But you have neglected the more important matters of the law—justice, mercy and faithfulness. You should have practiced the latter, without neglecting the former. You blind guides! You strain out a gnat but swallow a camel.

Woe to you, teachers of the law and Pharisees, you hypocrites! You clean the outside of the cup and dish, but inside they are full of greed and self-indulgence. Blind Pharisee! First clean the inside of the cup and dish, and then the outside also will be clean.

Woe to you, teachers of the law and Pharisees, you hypocrites! You are like whitewashed tombs, which look beautiful on the outside but on the inside are full of dead mens' bones and everything unclean. In the same way, on the outside you appear to people as righteous but on the inside you are full of hypocrisy and wickedness. (Matt. 23:23–28)

If the essence of the Christian life becomes conformity to rules, we will always be led into self-righteousness.

I have always liked to think of myself as a person who is free of legalism and self-righteousness. In fact, I have always been infatuated with the image of myself as a 'holy nonconformist.' But in spite of this little fantasy, I have been seduced into legalism and self-righteousness a number of times in my walk with the Lord.

Let me tell you how the Lord showed me this.

In the process of leaving my church in Fort Worth and leaving my job as a professor at the seminary, I began to go through a personal revival in my affections for the Lord Jesus. By the time we had moved to Anaheim, California, to be part of the staff at the Vineyard Christian Fellowship, I felt closer to the Lord than I had since the days just following my conversion.

One day in the fall of 1988, while I was driving to my church office, I noticed that I was in an unusually happy mood. I took a quick survey of my life and could not find any reason to account for the joy I was experiencing that day. I had no vacation or upcoming trip to look forward to. I had no new possessions to make me happy, nor any recent spiritual victories to account for the happiness in my life. I was just plain joyful on the way to an ordinary day of work. I began to ask the Lord why I felt such a sense of joy.

As I took a survey of my life, I realized that I was closer to the Lord than I had been in a long time. I was praying more than I ever had before and was actually enjoying it. I was meditating on the Scriptures more consistently and longer than I ever had before. I had always studied the Bible for lectures and sermons, but now there was something new about the quality of time I was spending just meditating for my own personal benefit. I was giving myself to people in a way that I hadn't done before in ministry. And for the first time in my life I was beginning to fast on a regular basis.

(One of the nice things about being a cessationist is that once you have that category of 'things that passed out of existence at the end of the first century,' you are free to dump things into that category that you don't like. I put not only the gifts into that category but also fasting.)

Without realizing it, I had begun to congratulate myself on my walk with the Lord, on my consistency and discipline. At just that point the Lord spoke to me as clearly as if he were speaking in an audible voice. He said to me, '*Do not rejoice in your commitment to the Lord Jesus—rejoice in the Lord Jesus himself. If you rejoice in your commitment to Jesus, it will lead you into self-righteousness.*'

With that revelation, I received a divine perspective on my life. I saw periods where I was growing close to the Lord, and then I saw that closeness interrupted as I began to rejoice in my commitment to the Lord.

A few days later I believe that the Lord showed me where this truth was in the Scriptures. It is found in the parable of the

Pharisee and the tax collector in Luke 18:9–14. In that parable the Pharisee prayed, 'God, I thank you that I am not like other men— robbers, evildoers, adulterers—or even like this tax collector. I fast twice a week and give a tenth of all that I get.' The Pharisee's prayer demonstrates that he was actually rejoicing in his commitment to God rather than rejoicing in God. If this is not interrupted, it will always lead to self-righteousness, and self-righteousness will cause us to despise others (see Luke 18:9).

Some people get seduced by putting spiritual gifts above the Lord Jesus. This seems to be what happened to the Corinthians. Others get seduced by emotionalism. They strive to obtain a certain level of feeling more than seeking after the Lord Jesus. These kinds of people are easily led into hype and emotional excess.

There is another even more subtle seduction. The church's style of worship has been undergoing a major change. In much of the church today people are using hymnals less frequently and opting for a more contemporary form of music. Instead of two or three hymns placed at the beginning of the service and viewed as part of the 'preliminaries,' many churches have an extended time of worship music. In my opinion, much of this is good, but even here I see some people getting seduced. Some people are actually worshiping worship rather than worshiping the Lord Jesus.

I have even found people who put the Christian life over Jesus. I have found churchgoers, even seminary students, who were converted to a way of life, but they were not converted to Jesus Christ. They love the Christian life: they love fellowship, going to church, going to meetings, giving to worthy causes, the stimulation that comes from reading the Bible, and even praying. It is possible to do all of these things and never have trusted Jesus Christ to forgive your sins and give you eternal life. I have seen seminary students led to Christ in their fourth year of seminary training. I have seen church deacons come to faith in Christ after years of faithful service in a conservative church.

What I am saying is that it is possible to put almost any good thing above Jesus Christ without realizing what we are doing. We can put the Bible and its commandments above the Lord. We can put the spiritual gifts and even various kinds of worship above the Lord. We can put various forms of ministry—witnessing, caring for the poor, praying for the sick—above the Lord. It is possible to be seduced by all of these things.

We must not equate Jesus with any of these good things. Jesus is not a doctrine, a theology, an abstract principle, a ministry, a church, a denomination, an activity, or even a way of life. Jesus is a *person*, a real person. And he demands that we put him above all of these good things. None of these things died for us; the Son of God did. None of these things controls our destiny; the Son of God does. Anytime I begin to give more attention to one of these things or pursue one of them more than I am pursuing the Son of God, it will become an idol in my life to take me away from him. We so easily confuse loving these good things with loving Jesus. We so easily confuse being committed to these good things with being committed to God.

More than anything else, a passion for God has to be guarded and cultivated or we will lose it. I find that almost every good thing in my life is all too ready to compete for my time and intimacy with God. The essence of all of life is loving God and then loving his people (Matt. 22:36–40).

A Passionate Love

I often speak of 'passion' for Jesus instead of love for Jesus because the word *love* has lost its biblical meaning in many religious circles today. As I said earlier, there has been a consistent attempt by theologians and popular preachers to define love primarily in terms of duty, without any reference to its emotional quality. A love for God that is devoid of emotion is a fictional

product created by the minds of modern teachers. The Bible never
defines love in that way.

I like the word *passion* because it stresses the emotional side of
love. Passion can be defined as 'any kind of feeling by which the
mind is powerfully effected or moved: a vehement, commanding,
or overpowering emotion.'[9] Passion is a feeling that moves the
mind and the will to action. The term *passion* covers a whole range
of feelings that are appropriate to loving God. I am referring to
such things as desire, longing, zeal, affection, craving, hunger,
and so on. These feelings are all characteristic of a person who is
deeply in love.

I want these passionate feelings to characterize my relationship
with the Lord Jesus. Of course, I want to be perfectly obedient to
the Lord, but I want that obedience to spring out of a passionate
love for him. I want to obey Jesus not simply out of discipline or
duty, or because of some reward or fear of punishment. I want to
serve him simply for the joy of being able to please the one I love
so much. If discipline is what *ultimately* drives us in our pursuit of
Jesus, eventually we will give up that pursuit. *But a man in love or
a woman in love will never quit.* That is the nature of love (Song
8:6–7). I want my life to be characterized by an unrestrained
affection for the Son of God.

Is this a realistic goal or just wishful thinking? I have heard
some people teach that at the beginning of our relationship to
God it is normal to have passion for him, and after a relatively
short time it is just as normal to have that passion replaced with
a more reliable sense of duty and discipline. I have even heard
some teachers say that the loss of passion is a mark of spiritual
maturity. I think the Bible presents just the opposite picture.

Think about those quotes from the Psalms at the beginning of
this chapter. The psalmists had not lost their passion for God.
They were filled with a hunger and a longing for him. They used
the most vivid metaphors to express their craving for God. Just as

the deer thirsted for streams of water, so the psalmist's soul thirsted for God (Ps. 42:1–2). David said that his greatest prayer was to be able to sit in the house of the Lord simply 'to gaze upon the beauty of the LORD and to seek him in his temple' (Ps. 27:4). If Old Testament saints felt passionate about God, how much more should New Testament saints, who live in the light of the cross and the power of the Holy Spirit?

Yet if we have lost that passion, how can we regain it? And how does our passion for God relate to our experience of his power? We will explore these questions in the final chapter.

14

Developing Passion and Power

One day Jesus came to the village of Bethany and decided to stay at the home of Mary, the sister of Martha and Lazarus (Luke 10:38–42). Mary had such desire and affection for the Lord that she sat at his feet listening to all that he said. It was dinner time, but she preferred to listen to Jesus than to eat.

According to the normal rules of hospitality in the ancient Near East, Mary was responsible, along with her sister Martha, for serving Jesus and his disciples a meal. But she felt a stronger desire to listen to him and be with him than to serve him. Her affection for the Lord overpowered the normal rules of etiquette. I am sure that if Jesus had told Mary to go and help her sister Martha, she would have done it in an instant. But there was no way she was going to leave his presence unless he commanded her to do so.

When Martha attempted to get the Lord to rebuke Mary for her lack of help in preparing the meal, Jesus not only refused to rebuke Mary, he commended her. Mary had chosen him, even above service to him, and the Lord said that she had chosen the best part, the one thing that would never be taken away from her.

Preachers often use this incident as an argument for the

necessity of Bible study. Yet Mary wasn't studying the Bible; she was sitting at the feet of her favorite person and listening intently to everything he said.

Mary's deep passion for the Lord was also seen six days before Jesus' last Passover. He knew that he had only six more days before his cross. Where do you think he chose to spend these last six days? He passed over all the 'politically correct' people and places in Jerusalem and went to the town of Bethany, about two miles southeast of Jerusalem. He chose the home of Lazarus, Martha, and Mary. Why? Because this was the place his heavenly Father had chosen before the foundation of the earth to anoint his Son for burial.

To whom would God give the honor of anointing his Son?

It happened like this.

Mary walked in during the middle of dinner with a pound of pure nard, a perfume worth at least a year's wages. Then she 'wasted' that expensive perfume by pouring it on the feet of Jesus. Next she let down her hair and wiped the feet of the Lord with her hair (John 12:1–3).

This was an extraordinary act. It was also an improper act. Mary interrupted the dinner, she approached a male guest, she let down her hair in the manner of an immoral woman, and she did the work of a slave. What led her to humble herself and transgress the bounds of propriety?[1] What led her to such an extravagant waste?

It was this: she recognized the greatness of Jesus, and she knew that he was worthy of all of the extravagance she could lavish on him. He was worthy of the deepest humiliation she could suffer on his behalf. Mary was driven by a holy passion for the Son of God. She wasted that perfume on Jesus, and she would waste her entire life on him if he would give her the opportunity. The gift was extravagant, but the gift only reflected the extravagance of her feelings for Christ.

Both John and Luke give us these 'snapshots' of Mary because they are presenting her life to us as a model to be copied. How do we copy such a life? How do we develop the same passion and devotion that Mary had for Jesus?

Developing a Passion for Jesus

There are three simple steps to developing passion for Jesus. The first step is obvious. You cannot love someone or have passion for someone you do not know. Like Mary, we must take time to get to know Jesus. The more we sit at his feet and listen to him, the better we will know him. And the more we know him, the more we will love him.

We must set aside a regular time for personal meditation in the Scriptures and prayer. We must never allow this time to become mechanical or ritualistic. We must remember that it is possible to read the Bible like a Pharisee and never hear the voice of God (John 5:37). It is possible to let our prayer time degenerate into nothing more than taking a shopping list to God.

In our regular times of meditation and prayer, we must remind ourselves that the purpose is to meet with a real Person. This Person speaks, guides, encourages, reveals, and convicts. He gets angry, and he forgives. We are capable of grieving him or making him rejoice. These are things the Scriptures teach us about this God we come to in prayer.

We should not presume that because we can read we can enter into his presence. A mechanical reading of the Bible or a ritualistic prayer will not get us into God's presence. The psalmist asked God, 'Open my eyes that I may see wonderful things in your law' (Ps. 119:18). He knew that without the presence of God to illumine the Word, he would never 'see wonderful things.' Ask for God's presence; don't assume it. Come to his Word desiring to meet and talk with a Person. Listen as you pray and meditate.

These are things that we all know. We have been taught them from the time of our conversion. The problem is not that we don't *know* them; the problem is that we don't *do* them. When I was the pastor of a Bible church, my main exhortation to the people was to read the Word and pray. The number-one confession I heard as I counseled people from my church was that they didn't read the Word, and they didn't pray on a regular basis.

For almost ten years now I have been traveling widely in the body of Christ. I would have to say that the majority of pastors and church members I meet do not have consistent personal times of meditation in the Bible and prayer. I have found this to be true in *all* branches of the church.

The Christians I talk to believe that the Word and prayer are important, and they actually want to mediate and pray, but they just don't. In most cases this is not due to a moral failure in their lives. Rather, they do not meet with the Lord because of a simple mechanical failure—they fail to schedule time with him.

People tend to live under an illusion that they will always have time to pray and meditate on the Word. That is one of the Devil's most successful lies. The Devil knows that if he can keep you out of God's presence, he will defeat you. Even if you have vast quantities of biblical knowledge, you will only become proud and clever at hurting people if you do not consistently come into God's presence. Even if you have powerful spiritual gifts, you will only wreak havoc in the church if you not come into his presence on a consistent basis. We will never grow in passion for the Son of God, nor be ultimately profitable for his service, if we do not come into his presence on a consistent basis.

There is not one biblical hero who did not come in to the presence of God on a regular basis. Follow Joshua's example and meditate in the Word day and night (Josh. 1:5–9). Follow Paul's example and pray continually (1 Thess. 5:17). Follow Mary's example and sit at the feet of Jesus (Luke 10:39). In order to follow their examples, we must learn to set aside a regular time, or we will never come before God on a regular basis. If we do these things on a regular basis, expecting to meet a Person, that Person will not disappoint us.

Here is the second key to acquiring passion for the Lord Jesus. In every relationship from time to time barriers are erected through misunderstandings and sometimes through wrongs. It is no different in our relationship with the Lord. Whenever we sin, that creates a barrier between us and him. The guilt of sin can keep us from going into the presence of the Lord. This is true in our horizontal relationships also. When I hurt someone that I love, I cannot really enjoy their company until that hurt has been made right.

There is only one thing that will remove the barrier between God and his disobedient children. It is the blood of his Son.

> But if we walk in the light, as he is in the light, we have fellowship with one another, and the blood of Jesus, his Son, purifies us from all sin.
>
> If we claim to be without sin, we deceive ourselves and the truth is not in us. If we confess our sins, he is faithful and just and will forgive us our sins and purify us from all unrighteousness. (1 John 1:7–9)

The guilt of sin is taken away whenever we confess that sin, trusting in the power of the blood of Jesus Christ to forgive us and cleanse us.

This is another truth that we have been taught from our conversion. Yet I encounter so many Christians who are weighed down by the guilt of sin and seem to spend more time living under condemnation than in the freedom of Christ. Many people tell me that they confess their sins and don't 'feel' forgiven. It is not enough simply to say some words about our sin; we must trust in the power of the blood of Jesus to forgive us. We will never be holy enough or disciplined enough to get into God's presence and be forgiven apart from the blood of his Son. The only thing the Father has given us to take away sin and guilt is the blood of his Son. Our good works, reformed lives, and best intentions will never take away the guilt of sin.

One more thing is absolutely essential if we are ever going to be consumed by passion for the Son of God. Most of my Christian life I have been making the same mistake over and over and over. I keep putting my confidence in my discipline, in my good intentions, in my knowledge of the Bible, in order to produce love for God. Yet I always end up in legalism and self-righteousness when I place my confidence in these things.

One day the Lord interrupted all of this when a dear friend of mine, Mike Bickle, told me that he had never recovered from the shock of something the Lord had said to him: 'If you ever make it in the Christian life, it won't be because you are a good follower. It will be because my Son is a good leader. Put your confidence in his ability to lead you, not in your ability to follow.' That divine revelation pierced my heart. I realized why self-righteousness and legalism were able to consistently get such strongholds in my life.

Please don't misunderstand me at this point. I'm not saying that we don't need discipline, or knowledge of the Bible, or godly behavior—we do. Nor am I saying that we are to be passive and simply let God do it all. I'm talking about our *attitude* and our *confidence*. We must do the right things, but we must never put our confidence in our ability to do those things. Our hearts are incredibly prone to deception (Jer. 17:9), and our feet are equally prone to wander off the path of righteousness (Rom. 3:10–18). In light of this, how could we ever trust in our ability to follow Jesus?

I have come to the point in my life where I realize that if I ever get passion for the Son of God it will not be because I earned it; it will be because he gave it to me as his greatest and most gracious gift. After all, isn't that how the greatest things come to us—as gifts? James says, 'You do not have, because you do not ask God' (James 4:2). The greatest gifts that God has to give us are ours for the asking. We can have anything from him that we are willing to labor for in prayer. I encourage you to spend more time asking God to grant you passion for the Son of God than you do asking him for anything else.

One prayer has done more to generate passion in my heart for the Lord Jesus than anything I have ever done before. This prayer is found within what is perhaps the greatest prayer in all of the Bible. I am referring to the high-priestly prayer of the Lord Jesus in John 17. I have turned the last verse of that prayer into my own personalized prayer.

> I have made you known to them, and will continue to make you known in order that the love you have for me may be in them and that I myself may be in them. (John 17:26)

Jesus said that he had declared the name of the Father to his disciples; that is, he showed them what the Father is like. Jesus did this for one overriding purpose: *he wanted his disciples to love him like his heavenly Father loves him.* He wanted the love that his Father has for him to be in his disciples.

I read this verse many times before I understood it. The first time I actually understood what Jesus was saying, I found it difficult to believe. How could I love Jesus like God the Father loves his very own Son? Of course, no one can love anyone to the same degree or quality that God loves them. But on the other hand, neither can we be as holy as God. Yet God says to us, 'Be holy because I, the LORD your God, am holy' (Lev. 19:2). It is through the power of his Spirit in us that we can walk in holiness. By that same power, we can live our lives with a consuming passion for our Lord.

The Father loves the Son more than anyone or anything else. He is devoted to the Son. His eyes never leave the Son. All that the Father does, he does for the Son. Jesus prayed that we would be driven by that same holy passion.

I have paraphrased John 17:26 in order to pray it like this: 'Father, grant me power from the Holy Spirit to love the Son of God like you love him.' I pray this in the morning when I get up; I pray it during the day when my mind slips into neutral; and I pray it when I fall asleep at night. My heart has been captured by this prayer. When I pray it, I am confessing to God that if he does not grant me a work of the Holy Spirit in my life, I will never acquire passion for the Son of God. I am confessing to him that my godliness, my discipline, my knowledge of the Word, though all good, are insufficient to produce passion for the Son of God. I can change my mind, but only the Holy Spirit can change my heart.[2] Divine love can only be divinely imparted.

If you begin to pray this prayer on a regular basis, passion for the Son of God will start flowing into your heart. It may take you months, even years, before you notice a significant difference. In fact, you will probably never be able to point to the day or the hour when you began to be consumed with passion for the Son of God, but others will notice. They will say you have changed; that you seem different. They will say there is a kindness, a gentleness in you they hadn't noticed before. There is an infectious quality in your love for the Son of God that didn't seem to be there before, and they will want to know what you have been doing.

Don't be passive about acquiring passion for the Son of God. Make it the focus of your life. Put your eyes on the Son of God and leave them there (Heb. 12:2), and you will find yourself becoming like him. You will find yourself falling in love with him as you ask God day after day to consume you with passion for his glorious Son. *And that passion, as it begins to occupy your heart, will conquer a thousand sins in your life.* You will begin to love what he loves and hate what he hates.

Passion and Power

What does all this talk about passion have to do with power and the miraculous gifts of the Spirit? Simply this: passionate love for God is the key to power. The apostles of the Lord Jesus were famous for miraculous power. The secret of their power is found in their call:

> Jesus went up on a mountainside and called to him those he wanted, and they came to him. He appointed twelve—designating them apostles—that they might be with him and that he might send them out to preach and to have authority to drive out demons. (Mark 3:13–15)

In Mark's version of the calling of the apostles, Jesus appointed the twelve for three purposes: (1) that they might be with him, (2) that he might send them out to preach, and (3) that they might have authority to drive out demons. The order of these purposes is highly significant. Before they attempted to minister for Jesus in preaching and casting out demons, they were called 'to be with him.' Out of that intimate experience of being with Jesus, he gave them power to preach and to drive out demons.

The most powerful people on earth are those who have been with Jesus (cf. Acts 4:13). Intimacy with Jesus, 'being with him,' always produces passion for him. Think about the most powerful people in the Scriptures. People like Moses, Daniel, Peter, John, and Paul were powerful in miracles, or in revelation, or in both. They were also people who were consumed with passion for God. As we have seen, however, passion and power are not confined to the Old Testament prophets and the New Testament apostles. Consider one more episode from Mary's life.

When Lazarus, Mary's brother, died, Jesus came to their home four days later. Martha was the first to greet him. She said to him, 'Lord, if you had been here, my brother would not have died' (John 11:21). Jesus responded to Martha by giving one of the greatest theological teachings in all of Scripture: '*I am the resurrection and the life*' (John 11:25, emphasis mine).

When Mary met the Lord Jesus just a few moments later, she said to him the very same words that Martha said, 'Lord, if you had been here, my brother would not have died' (John 11:32). When Mary said these words, however, Jesus wept. Then he walked to the tomb and raised Mary's brother from the dead. A person like Martha could get a great theological teaching out of Jesus. But a person like Mary could break his heart and move him to raise someone from the dead.

People who have Mary's passion for the Lord Jesus can move him in a way that others cannot. Passion for Jesus gave Mary access to the power of Jesus.

Let me give you a dramatic, contemporary example to illustrate what I mean.

Mahesh Chavda, an evangelist who is widely known for healings and miracles, faced a horrible dilemma in May of 1985. His son Aaron had just been born four months prematurely. The doctors gave Mahesh and his wife, Bonnie, no hope for little Aaron's survival. Death was certain and imminent. The physician said that even if he did survive, his brain had no chance to develop properly and that he would be a 'vegetable.'

Mahesh had given his word almost a year before to conduct several crusades in Africa. His wife and baby were in the hospital, and he was scheduled to leave for Africa. He felt that the Lord was telling him to go to Africa and keep his commitment. Yet his emotions told him to stay. How could he leave Bonnie to bury Aaron alone?

Bonnie persuaded Mahesh to go. 'Your job is to go when the Lord has called you to go,' she said. 'It doesn't matter whether or not you're here, but whether the *Lord* is here. And I know he is here. If Aaron lives, it will be because God intervenes, not because you are home.'

Mahesh left Bonnie and walked over to the intensive care unit where his tiny son lay fighting for his life. At this time Aaron weighed one pound and three ounces. Mahesh slid his hand under Aaron. He was so small that he fit easily within the palm of his father's hand. Mahesh watched Aaron gasp for each painful breath with his partially formed lungs. Then he anointed him with oil and prayed over him. Finally, he looked down at his little son and said, 'Aaron, it looks as though I may not see you again. I want you to know that your daddy loves you. But Jesus loves you even more than I do. If I never see you again here on this earth, I know I'll see you in heaven.' With that good-bye, he turned and left for the airport.

Weeks later, when Mahesh had finished the crusades in Zambia, he was finally able to reach Bonnie by phone, but only once. Miraculously Aaron was still clinging to life. Mahesh got on a plane for Zaire and landed in its capital city of Kinshasa on Sunday, June 9, 1985.

Mahesh did not know the local organizers of the crusade in Kinshasa, and he had received no word about the preparations for the meetings. He expected a small crowd of 700–800 people. On Monday morning at the leaders' meeting 2,300 people showed up. At the close of the meeting, an elderly woman whose body was covered with cancerous tumors was instantly healed in front of everyone. The tumors had completely disappeared.

The news of this miraculous healing spread like a forest fire in an August drought. That evening 100,000 people came to the meeting! They came with every disease imaginable; some were even brought in wheelbarrows. That night so many people were healed that even witches and sorcerers who had come to disrupt the meeting were converted, publicly repenting and declaring their faith in Jesus. By Wednesday, June 12, the morning crowd had swelled to 30,000.

That morning Mulamba Manikai was standing in the crowd,

and although his heart had been crushed, he was listening to Mahesh intently. Unlike most of his neighbors on Lumbi Street in the Mikondo section of Kinshasa, Mulamba and his family were Christians. When Mulamba had returned home from the meeting on Tuesday, he found his six-year-old son, Katshinyi, paralyzed and comatose. Mulamba and his older brother, Kuamba, carried the little boy to the medical facility at Mulamba's company. He was diagnosed with cerebral malaria, and Mulamba was told to take his son to the Mikondo Clinic for treatment.

At 4:00 a.m. on Wednesday morning as they neared the Mikondo Clinic, the six-year-old Katshinyi had a spasm and stopped breathing. Then his heart stopped beating and he died in his father's arms. Inside the clinic a physician gave the boy an injection and tried to revive him, but it was useless. 'Your son is dead,' the doctor said to Mulamba. 'I can do nothing for him. You must take him to Mama Yemo Hospital in Kinshasa and get a death certificate to bury him.'

When they brought the body to the hospital, the boy was again pronounced dead. Mulamba left his son's body at the hospital with Kuamba so that he could go borrow money to buy a burial permit.

As he stepped into the street, Mulamba began to pray that the Lord would raise his son from the dead if it would bring glory to God. Just as he remembered the story of Peter raising Dorcas from the dead, Mulamba heard God speak these words, 'Why are you weeping? My servant is in this city. Go to him.'

Mulamba knew the Lord was referring to Mahesh. He rushed to Kasavubu Square where Mahesh was preaching to 30,000 people. Mahesh was just concluding his message. At exactly 12:00 noon, eight hours after Katshinyi had died, Mahesh stepped back from the microphone.

Suddenly, Mahesh felt as if God had taken him into another realm. He was no longer aware of the throngs of people. He was enveloped in silence. The gentle voice of the Holy Spirit spoke clearly and unmistakably, 'There is a man here whose son died this morning. Invite him to come forward. I want to do something wonderful for him.' Mahesh spoke these exact words to the audience.

Mulamba ran forward shouting, 'It is I! It is I!' Immediately, Mahesh placed his hands on Mulamba's head and prayed, 'Lord Jesus, in your name I bind the powers of darkness and death that are at work in this man's son, and I ask you to send your Spirit of resurrection to bring him back to life.'

The crowd parted as Mulamba turned and began running to the hospital.

Here is what happened at the hospital at 12:00 noon, June 12, 1985, while Mahesh was praying over Mulamba at Kasavubu Square. Back at the Mama Yemo Hospital, Kuamba was holding the body of his brother's son in his arms. At noon he felt the body move, and then the boy sneezed. Katshinyi sat up and asked for food. Then he began to call for his father. God had brought him back from the dead.

Needless to say, the hospital was in an uproar. Mulamba walked into the room as Katshinyi was calling for his father. Mulamba grabbed his son and began to shout praises to God in the hospital room that just a few minutes earlier had served as the morgue for his son's lifeless body.

News of this great miracle spread through the city, and that weekend over 200,000 came in the evening to hear the gospel. Many were saved and healed.

I have seen a copy of the death notification for Katshinyi Manikai with its official seal and signed by Iwanga Embum. A skeptic might claim that Katshinyi's death had been misdiagnosed and that he was only in a coma. However, this would not explain the timing of the revelation (that a man's son had died and that God was going to do something for him) given to Mahesh eight hours later and the boy's immediate recovery.

I know Mahesh Chavda personally, and I am convinced of his integrity and the validity of his ministry. But so are thirty thousand residents of Kinshasa, Zaire, who witnessed the miraculous events of June 12, 1985.

Mulamba's brother, Kuamba, became a Christian after witnessing the power of God that morning. The Manikai family still lives at 26 Lumbi Street in Kinshasa.

God rewarded Mahesh for his faithfulness in two ways. First, he let him participate in a miraculous raising from the dead. Second, God remembered Mahesh's little Aaron and completely healed him. Today Aaron Chavda is a healthy normal eight-year-old.[3]

Spiritual maturity is not possessing vast quantities of Bible knowledge or possessing the most powerful spiritual gifts. Carnal people can have both of these things. Spiritual maturity is sharing the affections of God and discerning his voice. It is loving what God loves and hating what he hates. Spiritually mature Christians love God and his people passionately, and they hate anything that takes them away from God. Only in the context of such love will Bible knowledge and the gifts of the Spirit ever achieve their divine purposes. The power of the Spirit can flow unhindered through passionate love for God and his children.

Among the women in the Bible, I think Mary is the one who most exemplifies this passion for the Son of God. Among the men, it would have to be the apostle John. John is called 'the disciple whom Jesus loved.' The Living Bible refers to John as 'Jesus' closest friend' (John 13:23). That is a great translation. John was always one of the three disciples who were permitted to be on the 'inside.' But of the three, he was the closest to Jesus, and everyone knew it.

At the Last Supper, Jesus startled all the disciples when he told them that one of them was going to betray him. They were dying with curiosity to know which one it was, but no one had the courage to ask Jesus—not even Peter. So Peter turned to John and said, 'You ask him.' Peter knew what everyone else around that table knew, that John could get something out of Jesus that none of the rest of them could. Without a moment's hesitation, John turned to Jesus and put his head on Jesus' chest and asked, 'Who is it, Lord?' Jesus answered John immediately by giving the piece of bread to Judas. You see, John really was Jesus' best friend.

The next day, Jesus was hanging on a cross and looking out on a universe from which every visible trace of God seemed to have disappeared. All but one of his disciples had deserted him. Only John and four women were standing at the foot of the cross. Jesus looked down and saw his mother. Who would take care of her now? His brothers? The apostles? No, they had all deserted him. Then he looked at John. It is as though he said in his spirit, 'John, you're the only one I've got. No one else will do for my mother.' With tender affection, Jesus said to Mary, 'Dear woman, here is your son.' Then he said to his best friend, 'Here is your mother.'

John really was Jesus' best friend. But John doesn't have to be the *only* one who is his best friend.

We all have only one brief hour on the earth, and then we will stand before the Lord to give an account of our lives. Why not be like Mary and choose the best part, the one necessary thing, so that we can stand before him in confidence on that day? Why not be like John and make Jesus our best friend? The heart of Jesus is big enough to accommodate many more best friends and many more Marys.

Why would you want to settle for anything less?

Epilogue
Hearing God Speak Today

Kevin Forest became a Christian shortly after his gradua-
tion from high school. His 'past' had not been good. He
had grown up in an immoral climate, and various forms
of sexual immorality had enslaved him at one time or another.
For about a year after his conversion experience he managed to
stay out of immorality. Then he fell back into bondage.

About that time he met and married Regina. In many cases
marriage will stop immoral behavior, but it did not work that way
in Kevin's case. Even after marriage he continued his immoral
life—but Regina did not find out.

They began a family. A son and a daughter were born to them,
but Kevin continued his adulteries. Regina did find out about one
affair. It broke her heart, but she forgave Kevin. For Kevin's part
he lied about the other affairs, promised to be faithful, and
resumed his adulterous practices.

Then in 1986 their two-year-old daughter, Haylie, died from a
brain tumor. Kevin's grief turned into anger against the Lord.
Why would God take his baby girl? To punish him for his secret
sins? Yet not even the loss of his daughter could bring Kevin to
repentance. He continued to lead two lives. The one that everyone saw was the churchgoing, faithful husband and father. But in
secret he was entangled in sexual immorality.

As Kevin slid into deeper darkness, Regina got closer and closer to the Lord. Kevin started despising her for this closeness.

In July of 1989 the Forests were living in Santa Maria, California, and attending the Vineyard Christian Fellowship. With divine help Regina found out about a small part of Kevin's unfaithfulness. After the first confrontation, Regina called her pastors, Carl Tuttle and Ralph Kucera, for help. Carl's wife, Sonja, went to the Forests' home to comfort Regina, while Kevin ended up at Ralph and Linda Kucera's home.

Kevin had two alternatives in mind: he was either going to kill himself or run away to start a new identity. His pastors came close to using physical force in order to restrain him.

Paul Cain was in town that week to speak at a conference the Vineyard was hosting. The night of the blowup between Kevin and Regina, the Lord gave him a vision of the Forests. When he awoke the next morning, he called Carl Tuttle and said, 'There's a domestic problem in your church.'

'That's right,' Carl said.

'Her name is Regina. What's his name?' asked Paul.

'It's Kevin.'

'Listen, Carl, this guy wants to run. Don't let him do it. Make sure he's in the meeting tonight. The Lord may do something for him.' Then Paul hung up.

Both Kevin and Regina came to the church that night, but they were not sitting together. At the end of his message, Paul asked Kevin to stand up. A man named Kevin jumped up immediately, but it was not Kevin Forest. Paul said, 'No, you're not the Kevin I saw in the vision. There is another Kevin here.'

Then slowly Kevin Forest stood up.

'Kevin, I don't want to embarrass you, but your marriage is on the rocks,' Paul said. 'Last night I had a vision of you and Regina—that's your wife's name, isn't it? I don't want to embarrass you. I want to restore you. The Lord calls your wife "upright," but Satan has led you into sin. He has tried to destroy you. He has a contract on your life. You're twenty-eight years old, and the Devil plans to kill you before your thirtieth birthday. He hasn't been able to kill you yet, but he has killed your baby. *Satan* killed your baby, not God.'

Kevin felt as though his heart would break in two when Paul said this. He had been angry with God for Haylie's death, but it wasn't God who took Haylie. Kevin's agreement with evil had given the Devil an opening to hurt his family.

'Satan wants to kill you because he knows what God has for you and Regina.'

'Where's your wife?' Paul asked.

'There you are, Regina.'

Paul looked at Regina and appealed to her like a father.

'Regina, please trust me in what I'm about to say. You must forgive this man of all the things that were uncovered and revealed.'

Then Paul asked both of them to come down to the front of the church and stand before him.

'Regina, you must be upright. Satan is the one who is your enemy. Last night the Lord showed me that your baby is dead and your brother is dead. [Regina's brother had died three months before their daughter Haylie had died.] It's an all-out attack by the Devil. The devourer is at your doorstep now, but the Lord said that your lives and marriage are going to be restored.

'The only way out is total forgiveness and making your sacred vows over again. The Lord said that this is the *only* way out. Last night was the dark night of the soul, but things could be worse. The Lord showed me that you have two children who need you. Kevin, for God's sake repent tonight!

'The Lord is going to help you—Kevin, look at me—from this night on because you have repented. And Regina, you are going to have to forgive this man, because the Lord said after midnight tonight your husband will never again be called "Kevin," but he's going to be called "St. John." That happens to be his middle name.

'Let's praise the Lord for that. "Lord, I pronounce a blessing on every torn marriage, every sick and diseased life here. I pray that you'll heal them from the cancer of that marriage."

'I pronounce you all over again man and wife. I want you to meet all over again the all new St. John and Regina. Amen.

'I want you to thank the Lord for that!'

What I have just written does not come close to adequately describing what took place in the church that night. People were overcome by the presence of the Lord. Some were weeping uncontrollably. Some, afraid that their own sins were going to be revealed next, had begun repenting. Others were worshiping the Lord for his tender mercy and omniscient power.

There was an authority and power in the words that Paul spoke on that evening that cannot be captured in print. The only name that he knew through natural means was Kevin's. Everything else—all the other names, the events, and the restoration of the marriage—were revealed to Paul by the Lord.

This is one of the reasons that the words had such a divine impact. People in the room understood that these were truly prophetic words. These prophetic words did what Paul the apostle said they would do: they caused people to fall on their faces and declare that God was among them (1 Cor. 14:24–25)!

The next day Paul Cain told Pastor Tuttle that twelve other marriages in his church were in serious trouble and that the Lord would use Kevin's repentance and Regina's forgiveness to heal those marriages. Two weeks later, Kevin and Regina renewed their wedding vows on Sunday morning before the whole church. Afterwards Carl Tuttle said to the church that other marriages in the church were in danger, and the Lord would help them also if they were willing to repent and forgive as the Forests had done. Twelve couples rose and came to the altar of the church to receive prayer, to repent, and to forgive each other. As far as Carl knows, all twelve of these marriages are doing well.

Today, Kevin goes by 'John.' The Lord has given John and Regina two beautiful daughters in the place of the one Satan killed. Not only was the Forest's marriage saved, but also their lives were completely transformed by the grace that was communicated to them on the night of July 5, 1989. Today they are home-group leaders effectively pastoring people in their church.

The satanic power of sexual immorality over John was broken that night, and he discovered the power of the blood of God's Son to cleanse, restore, and set free. The Devil had convinced Kevin Forest that he only had two alternatives: either run or commit suicide. The prophetic ministry of the Holy Spirit gave him another and better choice.

The most difficult transition for me in my pilgrimage was not in accepting that Scripture teaches that God heals and does miracles today through gifted believers. The thing I resisted the most, was most afraid of, and which took the most convincing was accepting that God still *speaks* today.

Of course he still speaks today through the Scriptures, but that is not what I am talking about. I am referring to the other ways that God speaks, apart from the Bible, though never in contradiction to the Bible.

The Bible itself tells us that at various times God spoke in an audible voice, in a voice that was audible to only one person in a group of people, in inaudible sentences in the mind that were just as clear as the audible voice, in impressions, in visions, in dreams, in circumstances, in nature, through angels, and various other ways. But does the Bible teach that he *still* speaks in these ways, or were these forms of communication a sort of temporary stopgap measure until we received the completed Bible?

The problems associated with believing that God still speaks in these ways seemed overwhelming to me. First, and most repulsive to me, was the subjectivity involved in most of these various forms of communication.

Take dreams, for example. How do you even know if the dream came from God? What if an upset stomach the night before was the source of the dream? Even if you decided the dream *was* from God, how would you go about interpreting it? Do the Scriptures offer rules of interpretation for dreams? Even if you were fairly certain the dream was from God and that you knew what it meant, how do you know how much weight to give it? Would it have the same authority as the Bible, as a vision, an impression, an audible voice, and so on?

If it is true that there are always four voices competing for our attention—the voice of God, of the Devil, of others, and our own—where does the Bible teach how to discern which voice is which? How can you be certain, or is certainty an impossibility?

The subjectivity involved in trying to decide all this made it seem implausible that God would continue to speak in these ways after he had given us his clear, objective, inerrant Word.

Second, why would he even need to use these subjective means after he had given us the Bible? Or as someone once said to me, 'What's the purpose of all that other stuff now that we have the Bible?' Did not the Bible teach that it alone was all the Christian needed to be 'thoroughly equipped for every good work' (2 Tim. 3:17)?

Third, and this was the thing that frightened me most, if I admitted that God was still speaking apart from the Bible, wouldn't I be opening up the canon of Scripture again? Theoretically, what would keep someone from writing new books of Scripture? Or was I supposed to imagine that God spoke in two different ways: one way for the Bible that was errorless, and another way for private revelation that had mistakes in it!

Yet the Scriptures teach that God cannot lie (Heb. 6:19). If I accepted that God was still speaking today, it seemed inevitable that the authority of the Bible would be compromised.

Fourth, there was the abuse factor—'The Lord told me to tell you. . .' If we believe God still speaks today, aren't we opening up the door to controlling and manipulative people? If we disobey someone who says, 'God told me to tell you. . .,' would it be like disobeying one of the biblical prophets?

Fifth, there seemed to be decisive texts of Scripture against the idea that God is still speaking. Hebrews 1:1–2 seemed to say that prophets were part of an inferior way of revelation in the past, but now, in these last days, they were superseded because God has spoken to us through his Son. One possible interpretation of Ephesians 2:20 is that prophecy was a foundational gift that was no longer given after the foundation had been laid.

Finally, there seemed to be such a radical difference between prophecy in the Bible and contemporary prophecy. What was going on in the church under the name of prophecy could not begin to compare with the prophetic words of an Isaiah or a Jeremiah. One of my friends actually heard the following prophecy when he visited a rural charismatic church. A man stood up and said, 'Thus says the Lord, "Ah don't blame yew fer bein' scart [scared], sometimes ah git scart mahself.' ' Even when contemporary prophecy did not descend to this level, it seemed too dissimilar to scriptural prophecy to be taken very seriously.

These were the tensions I struggled with when I first began to study the subject with an open mind. There were so many problems associated with God speaking—and I did not even mention all the problems associated with tongues and their interpretation—that I wondered how I could ever find any resolution for them.

Today, after years of practical experience and intense study on the subject of God's speaking, I am convinced that God does indeed speak apart from the Bible, though never in contradiction to it. And he speaks to *all* of his children, not just to specially gifted prophetic people. And he will speak to us all in amazing detail.

I am convinced that this is what the Bible teaches and that the Bible has very clear and satisfying answers to all of the problems that seemed so overwhelming to me when I first began to study this subject.

I know that the Devil is giving demonic and occult revelation today. Some of his most successful and deceptive activity is occurring in the New Age movement. Many Christians seem afraid that if they 'open themselves up' to listening for God's voice, they will be deceived by New Age demons. In fact, too much of the church today has *more confidence in Satan's ability to deceive us than in God's ability to speak to us and lead us.*

There is a vast difference between the voice of God and the voice of Satan, and there are a number of scriptural safeguards to keep the sincere Christian from confusing the two. Furthermore, it is possible to believe that God still speaks today without diminishing, on a theoretical or practical level, one iota of the authority of God's inerrant Bible.

I started writing a chapter on hearing God's voice to be included in this book. I wanted to deal with the practical and theological problems related to the contemporary revelatory ministry of the Holy Spirit. That chapter quickly became two chapters, then three, and then I realized that I had begun another book altogether. I am now in the process of writing that book. To those who have found this present book helpful, I hope that the forthcoming book will be worth the wait.

Appendix A

Other Reasons Why God Heals and Works Miracles

When I began to study each of the healings and miracles in the Gospels and Acts, I discovered that there are many other reasons for those healings and miracles. The following examples are not meant to be exhaustive. But they do confirm the fact that miracles were meant to continue throughout the church age.

God heals because he is asked to heal. Sometimes the Bible gives no other reason for the healings of Jesus than simply he was asked to heal. To give a specific illustration, once in the region of Decapolis a man who was deaf and could barely speak was brought to Jesus. The text simply says that 'they begged him to place his hand on the man' (Mark 7:32). Jesus healed both his deafness and his speech impediment simply because he was asked. There is no other reason given in the text. No mention is made of faith, the compassion of Jesus, or the glory of God.

Later at Bethsaida a blind man was brought to Jesus, and the text says they 'begged Jesus to touch him' (Mark 8:22). Again, Jesus healed the man, but no reason is given for the healing in the context—except that he was asked. So apparently on some occasions a simple request is enough to motivate God to heal. This ought to encourage us to be much freer in our requests for healing and miracles from our heavenly Father.

Yet some people today tell us it is wrong—even sinful—to desire signs and wonders.[1] They base their claim on a statement Jesus made in Matthew 12:39, 'A wicked and adulterous generation asks for a miraculous sign! But none will be given it except the sign of the prophet Jonah.'

But are you really sinning if you ask God to do a miracle? If your loved one is dying and the physicians have given up all hope, is it really sinful of you to ask God for a miraculous healing of your loved one? If you have a friend to whom you have witnessed over the years and he has consistently rejected the gospel, is it really sinful and unbelieving of you to ask God to do a physical miracle in his presence that he might come to faith? Is it really sinful for a church to pray for an outpouring of the Holy Spirit with signs and wonders in their city that many people might be brought to faith in Jesus? Apparently some people feel that this is a sinful desire proceeding from an unbelieving heart.

On closer examination, however, this alleged reservation toward the value of miracles is found not in Jesus but in the minds of some modern writers. On two different occasions Jesus condemned those asking him for a sign as 'a wicked and adulterous generation.' The first request for a sign (Matt. 12:38) came immediately after Jesus had healed a demon-possessed man who was blind and mute (Matt. 12:22). The second request (Matt. 16:1) came right after Jesus had miraculously fed the four thousand (Matt. 15:32–39). In other words, in both contexts the Gospel writers are careful to show that when Jesus is asked for a sign, he has just done two amazing signs.

It is also important to note who asked Jesus for a sign. In Matthew 12:38, it is the Pharisees. In Matthew 16:4, it is the Pharisees and the Sadducees. This fact alone is enough to tell us that the request was not sincere. What kind of sign could these religious leaders want that would be more impressive than the healing of a demon-possessed man who was blind and mute, or more impressive than the feeding of four thousand people? In the parallel passage to Matthew 12:38, Luke makes it clear that the Pharisees were asking Jesus for a sign from heaven in order to test him (Luke 11:16). The same holds true for the second request for a sign (Matt. 16:1; Mark 8:11). We can understand why the Pharisees would want to test Jesus, but why did they ask for a sign from heaven?

Apparently they thought a sign from heaven would be incontrovertible proof that Jesus was the Messiah. It would be the one sign that could not be manipulated or faked. Maybe the blind person who had been healed earlier was not really blind. Or maybe his blindness was due to some psychosomatic cause. Maybe the feeding of the four thousand was due to some slight of hand trick, or perhaps the reports they had heard of this miraculous feeding were exaggerated. Even the raising of a dead person could not compete with a sign from heaven. Who can be sure that if the person was really dead after all? But there would be no way to fake some sort of cosmological sign in the heavens.[2] The Pharisees probably asked for this kind of sign because they were absolutely certain that it was beyond the capacity of Jesus to produce it.

What Jesus is rebuking here is not a desire for signs but the demand for signs from an evil and unbelieving heart. If it is really wrong to desire signs, or even to seek after them, why did the New Testament church pray like this:

> Now, Lord, consider their threats and enable your servants to speak your word with great boldness. Stretch out your hand to heal and perform miraculous signs and wonders through the name of your holy servant Jesus. (Acts 4:29–30)

If that prayer represented an evil desire, why did God answer it in this fashion?

After they prayed, the place where they were meeting was shaken. And they were all filled with the Holy Spirit and spoke the word of God boldly. (Acts 4:31)

God answers their prayer for signs and wonders with an immediate sign, an earthquake! And the following chapter in the book of Acts records an outpouring of signs and wonders (Acts 5:12ff.). And if it is truly wrong to seek after the miraculous, why does Paul exhort the Corinthians to eagerly desire spiritual gifts (1 Cor. 12:31; 14:1, 39)?[3] The truth is that God is pleased when we ask him for healing or miraculous signs in the right way and for the right reasons.

God heals to remove hindrances to ministry. After Jesus had come out of the synagogue at Capernaum, he went into Peter's house. He found Peter's mother-in-law lying sick with a fever. He 'took her hand and helped her up. The fever left her' (Mark 1:31). As soon as she was healed, Mark says that 'she began to wait on them' (Mark 1:31). In this case, her sickness was a hindrance to her service to the Lord Jesus, so the Lord healed her. On other occasions the Lord does not choose to remove a hindrance to ministry by healing but rather gives grace to bear the hindrance and serve anyway (cf. 2 Cor. 12:7; 1 Tim. 5:23). If an illness is an obstacle to your service to the Lord Jesus, the Bible gives you complete permission to ask him to remove it.

God does miracles in order to teach us. Theologians call this the pedagogical purpose of miracles (from the Greek word *paideuo*, 'to bring up, educate'). John had this in mind when he called the miracles of Jesus 'signs.' A sign is something that points beyond itself to something greater. Of course all of the miracles Jesus did teach us something about his nature and ministry. They also teach us something about the nature of the kingdom. When Jesus turned the water into wine, for example, he was not just demonstrating his power over nature; he was showing us a common characteristic about his kingdom. In his kingdom the ordinary would be turned into the extraordinary. The fact that the steward comments specifically that the best wine had been saved to last may tell us also something about the way in which the kingdom will culminate.

Jesus himself did not hesitate to draw lessons from his miracles. When he cursed the fig tree so that it withered, his apostles asked him about the meaning of this. He used that miracle to demonstrate the power of faith and the power of believing prayer (Matt. 21:18–22). I do not believe things are any different today. I think every miracle or answer to prayer that the Lord gives us today also has a teaching function. If we took the time to meditate on his present day works and to ask him for the illumination of the Holy Spirit, his miracles, healings, and special answers to prayer would all teach us something beyond the miracles themselves.

God does miracles to bring people to salvation. Theologians refer to this as God's soteriological (from Greek *soteria*, 'salvation') purposes. God's soteriological purposes can be divided into three categories. God does miracles to lead people to repentance. He also does miracles to open doors for evangelism. And, finally, he does miracles to authenticate his Son and the gospel message.

Miracles can lead people to repentance. When Jesus led Peter, James, and John to a miraculous catch of fish, Peter 'fell at Jesus' knees and said, "Go away from me, Lord; I am a sinful man!"' (Luke 5:8). This miracle served to convict Peter of his sinfulness and lead him to repentance. Jesus said this is what should have occurred in the cities where he had done most of his miracles (Matt. 11:20–24). Jesus made a similar claim for the religious leaders, 'If I had not done among them what no one else did, they would not be guilty of sin. But now they have seen these miracles, and yet they have hated both me and my Father' (John 15:24). The miracles of Jesus should have led the religious leaders to repent, but instead they hardened their hearts and their sin became even greater.

Miracles open doors for evangelism. Many times the Gospels record that after a miracle the report of that miracle went out through the land. It caused people to wonder greatly about Jesus and to want to hear him for themselves (Matt. 9:26, 31; Mark 5:20; Luke 5:15; John 4:30, 42; 6:2, 12:9–11, 17–19). This same thing occurred in the ministry of Philip: 'When the crowds heard Philip and saw the miraculous signs he did, they all paid close attention to what he said' (Acts 8:6). Likewise the Lord used Peter to raise up the paralytic Aneas and Luke tells us that 'all those who lived in Lydda and Sharon saw him and turned to the Lord' (Acts 9:35). There was the same response when Peter was used to raise Dorcas from the dead: 'This became known all over Joppa, and many people believed in the Lord' (Acts 9:42).

The New Testament teaches that miracles draw a crowd. They do not guarantee faith, but they will get an audience to hear the gospel preached.

What do you think would happen to the attendance at your church if in the next six months the Lord were to heal a paralytic and perhaps an AIDS victim during your services or in one of your home groups? The attendance at your church would probably quadruple. I am sure that many people would come for the wrong reasons. Some would come to your church for entertainment, the same way they go to the circus. I am sure you would also attract a group of orthodox cult watchers, who having heard of the miracles would come to disprove that any miracle had taken place, or failing that, to prove that the miracles had been done by the Devil. But in one respect it would make no difference why unbelievers came, as long as the gospel was preached with clarity and power, for then they would put themselves in a position to come under the convicting power of the Holy Spirit and be saved.

Miracles also authenticate Jesus Christ and the gospel message. I have already discussed the nature of authentication in chapter 8. In that chapter I concluded that God authenticated Jesus and the message about Jesus, but he did not authenticate the apostles. I also concluded from my study of the Scriptures that God did not have to authenticate Jesus or the message about Jesus with miracles in order to get people to believe in his Son. John the Baptist did no miracles (John 10:41), and yet he was used to bring many people to repentance. All the people held him to be a prophet. World religions and numerous cults are also flourishing in the world today, having begun without any miracles at all. So although God did not have to do miracles for the purposes of authentication, he graciously did do them.

Jesus himself appealed directly to the authenticating value of his miracles. He said to his disciples, 'Believe me when I say that I am in the Father and the Father is in me; or at least believe on the evidence of the miracles themselves' (John 14:11). In an incredible display of grace, Jesus said in effect, 'If you can't believe my words, believe on the evidence of my miracles.'

And the miracles of Jesus did produce belief. After the raising of Lazarus, John records, 'Therefore many of the Jews who had come to visit Mary, and had seen what Jesus did, put their faith in him' (John 11:45; 12:11).

This is not to say, however, that miracles always lead to faith. Sometimes they lead to a hardening of the heart. For example, in one group the raising of Lazarus produced faith, but in another group it produced something quite different. When the Pharisees heard that Jesus had raised Lazarus from the dead, they did not dispute that miracle or Jesus' other miracles (John 11:46–47). They even acknowledged that if Jesus continued doing miracles everyone would believe in him (John 11:48). But instead of believing in him themselves, they counseled together as to how they might kill him (John 11:49–53). They also wanted to kill Lazarus in order to remove all evidence of this miracle (John 12:10–11).[4]

Many people have no problem believing that miracles might

serve an authenticating function today—in China or Africa or some other remote place in the Third World. But if miracles could have an authenticating value in faraway places, why not in the westernized world also? If they had an authenticating function in New Testament times, why wouldn't they have an authenticating function today? Why put a geographical or chronological limitation on the authenticating value of miracles?

Someone might say, 'In the Western world we have the Bible, and they don't in Africa or China, and they didn't during the period of the Gospels and the book of Acts.' I would reply that this is not quite true, because at the very time the events of the book of Acts were occurring the church was also receiving the letters of Paul. So while the very events of the book of Acts were being written, the church was already in possession of some of the Epistles and perhaps some of the Gospels as well.

But even if this were not the case, the argument would still be invalid. For as we have seen before, miracles do not validate the Scriptures, the Scriptures validate miracles. No text of Scripture ever says that the Bible was given to replace the need for miraculous confirmation of the gospel message. Human nature has not changed in the last two thousand years. If the miracles of Jesus, the apostles, and others were helpful in authenticating the gospel message in the first century, miracles would also serve the same purpose in the twentieth century.

Miracles manifest the kingdom of God. Who could imagine a messianic kingdom without miracles and healings? The Old Testament prophesied that the Messiah would usher in a kingdom that would have both spiritual and physical healings. Isaiah wrote:

> Then will the lame leap like a deer, and the mute tongue shout for joy. Water will gush forth in the wilderness and streams in the desert. The burning sand will become a pool, the thirsty ground bubbling springs. In the haunts where jackals once lay, grass and reeds and papyrus will grow. (Isa. 35:6–7)

and also,

> The Spirit of the Sovereign LORD is on me, because the LORD has anointed me to preach good news to the poor. He has sent me to bind up the brokenhearted, to proclaim freedom for the captives and release from darkness for the prisoners. (Isa. 61:1)[5]

The coming messianic kingdom meant that the Holy Spirit would be poured out on all people, without distinction in regard to age, sex, or economic position (Joel 2:28–29). According to Joel's prophecy, the outpouring of the Spirit would result in an abundance of dreams, visions, and prophesying. Unlike the Old Testament period in which only a few prophesied or worked miracles in any one generation, these miraculous phenomena would be distributed widely across the people of God with the coming of the kingdom.

These miraculous phenomena were not simply signs of the kingdom of God; they were an essential part of it. The kingdom of God means the rule of God and his Christ. When Jesus came, the kingdom of God came. God began to exercise his rule in a new and more decisive fashion.

For example, Jesus brought an authority over demons that had never been seen or heard of before (cf. Mark 1:27). Jesus himself said, 'But if I drive out demons by the Spirit of God, then the kingdom of God has come upon you' (Matt. 12:28). After all, it would be a very hollow assertion to proclaim that the rule of God has come and not be able to cast out the demonic enemies of God's rule. The power to cast out demons is not simply a sign that the kingdom is here, but an essential part of the rule of God. For Jesus came to destroy the works of the Devil (1 John 3:8).

Among other things, the Devil employs supernatural power to blind the minds of unbelievers (2 Cor. 4:4–6), to hold people in bondage through the fear of death (Heb. 2:14–15), to cause physical illness (Luke 13:11; Matt. 9:32; 12:22), to cause mental illness

(Luke 8:26–39), and ultimately to cause demons to enter and dwell in a person (Matt. 12:45; cf. Judas in John 13:27). These are some of the works of the Devil that Jesus came to destroy. The works of the Devil cannot be destroyed by mere human power. When demonic power is the source of a person's illness, no amount of medical treatment will make that person well. The woman that Jesus met in the synagogue, who was bent over for eighteen years and could not straighten up at all, could have gone to the finest surgeons without ever being healed, because ultimately her illness was demonic (Luke 13:10–17). Only a miracle from God could have healed this woman. The power to heal her was not just a sign that the kingdom was here; it was an *essential* part of the kingdom rule, without which kingdom rule would not have been asserted, and this particular work of the devil would not have been destroyed.[6] Without the miraculous power to free those bound by the Devil, all discussion of the kingdom is just empty talk.

Another line of evidence that demonstrates that miracles were viewed by the New Testament writers as an essential part of the kingdom is the consistently close relationship between the preaching of the kingdom and the occurrence of miracles. This was true in the ministry of Jesus.

> Jesus went throughout Galilee, teaching in their synagogues, preaching the good news of the kingdom, and healing every disease and sickness among the people. News about him spread all over Syria, and people brought to him all who were ill with various diseases, those suffering severe pain, the demon-possessed, those having seizures, and the paralyzed, and he healed them. (Matt. 4:23–24; see also Matt. 9:35)

Jesus is not content to preach about the kingdom; he also demonstrates the kingdom with works of power.

The same can be said of the apostles. When Jesus sent them out to proclaim the kingdom, he also gave them authority over demons and all diseases (Matt. 10:1, 7–8; Luke 9:1–2). In this context Jesus views both demons and disease as enemies of his kingdom. The apostles overcame both demons and disease by proclaiming the kingdom and by using their delegated authority to do miracles.

Miracles also occur in the ministry of those who are not apostles when they proclaim the kingdom of God. The seventy sent out by Jesus proclaim the kingdom of God and heal the sick (Luke 10:9, 17). Philip proclaims the kingdom of God to the Samaritans and also works miracles (Acts 8:6–7, 12).

This pattern makes perfect sense when we remember that the kingdom of God means the rule of God. God rules over our spirits and our bodies and over those forces of evil that can wound both our spirits and our bodies. Whatever Satan can wound, Christ can heal. Miracles and the kingdom of God are inseparably linked.[7]

God heals for sovereign purposes. I mentioned this several times in chapter 11, but the point is worth repeating. There are a number of healings in the New Testament where no explanation is given for them. We can find no evidence of faith on the part of those being healed, no faith on the part others bringing them, no statement concerning the glory of the Lord or the compassion of the Lord. In short, he healed simply because he wanted to. This is especially true of a group of miracles that take place on the Sabbath day (Matt. 12:9–13; Mark 3:1–5; Luke 6:6–10; 14:1–4; John 5:1–9). And there is also the healing of Malchus' ear (Luke 22:50–51), where Jesus refuses to accept the consequences of Peter's rash act.

Today there are times when the Lord heals someone that we would never have expected him to heal, or he does it in a way we would not expect, and he gives no reason for it. Conversely, there are times when we would expect him to heal and he doesn't, and again he gives no reasons for it. All of this points to the fact that God truly is sovereign and that he does not reveal all of his purposes to us.

Our survey of the various purposes for healings and miracles ought to make it clear that the New Testament ministry of healing is quite a bit more complex than some writers have led us to believe. Yes, God did heal to authenticate the ministry of Jesus and the gospel message, but this was not the only reason that he healed. He had other saving purposes for his miracles, namely, to lead people to repentance and open doors for the gospel. He healed simply because people asked him. He healed to remove hindrances to ministry and service. He healed to teach us about God and the nature of his kingdom. He healed and did miracles to manifest his kingdom. And finally, he healed for sovereign purposes without giving any reason at all except that he is God.

Appendix B

Did Miraculous Gifts Cease With the Apostles?

Benjamin Breckinridge Warfield, a professor at Princeton Seminary, popularized the argument that miraculous gifts of the Spirit were given only to a few, namely to the apostles and Stephen and Philip. The purpose of these gifts, according to Warfield, was to authenticate the apostles as trustworthy teachers of doctrine. When the apostles died, therefore, the gifts necessarily passed away with them.

Warfield wrote in 1918,

> It is very clear from the record of the New Testament that the extraordinary charismata were not (after the very first days of the church) the possession of all Christians, but supernatural gifts to the few.[1]
>
> These gifts were not the possession of the primitive Christian as such: nor for that matter of the Apostolic Church or the Apostolic age for themselves; they were distinctly for the authentication of the Apostles. They were part of the credentials of the Apostles as the authoritative agents of God in founding the church. Their function thus confined them to distinctively the Apostolic Church, and they necessarily passed away with it.[2]

Even today Warfield's modern theological descendants are still arguing in essentially the same way. Listen to how Peter Masters formulates this argument. He writes:

Every example of healing (by the instrumentality of a person) in the Book of *Acts* is performed by an apostle, or an apostle's deputy, and if we go *strictly by the biblical record*, the only three 'deputies' who had any involvement in healing were Stephen, Philip and possibly Barnabas if *Acts* 14:3 includes him. (We shall comment in a moment on the hypothetical possibility that there were others also.) Outside this select group there are no 'gifted' healing activities actually recorded in *Acts* or the epistles. . . .

In these days of charismatic confusion we need constantly to draw attention the texts which prove that signs and wonders were peculiar to the apostolic band, and were not bestowed generally.[3] (author's emphasis)

At first sight, both Warfield's statement and Masters' argument seem to carry conviction. On close examination, however, both of these arguments fall apart.

Were Supernatural Gifts Limited to a Few?

I mentioned the following earlier in the book, but it bears repetition. The first difficulty with the argument that only the apostles and their close associates did signs and wonders is that it *ignores* an insurmountable exception. Everyone admits that Stephen and Philip did signs and wonders.[4] Everyone admits that the apostles laid hands on Stephen and Philip. And although Acts 6:6 does not say that Stephen and Philip were given miraculous powers when the apostles laid hands on them, I would be willing to grant that for the sake of the argument.[5]

In each instance when the book of Acts uses the expression 'signs and wonders' it refers to an *abundance* of miracles done by those who are preaching Jesus. Who engages in a ministry of signs and wonders in the book of Acts? Luke tells us twice that the apostles were doing 'many signs and wonders' (Acts 2:43; 5:12). When he gives us specific illustrations of apostolic miracles, he only shows us miracles worked through Peter or Paul. The only other specific examples of a ministry of signs and wonders are the ministries of Stephen and Philip.

Why does Luke pick two apostles and two nonapostles to illustrate the signs and wonders ministry? Doubtless there were many stories of signs and wonders on the part of other apostles, but Luke has passed over these stories because they did not suit his purposes. If Luke had really wanted to teach us that the signs and wonders ministry, as well as the ministry of the miraculous gifts of the Spirit, were distinctively apostolic, wouldn't he have given more attention to miracles by the other apostles? Indeed, if that were his intention he would have suppressed the stories about Stephen and Philip and substituted apostolic healing stories.

If, as Warfield and his theological descendants maintain, the primary purpose of signs and wonders was to authenticate the apostles, why do Stephen and Philip do signs and wonders? If they reply that it is because the apostles laid hands on them and that they were close associates with the apostles, they have still not answered the question. Why did the apostles lay hands on them to give them the power to do signs and wonders? If signs and wonders were meant to authenticate the apostles, there is absolutely no reason for Stephen and Philip to do miracles. Permitting anyone other than apostles to do signs and wonders actually weakens the value of signs and wonders as an authenticating tool of the apostles' ministry. Here is a serious inconsistency to which I have not found even a remotely satisfactory answer among those who teach cessationism.

These authors have a much deeper problem, however, than ignoring the exception that disproves their interpretation. Those who argue like Masters are using a flawed method of interpreting the Bible's narrative literature,[6] a method that is virtually guaranteed to lead to wrong conclusions.

Let me illustrate what I mean.

Even if it were true that we could only find a few people in the book of Acts who actually displayed supernatural gifts, that would not mean that only a few people in the New Testament received supernatural gifts. The narrative literature of the Bible only tells the story of the few. The book of Acts, for example, has Peter for its main character in the first twelve chapters, with a very small role played by John and somewhat larger roles played by Stephen and Philip. From chapter thirteen to the end of the book, Paul is the dominant character. The narrative literature of the Bible is *the story of special people*, people who play significant roles in God's redemptive history. The overwhelming majority of biblical examples of both godly ministry and passionate devotion are drawn from the lives of the few, very special, and exceptional characters who became prominent in salvation history. It is impossible, therefore, to justify logically or biblically a hermeneutical principle (1) which is *primarily based* on the *observation* that only a few in the Bible possess or do certain things, and (2) which functions to justify the cessation of these things.

For instance, Paul is the only truly significant church planter in the New Testament, and most of the apostles seem to stay in Jerusalem rather than going out to plant churches. Does that mean that only the few were intended to plant churches, and that when Paul died, church planting also died? Even though the observation is correct, the conclusion is false, because it contradicts New Testament commands to evangelize and disciple the world (see Matt. 28:18–20; Luke 24:47; and Acts 1:8). The fact that only a few possess or do certain things, therefore, is irrelevant *in itself* to determine whether such things were meant to be temporary or permanent in the life of the church.

Scripture presents the lives of special people to Christian readers as examples to copy (see Heb. 11:4–12:3; 1 Cor. 4:16–17; 11:1; Phil. 3:17; 4:9; and 1 Thess. 1:6). Modern interpreters, however, who have no experience of the miraculous, assume an antisupernatural method of interpretation at this point. They read the stories of the apostles, Stephen, Philip, Agabus, and others in the book of Acts and assume that the divine guidance and miracles associated with their lives are not to be copied or even hoped for in modern Christian experience. On a theoretical level this assumption may or may not be true, but in order for it to carry conviction it needs to be based on clear statements of Scripture, not simply on the observation that only a few people did miracles in the New Testament.

In the book of Acts only five people are mentioned by name as doing signs and wonders: Peter, Paul, Barnabas, Stephen, and Philip. Should we conclude from this that these were the only five to do signs and wonders? No, because we are told the other apostles also did signs and wonders, even though they are not mentioned by name (Acts 2:43; 5:12). Is it fair to draw the conclusion that only the apostles did signs and wonders? No, because we have the examples of Stephen and Philip to contradict this conclusion, and more importantly, we lack a specific statement in Acts or anywhere else that the ministry of signs and wonders is limited to the apostles. Or to put it another way, historical examples, such as those found in narrative literature, must be interpreted by clear statements from Scripture itself, not from our own experience or what seems logical to us as readers.

When we look at the Scriptures, we will find that Warfield's assertion that only a few received supernatural gifts is completely false. Masters was more careful in his assertion. He said that

> every example of healing (by the instrumentality of a person) in the Book of *Acts* is performed by an apostle, or an apostle's deputy, and if we go *strictly by the biblical record* the only three 'deputies' who had any involvement in healing were Stephen, Philip and possibly Barnabas. *Acts* 14:3 includes him.[7] (author's emphasis)

Masters limits his argument to the specific examples of *healing* in Acts. Depending on how we view Ananias' ministry in Acts chapter 9, Masters' statement is open to question, for Ananias was used to heal Paul's divinely caused blindness (Acts 9:17–18). But even if Masters' statement about Acts were true, it is only an observation about healing in the book of Acts, not about the other miraculous phenomena or the rest of the New Testament, and the conclusion he draws from his interpretation of the evidence in Acts is contradicted by the rest of the New Testament.

A Survey of Sings, Wonders, and Miracles

The following is a brief survey of both the occurrences of signs and wonders in the New Testament and the occurrences of miraculous gifts of the Spirit. Remember that the reason Warfield and others want to argue that supernatural gifts are only given to the few is that they see their purpose as authenticating the apostles. Every example of these gifts given outside the circle of the apostles, therefore, challenges the theory that the gifts were only given to the few and for the authentication of the apostles.

In Luke 10:9 Jesus grants authority to the *seventy-two* to heal the sick in their preaching mission. In verse seventeen they return full of joy, saying, 'Lord, even the demons submit to us in your name.' Jesus acknowledges in verses nineteen and twenty that he had given them special power over demonic forces. Just for the sake of argument, I am willing to grant that this may have been a temporary mission and a temporary empowering. But this is still a tremendous exception to the theory that only a few received miraculous gifts, and then only for the purpose of authenticating the apostles. Why did Jesus ever give the seventy-two authority to heal the sick and cast out demons if he intended only a few to do miracles and only for the purpose of authenticating the apostles?

There was also the anonymous man who was the subject of the interchange between John and Jesus in Mark 9:38–39:

'Teacher,' said John, 'we saw a man driving out demons in your name and we told him to stop, because he was not one of us.' 'Do not stop him,' Jesus said. 'No one who does a miracle in my name can in the next moment say anything bad about me.'

This is an extremely interesting case. Here we have an anonymous man in the Gospels who was doing something that only Jesus and the apostles thus far had been empowered to do—driving out demons. Yet neither Jesus nor the apostles had laid hands on this man and recognized him as an official member of the apostolic band. Why does Mark include this story? What is he trying to tell us? This certainly is a significant exception to the theory that only the apostles and their followers did miracles and only for the purpose of authenticating apostolic ministry. Thus even in the Gospels the ministry of the miraculous is not limited to the twelve apostles nor distinctively for their authentication.

When we turn to the book of Acts, we discover that many people exercise various miraculous gifts of the Holy Spirit. For example, there are many people who speak in tongues:

1. The one hundred twenty (Acts 2)
2. The Samaritans (They almost certainly spoke in tongues, for Acts 8:18 says that Simon 'saw' the Samaritans receiving the Holy Spirit.)
3. Cornelius and the Gentiles with him (Acts 10:45–46)
4. The twelve disciples at Ephesus (Acts 19:6)

There are also a number of people mentioned in Acts who had received the gift of prophecy:

1. The prophet Agabus (Acts 11:28; 21:10–11)
2. The individuals in Acts 13:1
3. The prophets Judas and Silas (Acts 15:32)
4. The disciples at Tyre who 'through the Spirit. . . urged Paul not to go on to Jerusalem' (Acts 21:4)

5. Philip's four unmarried daughters who prophesied (Acts 21:9)
6. Ananias (Acts 9:10–18)

When Stephen and Philip are added to the list just mentioned, there is an impressive variety of nonapostolic figures receiving and exercising miraculous charismata in a book that is almost exclusively devoted to the ministries of Peter and Paul.

Ananias is one of the more interesting examples of a nonapostolic character who has a miraculous ministry. His relative obscurity makes him all the more interesting. The only thing we know about him is that he was 'a devout observer of the law and highly respected by all the Jews living there' (Acts 22:12).

In Ananias's ministry to Saul, he exercised both a healing gift and a prophetic gift (Acts 9:10–18). But more than this, it was at the hands of Ananias that Saul was filled with the Holy Spirit (Acts 9:17). God used Ananias, a nonapostolic individual, to confer the Holy Spirit on an apostle! It is likely that the apostle Paul was given his 'miracle-working powers' at this very instance, because he not only received the Holy Spirit at this time, but he was also to be *filled with the Holy Spirit* when Ananias laid hands on him (Acts 9:17).[8]

In the book of Acts we find so many exceptions to the idea that only a few received supernatural gifts and that the supernatural gifts were exclusively for the authentication of the apostles that we are forced to abandon this theory.

Masters wants to draw a conclusion about healing based on his *observation* that only the apostles and three others are presented as healing in the book of Acts. However, his conclusion is not justified. First, he limits his examples to only the miraculous gift of healing, and even here Ananias (Acts 9:10–18) is an exception to his observation, for Ananias is used to heal Paul.[9] But more importantly, the book of Acts abounds in other miraculous charismata. I have already mentioned the examples of tongues and prophecy in the book of Acts that occur in people who are not apostles. If Masters wants to argue that the miraculous gifts have ceased because they were tied exclusively to the apostles, he cannot limit his conclusions to one gift. Nor can he limit his observations only to the book of Acts. When we examine the rest of the New Testament, we find that the evidence for miracles, healings, and the other miraculous gifts of the Spirit is significantly broader than the book of Acts.

All of the gifts of the Spirit were in operation at the church in Corinth (1 Cor. 12:7–10). Some have argued that 1 Corinthians 12:8–10 contains a summary of the gifts given to the whole church rather than gifts that were actually present in the Corinthian church. Their goal in asserting this is to suggest that only the apostles and a few others experienced the miraculous gifts. They would like us to believe that the average Corinthian Christian only had the nonmiraculous gifts. Paul specifically contradicts this suggestion when he tells the Corinthians that none of the spiritual gifts (*charismata*) were lacking among them (1 Cor. 1:7). The description in 1 Corinthians 14:26 where tongues and prophecy are present in the normal Corinthian worship service also contradicts this interpretation. The gift of prophecy was also in use in Rome (Rom. 12:6), Thessalonica (1 Thess. 5:20), and Ephesus (Eph. 4:11). The casual way in which Paul mentions miracles in Galatians 3:5 suggests that miracles were common among the Galatian churches.[10]

The Role of the Apostles in Conferring Spiritual Gifts

Warfield argued that

> only in the two initial instances of the descent of the Spirit at Pente-
> cost and the reception of Cornelius are charismata recorded as

conferred without the laying on of the hands of the apostles. There is no instance on record of their conference by laying on of the hands than anyone else than an apostle.[11]

It should be noted that this is not an argument based on a specific statement of Scripture about the impartation of the gifts of the Spirit. It is ultimately an argument from silence. Warfield has already noted a major exception to his theory, namely, the case of Cornelius. This is a significant exception because Peter was present. If it is truly necessary to receive spiritual gifts through the laying on of the hands of the apostles, why didn't Peter have to lay hands on Cornelius?

There are other exceptions as well. Many people appear in the book of Acts who have the gift of prophecy, and yet there is no recorded instance of an apostle laying hands on them. I am referring to Agabus (Acts 11:28; 21:10–11), the individuals in Acts 13:1, the prophets Judas and Silas (Acts 15:32), and Philip's four unmarried daughters who prophesied (Acts 21:9). There is no evidence in the book of Acts that any of the apostles laid hands on the previously mentioned people in order for them to receive the miraculous charismata which they exercised. There is also the case of Ananias, who laid hands on an apostle that he might receive the Holy Spirit and be filled with the Spirit as mentioned previously.[12] Outside the book of Acts we find similar evidence. Timothy, for example, is an individual who received one of the charismata through the laying on of the *elders* hands (1 Tim. 4:14).[13]

Edward Gross formulates Warfield's argument in a slightly different way. He writes:

> Both the direct statements and the implications of the Scriptures support the teaching that miraculous gifts were bestowed only through the agency of an apostle. The conclusion, then, is that when the apostles ceased living, the miraculous gifts ceased being conferred. The one was dependent upon the other.[14]

Whereas Warfield argued that the gifts were conferred only through the 'laying on of the apostles hands,' Gross substitutes 'only through the agency of an apostle.' In this way, Gross can claim that Cornelius and his friends received the gift of tongues through the 'agency' of Peter even though Peter did not lay hands on them.

For Gross the most important text is Acts 8:5–19. This is the story of the Samaritans' conversion. Philip does great signs among the Samaritans and preaches Christ to them so that many are converted, but they do not receive the Holy Spirit at their conversion. This is the only place after Pentecost where someone clearly believes in the Lord Jesus and does not receive the Holy Spirit immediately on their belief. The Samaritans did not receive the Holy Spirit until Peter and John came down from Jerusalem and prayed for them. Why was there a delay in giving the Holy Spirit to the Samaritans?

Gross answers the question in the following way:

> Philip was a miracle worker (Acts 7, 13). So why could he not confer these like signs upon the Samaritans through the prayer in Jesus name? The simple and obvious answer is: Philip was not an apostle. Philip could preach and perform miracles; but it was God's will that only the apostles could bestow miraculous gifts.[15]

Gross is right. The answer he gives is simple, but it is too simple. The question does not primarily concern the bestowal of miraculous gifts but the bestowal of the Holy Spirit.[16] Consider Professor Turner's evaluation of the position that Gross takes. He writes:

> To say the Samaritans in Acts 8:14–17 'all receive the power of working signs by the laying on of Apostolic hands,' and that this was paradigmatic, is sheer nonsense and needs to be labelled as such: it totally misses Luke's point. Laying on of hands indeed there was, and signs there were too—both at the same time and possibly later—but Luke is concerned to depict the Samaritan reception of the Spirit promised

in Acts 2 (vv. 17–21, 33, 38ff.) *to all*; not a special charism for working apostolocentric authenticating signs![17]

The answer to the delay in the Samaritans' reception of the Holy Spirit is more likely found in the history of the Samaritans. Throughout their history they refused to submit to the authority of the divinely chosen leaders of Israel. They even produced their own sectarian edition of the first five books of the Bible, and they refused to acknowledge the rest of the Old Testament. In short, they had always refused to submit to God's ordained leadership. By delaying the gift of the Spirit until the apostles could lay hands on them, God was once for all correcting this problem. The Samaritans would be taught from here on out that they must submit to the leadership of the apostles at Jerusalem. They had always refused to acknowledge the authority of Jerusalem and instead had substituted their own centers of worship. This problem was now corrected.

It was not simply miraculous gifts that were at issue. It was the giving of the Holy Spirit and submission to apostolic authority. The Acts 8:5–19 example is not only capable of another explanation than that given by Gross, it demands another explanation.

There are two other insurmountable obstacles to Gross's theory that the 'miraculous gifts were bestowed only through the agency of an apostle.' The church at Rome had not been founded by an apostle nor ever visited by an apostle as far as the biblical record is concerned. In spite of the lack of apostolic presence, however, the church at Rome had the gift of prophecy functioning there (Rom. 12:6–8). If the miraculous gifts can only be given through the agency of an apostle, how did Rome get it? All Gross can say about the presence of prophecy at Rome is, 'This could have been conferred by the apostles on the Roman leaders while they were still in Jerusalem, shortly after their conversion to Christianity.'[18]

We can always suggest an explanation of this sort when the facts contradict our theory. It is also possible, for example, that Peter could have visited Rome, and the Scriptures are simply silent about his visit. Gross's explanation of how the gift of prophecy came to the church at Rome is not really an explanation. It is an *explaining away* of an example that overturns his theory. You cannot base your theology on what 'could have been' nor on arguments from silence. If you are content to base your theology on examples rather than clear statements of the Scripture, then you must accept counter examples as well.

Gross argues that 'the direct statements . . . of the Scripture' support his theory. Yet he never produces one simple direct statement from Scripture that teaches that the miraculous gifts were bestowed only through 'the agency of an apostle.' In fact, there is no clear statement in Scripture that teaches the spiritual gifts could only be given through the agency of an apostle. In the church at Rome we have a clear exception to such a rule—an exception of such magnitude that it undermines the rule altogether. Nor is the church at Rome the only exception. Another clear exception to Gross's rule is found in 1 Timothy 4:14. Paul writes, 'Do not neglect your gift, which was given you through a prophetic message when the body of elders laid their hands on you.' Timothy was given a *charisma* through the supernatural gift of prophecy and the laying on of elders hands, not the laying on of Paul's hands. At another time, Timothy received a gift through the laying on of Paul's hands (2 Tim. 1:6). To allege that 1 Timothy 4:14 and 2 Timothy 1:6 refer to the same incident is unconvincing because there is no evidence for such an assertion.

The Alleged Loss of Paul's Gift of Healing

Paul's failure to heal Epaphroditus (Phil. 2:25–27), Timothy (1 Tim. 5:23), and Trophimus (2 Tim. 4:20) indicates to some people that his healing gift must have ceased before the end of his life.[19] Geisler thinks that this conclusion is warranted by other indications in Scripture. He thinks that the Scripture which deals with the 'early period,' A.D. 33–60, abounds in the miraculous, while the Scripture dealing with the 'later period,' A.D. 60–67, has no instances of tongues, healings, exorcisms, or raisings from the dead.[20] To illustrate his point Geisler offers this specific example: 'The same apostle who exorcised a demon on command (Acts 15) [sic] could only hope for repentance that Hymenaeus and Philetus would "escape from the trap of the devil" (2 Timothy 2:26).'[21]

First of all, the example of Hymenaeus cited by Geisler hardly means that Paul lost the ability to cast out a demon. Who seriously believes that the most eminent of all the apostles lost his authority to cast out demons before the end of his life? In the case of Hymenaeus, Paul had turned this man over to Satan for his blasphemous teaching (1 Tim. 1:20). The Scripture does not say anything about Paul attempting or even wanting to cast a demon out of Hymenaeus. And it was never the practice of New Testament apostles to cast demons out of heretics and false teachers. Their practice, and their advice to the church, was to avoid these kinds of people (Titus 2:9–11; 2 John 10–11). For Geisler's example to carry any conviction at all, he would have to show that Paul attempted to cast the demon out of Hymenaeus and could not do so. This leads us to the major problem, not only of this specific example, but of the whole argument concerning the lack of the supernatural in Paul's final epistles.

Geisler's argument carries no conviction at all because it is an argument from silence. Geisler argues that 'from Ephesians to 2 Timothy we have no mention tongues, healings, exorcisms, or raisings from the dead.'[22] He concludes, therefore, that since these things are not mentioned, they must not be occurring during the period of these epistles (roughly A.D. 60–68).[23] For Geisler's argument to be believable, he would have to show that

if these miraculous gifts were still in existence Paul would have
had to mention them in these epistles.[24]

I could use Geisler's same methodology to 'prove' that Paul had
lost his gift of celibacy by A.D. 60–67. Paul referred to his celibacy
as a charisma (1 Cor. 7:7), and it is evident that he highly valued
this gift. Yet he does not mention it in his latter epistles (from
Ephesians to 2 Timothy). Would I be justified in concluding that
he no longer had the gift of celibacy? Of course not. I would have
to prove first that he should have mentioned it if he still had it.
Likewise, Paul does not mention from Ephesians to 2 Timothy
any success that he has had during that time in personal evangelism. Should we therefore conclude that his evangelistic gift has
ceased? I hope you can see by now the inability of an argument
from silence to prove anything from Scripture.

But there is more wrong with Geisler's argument than just
being an argument from silence. Ultimately, Geisler is comparing
apples and oranges. He is contrasting narrative literature with
didactic literature. By definition, these two kinds of literature deal
with different themes. The book of Acts is composed of stories,
while the Epistles deal with particular problems in individual
churches. One of the purposes of the book of Acts is to show the
continuing works of Jesus in his miraculous power ministry.[25] Of
course the book of Acts is going to be filled with stories of miraculous deeds, while the Epistles will generally mention these things
only when they are the source of a problem, as in Corinth.

Paul was in prison when he wrote Ephesians, Philippians,
Colossians, and Philemon. That is why they are called the prison
Epistles. Obviously, they are not going to be filled with narrative
stories about his miracle-working ministry nor his evangelistic
ministry—he is in prison! His last three letters at the end of his life
to Timothy and Titus center on advice to these young men in
shepherding the flock under their charge. He is not writing to
them narrative stories about his exploits. Why should we expect

him to tell Timothy and Titus about miracles in his own life which they had witnessed numerous times?

There is another problem with Geisler's observation about the later portions of Scripture. He fails to mention that the most graphic visions and explicit prophetic revelation do not come in the book of Acts. They come some thirty years after Paul's death. I am referring to the visions and prophesies that were given to the apostle John around A.D. 95, which were recorded in the book of Revelation. The revelatory charismata, therefore, were still functioning in great strength thirty years after Geisler says they ceased.[26]

Yet there were three close associates of an apostle famous for his healing gift who did not get healed. How are we to account for this? First of all, it is impossible to account for the lack of healing of these three men by the loss of Paul's healing gift. Why? Because no one can give a *scriptural* reason why Paul should have lost his gift of healing six or seven years before the end of his life.

Why would God have withdrawn Paul's healing gift? No cessationist can give a consistent reason for this withdrawal. The cessationist believes that the healing gifts authenticated the apostles and their ministry, especially their ministry of writing Scripture. On this theory, does Paul no longer need divine authentication? This would mean that the letters written at the end of his life do not have the same miraculous authentication that the other letters had. And what of his evangelistic ministry? Does he no longer require divine authentication for his evangelistic ministry during the years after his release from his first Roman imprisonment (A.D. 63–65)? In reality, wouldn't the withdrawal of Paul's healing gift show that God was lifting his approval, since according to the cessationist theory the miraculous gifts were meant to show God's divine approval of the apostles?

There is yet another inconsistency in Geisler's theory. Why did God leave Paul's prophetic gift and his revelatory gift (for writing

Scripture) and take away his healing gift? He is still making prophetic statements in his last letter (see 2 Tim. 4:6–8 where Paul prophesies his death and future reward; see also his prophetic statement about Alexander in 4:14). Why would God withdraw healing and miracles but leave the prophetic and revelatory gifts?[27]

It is far simpler to believe that the apostle Paul prayed for these three men and God simply said, 'No.' Since it has already been demonstrated that neither Jesus nor the apostles could heal at will, why not simply assume that God, for his own sovereign purposes, chose not to heal these three men through Paul's healing gift? This is much easier to believe than the theory that by A.D. 60, seven to eight years before the end of his life, God had withdrawn the healing gift of the most eminent of his apostles.

Do the Scriptures Teach that Apostleship Has Ceased?

Most cessationists assume that apostleship is one of the charismata. Then they attempt to prove from Scripture that apostleship has ceased and consequently draw the conclusion that at least one spiritual gift was temporary. This conclusion admits to the possibility of other gifts being temporary.

Others, as we have seen, go beyond this conclusion and view the passing of the apostles as *necessarily* demanding that the miraculous spiritual gifts have ceased. They claim the miraculous gifts were given only to the apostles and their close associates, they were capable of being imparted only by the apostles, and they were only for the distinct purpose of authenticating the apostles.

The passing of the apostles, however, (assuming for the sake of argument that they have ceased) may have little relevance to the question of whether or not the miraculous gifts of the Spirit have ceased. In reality, there are many people who believe that the gifts of the Spirit are presently being given, even though they also think that Scripture teaches that apostles ceased at the end of the first century.[28] They, as well as others, become nervous when the conversation turns to the possibility of present-day apostles.

Their concern revolves around two issues: apostles wrote Scripture, and they had an authority so great that to disobey them was equal to disobeying God. No one—at lease no one that I know—wants to open up the possibility of someone adding to the Scriptures. I certainly don't. And it is difficult to imagine anyone in the contemporary church who has the character to bear the authority that was given to the apostles. Do you know a church leader who does all things for the sake of the gospel (1 Cor. 9:23)? Or a leader for whom living simply means Christ (Phil. 1:21)? These kinds of issues naturally make us reticent to identify any- one today as an apostle in the same sense that Paul and the Twelve were apostles. Before we draw a hasty conclusion, how- ever, there are a number of issues we must consider.

Is Apostleship a Spiritual Gift?

Many writers assume that apostleship is a spiritual gift. But that assumption has not been proven. Paul himself does not call apos- tleship a spiritual gift, either in 1 Corinthians 12 or in Ephesians 4:11. What I mean is that he never applies the term *charisma* to apostleship, nor does he speak of apostleship in the same way he speaks of the other spiritual gifts.[29] If apostleship is not a spiritual gift in the same sense that healing or miracles are spiritual gifts, what is it then?

Apostles were not mentioned in the list of miraculous charis- mata in 1 Corinthians 12:8–10. Paul does not mention apostles until his concluding list beginning at 1 Corinthians 12:28. Fee remarks, 'It is no surprise that Paul should list "apostles" first. The surprise is that they should be on this list at all, and that he should list them in the plural.'[30] An apostle can hardly be thought of as a 'spiritual gift' like healing, miracles, teaching, and so on. Technically, however, the list beginning in verse 28 is not only a list of spiritual gifts. The first three items are not gifts but persons who represent ministries—apostles, prophets, and teachers. The remaining items are gifts—miracles, gifts of healing, helps, administrations, and tongues. The mixture in this list of persons and spiritual gifts was probably intended to indicate that the wide diversity in the body—from apostles to the gift of tongues and everything in between—has been appointed by God, and therefore, empowered by him. Strictly speaking, Paul has not called apostles 'spiritual gifts.'

It is virtually impossible to define the 'gift' of apostleship in the same way that the other gifts can be defined. We can easily conceive of someone exercising the gift of prophecy without being a prophet. The same is true for all the other gifts. But how could someone come to a meeting of a local assembly and exercise the gift of apostleship in that meeting without actually being an apostle? An apostle in an assembly might teach, or prophesy, or heal, or lead, or administrate. But what would it mean to exercise the gift of apostleship? We simply cannot think of apostleship apart from the historical apostles. In the New Testament an apostle is not a spiritual gift but a person who has a divinely given commission and ministry.

Who Were the New Testament Apostles?

The first people to be called apostles in the New Testament were the original twelve disciples of Jesus (Matt. 10:2). When Judas defected from this group by betraying Jesus, Matthias was taken by lot to fill Judas' place (Acts 1:21–26). This group of twelve is unique and could not be expanded beyond the twelve. The original twelve were specifically called and appointed for this task by the Lord himself during his earthly ministry (Mark 3:13ff.). Even

Matthias was divinely chosen by the Lord (cf. Acts 1:24). The requirement for membership in the original twelve was to have been with Jesus since the baptism of John and to have been an eye witness of his resurrection (Acts 1:21ff.). The names of these twelve are inscribed on the twelve foundation stones of the wall of the New Jerusalem (Rev. 21:14). These twelve, therefore, make up a closed circle to which no new additions were possible after the inclusion of Matthias.

There were, however, other apostles, but they were never counted as part of 'the Twelve.' It is clear that the New Testament viewed both Paul and Barnabas as apostles (Acts 14:4, 14). James, the Lord's brother, is clearly called an apostle by Paul (Gal. 1:19,[31] cf. 1 Cor. 15:7), and James also appears, along with Peter, as one of the major leaders of the church at Jerusalem during the council at Jerusalem (Acts 15:13–19).

Are there other apostles? It is possible that Paul also refers to Silas as an apostle (1 Thess. 2:7).[32] Romans 16:7 may also indicate that Andronicus and Junias were apostles, but there are a number of interpretive difficulties with this passage that keep us from being certain about its meaning. Finally, the phrase 'all the apostles' in 1 Corinthians 15:7 may refer to an unspecified number of apostles in addition to 'the Twelve' already mentioned in 1 Corinthians 15:5.[33]

To summarize all of this, the New Testament clearly teaches that there were fifteen apostles: the Twelve plus Paul, Barnabas, and James. Very likely Silas was a sixteenth apostle. Perhaps Andronicus, Junias, and some other unnamed apostles (1 Cor. 15:7) ought to be added to this list. The fact that there were false apostles (2 Cor. 11:13) indicates that the number of apostles could not have been fixed in New Testament times, or else there would be no possibility for these men to masquerade as apostles.[34]

The Requirements for Apostleship in the New Testament

Under this section I am not discussing the requirements for membership in 'the Twelve.' We have already seen that this was a unique circle which would not admit any additions beyond Matthias. Here we are concerned with those who became apostles after the Twelve. Even though the Twelve have a unique place in the history of redemption, the New Testament does not teach that this second group of apostles had any less authority than the Twelve. The requirements, however, for membership in this second group of apostles are slightly different than in the original twelve, because these men were not with the Lord Jesus from the beginning of his ministry, starting with the baptism of John.

In what follows we are basically dependent on Paul's description of his own apostleship. Paul set forth the *requirements* and *characteristics* of apostleship. We must be careful not to confuse these two. On the one hand, many people may share certain characteristics with the apostles, but that would not make them apostles. The apostles do signs and wonders (Acts 2:43), for example, but so do Stephen and Philip (Acts 6:8; 8:6), who are not considered apostles.

If we confuse the requirements of apostleship with the characteristics of apostleship, we could multiply the list of requirements indefinitely. We might also end up excluding some true apostles from the list. For instance, if we say that writing Scripture is a requirement for apostleship, then we would have to exclude all those apostles who did not write Scripture.

Paul sets forth three requirements for apostleship. The first and most important requirement is the specific call and commission from the Lord Jesus Christ (Gal. 1:1; Rom. 1:1, 5; 1 Cor. 1:1; 2 Cor. 1:1). The other two requirements are set forth in 1 Corinthians 9:1–2:

> Am I not free? Am I not an apostle? Have I not seen Jesus our Lord?

Are you not the result of my work in the Lord? Even though I may not be an apostle to others, surely I am to you! For you are the seal of my apostleship in the Lord.

The second requirement that Paul very clearly sets forth is that an apostle must have seen the Lord Jesus Christ. In Paul's case this requirement was met on the Dan ascus road when he saw the risen Christ (Acts 9:1–9). The third requirement is perhaps not really a requirement but rather a characteristic or proof of apostleship. Here I am speaking of his appeal to the Corinthians that they are the seal of his apostleship. In other words, Paul is appealing to his effectiveness in ministry, specifically in planting churches.

It is at once apparent that the only unique requirement of apostleship is the personal call and commission of the Lord Jesus Christ. Others had seen the risen Lord (1 Corinthians 15:6 mentions more than five hundred who had seen the risen Lord), but this did not make them apostles. Likewise, others were effective in ministry and even in planting churches (cf. Philip's ministry in Samaria), but this did not make them apostles. The foundation then of apostleship is the personal call and commission of the Lord Jesus Christ.[35]

The Characteristics of New Testament Apostleship

There are five characteristics which Paul stresses so commonly in his writings that we would have to list them as definite characteristics of an apostle. Others may share these characteristics, however, without being an apostle, but it would be difficult to imagine any apostle who did not have these characteristics.

First on this list is the suffering of an apostle. The most important texts here are 1 Corinthians 4:9–13; 2 Corinthians 4:7–12; 6:3–10; 11:23–33; and Galatians 6:17. The theological purpose behind this suffering is given in 2 Corinthians 4:7: 'But we have this treasure in jars of clay to show that this all-surpassing power is from God and not from us.'

The suffering of the apostles, then, is not accidental but divinely intended. God publicly displayed their weakness by allowing them to suffer and be persecuted. He allowed them to be misunderstood and to appear as unprotected (they go hungry, cold, and naked), so that no one would put their confidence in the 'jars of clay' but rather in the power of God to use those earthen vessels. Time and time again the Lord displays the apostles as mere men and as weak men (2 Corinthians 12:9–10) so that glory may be given to God for the surpassing greatness of his power and not to men for the greatness of their power. According to the New Testament, it is impossible to conceive of an apostle who was not intimately acquainted with suffering and persecution.

Today there are those in the church who are claiming to be apostles, but they seem to want no part of apostolic suffering. They not only live lifestyles of lavish ease, but they accept and encourage an incredible deference that is paid to them by ordinary Christians in the body of Christ. They effectively put themselves beyond the rebuke of fellow Christians, as though this were part of their apostolic calling. They also teach that God wants Christians to live lives of wealth and comfort with little, if any, experience of suffering.

A second characteristic is the special insight into divine mysteries given to the apostles. They have divine insight into the mystery of Christ (Eph. 3:1–6), into the mystery of godliness (1 Tim. 3:16), into the mystery of Israel's conversion (Rom. 11:25–32), and Paul had even seen visions and heard revelations which he was not permitted to speak on earth (2 Cor. 12:1–4, 7). Insight into divine mysteries, however, is not unique to the apostles. Prophets also have insight into divine mysteries (Eph 3:5).[36]

A third characteristic of apostolic ministry is the presence of signs and wonders as they proclaim the Lord Jesus. Jesus promised the apostles that they would be clothed with power from on high (Luke 24:49; Acts 1:8). This was fulfilled in the Twelve (Acts 2:43; 5:12) and in the ministry of the apostles who came after the Twelve (note the miracles done through Barnabas and Paul in Acts 14:3 and 15:12 and through Paul alone in Romans 15:19 and 2 Corinthians 12:12). Again, although this is a characteristic of apostolic ministry, it is not uniquely apostolic, because Stephen and Philip did signs and wonders also.

A fourth characteristic is the blameless integrity of the apostles (1 Cor. 1:12; 2:17; 4:2; 7:2). Others, of course, may have blameless integrity without being an apostle, but who could imagine an apostle who was not blameless in his integrity?

The last characteristic is apostolic authority. The Twelve were given authority over demons and all diseases (Matt. 10:1; Mark 3:15; 6:7; Luke 9:1). This authority was not unique to the apostles alone, however, it was also given to the seventy when Jesus sent them out (Luke 10:19). And the anonymous man mentioned in Mark 9:38–41 apparently had authority over demons.

Sometimes the nature of apostolic authority is misunderstood. It is not uncommon for people to view this authority as primarily authority over believers to direct their lives and make decisions for them. When authority is mentioned in the New Testament in connection with the apostles, it is primarily authority over the antikingdom forces. It is, of course, true that Ananias and Sapphira dropped dead while Peter was exposing their sin (Acts 5:1–11). But did Peter really have the authority to kill sinning believers? I don't think so. I think it is more likely that God showed him the sin of these two and what *he* intended to do to them.

Paul also had an authority to impart spiritual gifts. He reminded Timothy to stir up the gift that was in him through the laying on of Paul's hands (2 Tim. 1:6; cf. Rom. 1:11). Yet even this is not uniquely apostolic, for the elders also have power to impart spiritual gifts (1 Tim. 4:14).

Paul claimed that he was given authority to build up rather than tear down (2 Cor. 10:8; 13:10). The idea of building up probably refers to the foundational role the apostles had in establishing the first-century church (Eph. 2:20). It was clearly Paul's intention to emphasize the positive aspect of his authority—the authority to build up. But the reference to 'pulling you down' was not simply an idle threat or a figure of speech. Paul had the authority to deliver church members over to Satan in particular instances (1 Cor. 5:5; 1 Tim. 1:20). Paul warned the Corinthians that if they did not change their attitude he would have to come to them 'with a whip' (1 Cor. 4:18–21). There is an ominous tone in these words. Paul was clearly claiming a divine power to bring judgment on the Corinthian church if they did not repent.

Is this kind of authority unique to the apostles? I do not think so because the Scripture does not say that it is unique to the apostles. Conceivably God could use someone today to give a prophetic word of judgment to an individual, to a church, a city, or a nation. I actually know of several cases where Christians have been warned to repent or their lives would be taken. I know of two instances where lives were taken just as the prophetic word said they would be.

Some would perhaps object that I have not listed the ability to write Scripture as part of apostolic authority. The reason I have not listed it is that not all apostles wrote Scripture. In reality, only three of the original twelve apostles wrote Scripture—Matthew, John, and Peter. And some who were not apostles wrote Scripture. In fact, we do not even know who wrote the book of Hebrews, yet it is still Scripture. This is not to say that I believe someone can write Scripture again today. I do not think anyone has that ability today. I think that our Bible, the Old and New Testament, is complete and sufficient and that it will never have any additions. It is also my personal conviction that the Bible, both the Old and New Testament, is the inerrant Word of God. We do not, however, safeguard the Bible from any further additions by claiming that there are no more apostles, since apostolic authorship was clearly not divinely intended as a test for canonicity.

Arguments That the Apostolic Office Has Ceased

MacArthur lists six reasons why the apostolic office has ceased:

1. The church was founded upon the apostles.
2. Apostles were eyewitnesses to the resurrection.
3. Apostles were chosen personally by Jesus Christ.
4. Apostles were authenticated by miraculous signs.
5. Apostles had absolute authority.
6. Apostles have an eternal and unique place of honor.[37]

The first thing to notice about these arguments is that neither MacArthur, nor anyone else, can produce a specific text of Scripture that says the apostolic office has ceased or would cease during the church age. All of these arguments are based on theological deductions, not on specific statements of Scripture. None of these arguments, nor the passages used to support these arguments, teach that the Lord could not give additional apostles to the church after Paul, Barnabas, and perhaps others in the first century.

Reply to number 1: The fact that the apostles had a foundational role in the establishing of the church (Eph. 2:20) does not mean that the Lord could not, or would not, give more apostles. Someone had to found the church. Would we argue that just because they founded the church their ministry must be temporary? The founding director of a company or corporation will always be unique in the sense that he or she was the founder, but that does not mean the company would not have future directors or presidents.

On the other hand, Ephesians 4:11–13 *may* indicate that God intended apostles to continue until the return of Jesus. Five ministries—apostles, prophets, evangelists, pastors and teachers—were given to the church (v. 11). Why? Paul says that these ministries were given to equip the believers so that the believers can do the work of the ministry (v. 12). How long is this arrangement supposed to continue? Paul answers this question in verse 13:

> *Until* we all reach unity in the faith and in the knowledge of the Son of God and become mature, attaining to the whole measure of the fullness of Christ. (Eph. 4:13, emphasis mine)

The only reference in Paul's writings that I have found that specifically mentions the 'duration' of the apostles' ministry is the 'until' of Ephesians 4:13. If taken literally this would mean that the church will have apostles present until it reaches the maturity described in verse 13.

I know, however, that there are other interpretations of Ephesians 4:11–13. I plan to discuss them and Ephesians 2:20 in detail in my next book. My present point is simply this: we do not have a specific statement from Scripture to the effect that there would only be 'one' generation of apostles. We do, however, have a specific statement that says we will have apostles at least until the church comes to maturity. At present it is difficult to view the church as having reached the level of maturity described in verse 13.

Reply to number 2: It is true that an apostle had to be an eyewitness of the resurrection. In Paul's case this was fulfilled after Jesus had ascended into heaven. The Lord appeared to Paul on the Damascus road (Acts 9:1–9). Later, in Paul's testimony, he refers to this as 'the vision from heaven' (Acts 26:19). Elsewhere, Luke uses this word for angelic visions (Luke 1:22; 24:23). What is to prevent the Lord from appearing to others in this same fashion? I know of no scriptural reason why the Lord has not, or could not, appear to others in his church.

Reply to number 3: What is to prevent the Lord from personally choosing and commissioning others to be apostles? He did this to Paul, James, Barnabas, and most likely Silas. Why couldn't he do that today? MacArthur writes, 'When the pastoral epistles set forth principles for lasting church leadership, they speak of elders and deacons. They never mention apostles.'[38] Again, this is an argument from silence. Why should the pastoral epistles have mentioned apostleship? Elders, deacons, and apostles existed side by side in the New Testament church. The church needed rules governing the selection of elders and deacons, because Jesus had left their selection to his church. On the other hand, the church never chose its apostles. Jesus himself did that personally. Why then would he write Timothy or Titus and give them rules for choosing or electing apostles?

Reply to number 4: I have already shown that apostles were not authenticated by signs and wonders. To be sure, they did signs and wonders, but these signs and wonders did not authenticate them; rather the signs and wonders authenticated the Lord Jesus and the message about him. There is no scriptural reason, certainly no specific text, that would prevent Jesus from granting an outpouring of signs and wonders to his church in this century or any other century for that matter. And as we have seen, the ministry of signs and wonders is not a unique characteristic of the apostolic office. Others also do signs and wonders.

Reply to number 5: I do not think MacArthur, or others, are correct when they say apostles had 'absolute authority.' MacArthur writes, 'When the apostles spoke, there was no discussion.'[39] This simply is not true. Peter's hypocrisy was so great at Antioch that even Barnabas was carried away by it, along with a number of other Jewish Christians, so that Paul had to oppose Peter before the whole group (Gal. 2:11–21). On another occasion, Paul and

Barnabas could not convince Jewish believers from Judea that circumcision was unnecessary. It took a church council at Jerusalem to settle the issue (Acts 15:1–35).

There is a tendency among some protestant writers to almost deify the apostles. Gross maintains that an apostle 'taught nothing contradictory to the Word of God (Galatians 1:8, 9).'[40] But Peter did teach something contrary to the Word. Paul said that when Peter came to Antioch, his example led a number of people into hypocrisy. This was certainly a form of teaching, and Paul had to oppose it. I do not believe the apostles ever made a mistake writing under the inspiration of the Holy Spirit, but they did not live under constant inspiration of the Holy Spirit. As Peter's example shows, they were capable of significant sin, just like any other believer in the church.

The doctrine of inspiration only extends to the portion of the written Word of God that was given to each of the apostles. The doctrine of inspiration does not extend to their other interpretations or opinions. In my opinion, MacArthur, Gross, and others have gone significantly beyond what the Bible says about the authority of the apostles. They have done this, I am sure, in order to preserve the uniqueness of the apostles and ultimately the unique authority of the Word. But we do not protect or honor the Word when we go beyond what it says and claim for it something it does not claim for itself.

I might also point out that the Scriptures do teach that before Christ returns the Lord will commission two witnesses who will have greater power and authority than the apostles ever enjoyed. I am referring to Revelation 11:3–6:

'And I will give power to my two witnesses, and they will prophesy for 1,260 days, clothed in sackcloth.' These are the two olive trees and the two lampstands that stand before the Lord of the earth. If anyone tries to harm them, fire comes from their mouths and devours their enemies. This is how anyone who wants to harm them must die.

These men have power to shut up the sky so that it will not rain during the time they are prophesying; and they have power to turn the waters into blood and to strike the earth with every kind of plague as often as they want.

These two men are called 'witnesses' like the apostles (Acts 1:8). They also prophesy. They will enjoy a protection and an authority that not even the apostles enjoyed: they will be able to kill anyone who wishes to harm them. And they will have a greater signs and wonders ministry than any Old Testament prophet or any New Testament apostle. Yet neither their ability to prophesy, their authority, nor their signs and wonders ministry will in any way endanger the unique authority of the canon of Scripture. This demonstrates that God could give apostles at any time in history (or those with more power and authority than the apostles) without doing violence to his Word or the gospel.

I find it ironic that some who are most insistent on the cessation of the apostles have, in fact, their own modern apostles. Just to cite one example, I recently spent several hours discussing theological differences with a man who is completely committed to Reformed theology. He was most concerned about my belief that God still speaks to us today, that he will give us dreams, visions, words of knowledge, guidance, warnings, and so on. He sees this as endangering the unique authority of the Bible. He sees it as contradicting the Reformation's cry of *sola Scriptura* and the Reformation's doctrine of the sufficiency of Scripture.

When we were discussing our differences on this point, I was citing Scripture as my reason for believing that God still speaks. Rather than interact with me on a scriptural basis, he continually cited theological writings from the Reformation period. This was true for most of our discussion. In fact, I don't think it would be an overstatement to say that this man was more at home in the writings of Calvin and Calvinists than he was in the literature of the Bible.

It was apparent as I listened to him talk that he had more practical confidence in Calvin's interpretation of the Bible than in the actual writings of Paul. On a practical level, Calvin was a greater authority for him than even the apostle Paul. On a theoretical level he would never admit this, and he would be highly offended at my even suggesting it. Yet I cannot help believing that on a practical level it really is true.

This case is not unusual. I find that others are also more confident in citing their theological traditions rather than citing and arguing from specific texts of Scripture. In effect, this makes the originators of those traditions, whether they be Calvin, Luther, or someone else, equal if not greater in authority than the apostolic writers of Scripture. Calvin may not be an apostle to some, but I can certainly show you people to whom he is *the* apostle.

Reply to number 6: MacArthur's argument that 'apostles have an eternal and unique place of honor' is supported by Revelation 21:14, which says that the names of the twelve apostles are inscribed on the twelve foundations stones of the wall of the new city. But the argument does not take into consideration Paul, Barnabas, or other potential New Testament apostles after the Twelve. Everyone admits that the Twelve have a unique place in the history of salvation. That is not at issue. But after the Twelve, God saw fit to add at least three others and possibly more. If he could add three or four others during the lifetime of the Twelve, why couldn't he add others after the first century? The Scriptures do not teach that apostles have ceased.

I believe that the twelve apostles were unique and formed a closed circle. However, the addition of Paul, Barnabas, James, and possibly others opens the possibility of God giving additional apostles at any time in history. No specific text of Scripture prevents Jesus from appearing to and commissioning others in an apostolic office. In the future, he is going to give two witnesses to the church who will have even greater power than the first-century apostles (Rev. 11:3–6), and this will not endanger the authority of the Scripture. If at the end of church history the Lord is going to give two witnesses to the church who will be greater in authority and power than the New Testament apostles, why couldn't he give more apostles to the church before the time of the two witnesses?

I do not know of anyone today whom I would want to call an apostle in the same sense that I would call Paul an apostle. I am not willing, however, to rule out this possibility, because I do not think the Scriptures rule it out.

Even if apostles have ceased, that would prove nothing in regard to the ministry of signs and wonders or of the miraculous gifts of the Spirit. This is true because neither signs and wonders nor the miraculous gifts of the Spirit were limited to the apostles. Neither by *example* nor *statement* of Scripture can anyone prove that the miraculous gifts of the Spirit were limited to the few. Just the converse is true. The attempt to prove that miraculous gifts were *exclusively* imparted through the apostles has no scriptural basis, but rather is an illusion birthed by theological prejudice. Perhaps, the worst example of this kind of prejudice is seen in the attempt to prove that the apostle Paul lost his gift of healing around A.D. 60, a full seven or eight years before the completion of his ministry.

The attempt, therefore, to connect the alleged cessation of the gifts with the passing of the apostles is futile on both levels of the argument. On the one hand, it cannot be proved scripturally that apostles have ceased, and on the other hand, it cannot be proved that signs and wonders or the miraculous gifts of the Spirit were exclusively connected to the apostles.

Appendix C

Were There Only Three Periods of Miracles?

John MacArthur is a modern-day proponent of the view that there were only three periods of miracles in the biblical record. He formulates the argument in the following way:

> Most biblical miracles happened in three relatively brief periods of Bible history: in the days of Moses and Joshua, during the ministries of Elijah and Elisha, and in the time of Christ and the apostles. . . .
>
> Aside from those three intervals, the only supernatural events recorded in Scripture were isolated incidents. In the days of Isaiah, for example, the Lord supernaturally defeated Sennacherib's army (2 Kings 19:35–36), then healed Hezekiah and turned the sun's shadows back (20:1–11). In the days of Daniel God preserved Shadrach, Meshach and Abednego in the furnace (Daniel 3:20–26). For the most part, however, supernatural events like those did not characterize God's dealings with his people. . . . All three periods of miracles were times when God gave his written revelation—Scripture—in substantial quantities. Those doing the miracles were essentially the same ones heralding an era of revelation. Moses wrote the first five books of Scripture. Elijah and Elisha introduced the prophetic age. The apostles wrote nearly all of the New Testament.[1]

There are a number of difficulties with this argument, and it seems that most cessationists no longer use it. The first difficulty is with the alleged purpose of three periods of miracles. The reason for each period of miracles according to the theory is that they authenticate the written revelation God was giving at the time. In the case of Moses and Joshua, and Christ and the apostles, there was written revelation being given. But in the case of Elijah and Elisha there was no written revelation being given. The first written prophetic revelation does not come until the time of Isaiah, Micah, and Amos, almost a hundred years after the death of Elijah, and fifty years or more after the death of Elisha.

The idea that miracles were common only at the time of Moses to Joshua and Elijah to Elisha is also contradicted by a specific statement of Scripture. Jeremiah claimed,

> You performed miraculous signs and wonders in Egypt and have continued them to this day, both in Israel and among all mankind, and have gained the renown that is still yours. (Jeremiah 32:20)

If Jeremiah's statement is to be taken literally, he quite clearly sees signs and wonders occurring in his own time (his ministry began in 626 B.C. and ended some time after 586 B.C.) both in Israel and in other nations.[2]

There is another inconsistency in this theory. MacArthur claims that Elijah and Elisha introduced the prophetic age. This is an inaccuracy. It is Samuel who introduced the prophetic age. He was the prophet of whom it was said, 'None of his words fall to the ground' (1 Sam. 3:19–21). Furthermore, at the time of Samuel there were already groups of prophets prophesying (1 Sam. 10:5). If the theory that MacArthur puts forth were accurate, we would expect the period of Samuel to be introduced with an outbreak of miracles.

Finally, I do not dispute that the New Testament age was clearly an age of new revelation, but MacArthur is certainly in error when he claims that 'the apostles wrote nearly all of the New Testament.' Mark, Luke, and Jude were not apostles, and

Hebrews is anonymous. These books comprise approximately forty-two percent of the New Testament.

Another fault with the theory is that there are simply too many supernatural events occurring outside of these three periods for the theory to be meaningful. A quick survey of the Old Testament will reveal how commonly miraculous events occurred. We won't even look at the books of Exodus through Joshua, because these books deal with the period of Moses and Joshua, nor will we consider any supernatural occurrences from 1 Kings 17 through 2 Kings 13 (nor 2 Chron. 17–24), because these books deal with the period of Elijah and Elisha.

Just for fun, let us consider that these portions of Scripture have been cut out of our Bibles. This will mean, of course, that we will not have the ten plagues that the Lord visited upon Egypt. We will also be missing the parting of the Red Sea and Elijah ascending in the chariot of fire into heaven.

What kinds of miracles and supernatural events will be left? According to MacArthur, our new Bible should be fairly purged of the supernatural, and all we should find are a few 'isolated incidents' of supernatural events. You be the judge of how accurate this theory is as you consider the events from the following table.

Scripture	Description
Genesis	
1–3	The creation of the earth and the fall of man
5:24	The rapture of Enoch
6:2ff.	The sons of God (angelic/demonic beings) married the daughters of men
6:9–8:19	The Noahic flood
11:1ff.	The confusing of human language at the Tower of Babel
12:1–3	The supernatural call of Abraham

Scripture	Description
12:17	The plague on Pharaoh's house
15:12–21	Abraham's trance, the smoking firepot, and blazing torch
16:7	The angel of the Lord appears to Hagar
17:1ff.	The Lord appears to Abraham
18:1ff.	The Lord and angels appear to Abraham and eat a meal with him
19:11	The angels blind the men of Sodom
19:23ff.	The Lord destroys Sodom and Gommorah
19:26	Lot's wife is turned into a pillar of salt
20:3ff.	God warns Abimelech in a dream not to touch Sarah
20:17ff.	God supernaturally saves the life of Hagar and Ishmael
21:1ff.	Sarah miraculously conceives Isaac
22:11	The angel of the Lord prevents Abraham from sacrificing Isaac
24:12ff.	Abraham's servant is supernaturally led to Rebekah
25:21	Rebekah supernaturally conceives twins
25:23ff.	The Lord speaks to Rebekah concerning the destiny of the twins in her womb
26:2	The Lord appears to Isaac
26:24	The Lord appears to Isaac again
28:12ff.	The Lord appears to Jacob
31:3	The Lord speaks to Jacob, commanding him to return to Palestine
32:1	The angels of God meet Jacob
32:24ff.	Jacob wrestles with the angel of the Lord all night
35:9	God appears to Jacob and blesses him

Scripture	Description
37:5ff.	Joseph's dreams
38:7ff.	The Lord kills Er and Onan
40:1ff.	Joseph interprets the dreams of the cupbearer and the baker
41:1ff.	Joseph interprets Pharaoh's dream
Judges	
2:1–5	The angel of the Lord appears to all Israel
3:9ff.	The Spirit of the Lord empowers Othniel to deliver Israel
3:31	Shamgar kills 600 Philistines with an oxgoad
4:4ff.	Deborah prophesies to Barak
6:11.	The angel of the Lord appears to Gideon
6:36	The miracle of Gideon's fleece
7:1ff.	The Lord sends divine panic against Midian so that Gideon can defeat them with only 300 men
11:29ff.	The Spirit of the Lord comes upon Jephthah to deliver Israel from the Ammonites
13:3ff.	The angel of the Lord appears to Manoah and his wife
14–16	Samson's supernatural feats
1 Samuel	
1:19ff.	Hannah supernaturally conceives Samuel
3:1ff.	The Lord appears to Samuel the first time
3:19–21	The Lord lets none of Samuel's words fall to the ground
5:1–5	The destruction of the idol Dagon
5:6ff.	The Lord strikes the Philistines with tumors
6:19ff.	The Lord kills some of the men of Bethshemesh
9–10	Samuel's prophetic ministry to Saul

Scripture	Description
10:20ff.	Saul is chosen by lot to be king over Israel
11:6ff.	The Spirit of the Lord empowers Saul to deliver Israel from the Ammonites
16:1ff.	Samuel's prophetic ministry to David
16:13	The Spirit of the Lord comes upon David
16:14	The Spirit of the Lord leaves Saul, and an evil spirit from the Lord terrorizes him
18:10–11	An evil spirit causes Saul to try to kill David
19:9–10	Again an evil spirit causes Saul to attempt to kill David
19:20ff.	Three times the Spirit of the Lord comes upon Saul's messengers and they prophesy
19:22ff.	The Spirit of the Lord comes on Saul and he prophesies
23:4, 10–12; 30:8	The Lord repeatedly gives supernatural guidance to David
28:12ff.	Samuel appears from the dead to Saul
2 Samuel	
2:1	The Lord gives supernatural guidance to David
5:19	The Lord gives supernatural guidance to David
5:23–24	The Lord gives supernatural guidance to David
6:7	The Lord kills Uzzah
7:5ff.	Nathan prophesies to David
12:1ff.	Nathan exposes David's sin
12:15ff.	The Lord kills David's child
12:25	Nathan prophesies concerning Solomon
21:1	The Lord explains the cause of the famine to David

Scripture	Description
24:11	The Lord speaks to David through Gad and kills 70,000 Israelites
1 Kings	
3:3ff.	The Lord appears to Solomon and grants him great wisdom
8:10ff.	The glory of the Lord fills the temple
9:2ff.	The Lord appears a second time to Solomon
11:11ff.	The Lord tells Solomon that he will take the kingdom from him
11:29ff.	The prophet Ahijah tells Jeraboam that the Lord has given him the tribes of Israel
13:1ff.	A man of God prophesies the birth of Josiah, the Lord splits the altar at Bethel, and the Lord withers Jeraboam's hand and then heals it
13:20ff.	An old prophet prophesies the death of the man of God, and the Lord kills the man of God with a lion
14:5	The Lord prevents Jeraboam's wife from deceiving the prophet Ahijah, and he prophesies judgment on Jeraboam's house
16:1ff.	Jehu prophesies judgment against Baasha
2 Kings	
15:5	The Lord strikes Azariah with leprosy
19:20ff.	Isaiah prophesies to Hezekiah concerning Sennacherib
19:35	The angel of the Lord kills 185,000 Assyrians
20:5ff.	Isaiah prophesies to Hezekiah that the Lord will add 15 years to his life
20:10ff.	The Lord causes the sunlight to go back ten steps on the stairway of Ahaz

Scripture	Description
20:16ff.	Isaiah prophesies judgment to Hezekiah
21:10ff.	The Lord prophesies judgment on Judah through his prophets
22:14ff.	The prophetess Huldah prophesies judgment on Judah but blessing on Josiah
1 Chronicles	
12:18	The Holy Spirit prompts Amasai to prophesy to David
21:1	Satan incites David to take a census of Israel
21:16	David sees the angel of the Lord
21:20	Araunah sees the same angel
21:26	The Lord sends fire from heaven to David's altar
2 Chronicles	
7:1	Fire comes down from heaven and consumes Solomon's offerings
11:2	Shemaiah prophesies to King Rehoboam not to fight against Israel
12:5	Shemiah prophesies against Rehoboam
12:7	Shemiah prophesies again to Rehoboam that God will have a measure of mercy on him
13:15ff.	God supernaturally delivers Judah
13:20	The Lord kills Jeroboam
14:12ff.	The Lord supernaturally delivers Judah from the Ethiopians
15:1ff.	Azariah prophesies to King Asa
16:7ff.	Hanani, the seer, prophesies judgment on King Asa
25:7ff.	A man of God prophesies to Amaziah not to take the army of Israel into battle with him
25:15ff.	A prophet prophesies judgment on Amaziah for his idolatry

Scripture	Description
28:9ff.	Oded prophesied judgment against the Israelite army if they refuse to release their captives from Judah
Ezra	
5:1	Haggai and Zechariah prophesy to the Jews who are in Judah
Job	
1–2	Supernatural satanic persecution of Job by God's permission
38–42	God's conversation with Job and the restoration of Job's fortune
Daniel	
2:1ff.	God supernaturally reveals Nebuchadnezzar's dream and its interpretation to Daniel
3:1ff.	Daniel's three friends walk in the fiery furnace with the preincarnate Christ and are preserved
4:19–27	Daniel interprets a second dream of Nebuchadnezzar
4:28ff.	God afflicts Nebuchadnezzar with insanity
5:5ff.	A hand supernaturally appears and writes Belshazzar's judgment on the wall
5:17ff.	Daniel interprets the writing
6:1ff.	Daniel is supernaturally preserved in the lions' den
7–12	Supernatural visions of the last days and angelic visitations are given to Daniel

Just a casual glance at the previous table will demonstrate that neither MacArthur, nor anyone else, can purge the abundance of supernatural events from the Old Testament by trying to cram them all into two brief time periods. Supernatural events are consistently spread over the entire Old Testament.

What kind of supernatural events are we talking about here? The previous table can be summarized in the following way:

1. Many appearances of the Lord to individuals
2. Many appearances of angels to individuals and even to groups of people
3. Supernatural rescues of individuals
4. Supernatural deliverances of groups and even the whole nation
5. Supernatural empowerings for:
   a. superhuman strength
   b. prophetic understanding and prophetic words for people who are not prophets
   c. supernatural guidance and direction in a variety of ways
6. Supernatural judgments:
   a. the destruction of individuals
   b. the destruction of armies
   c. the destruction of cities
   d. the destruction of the earth
   e. other supernatural judgments such as illness, blindness, insanity, and plagues
7. Supernatural dreams, trances, and visions
8. Supernaturally given interpretation of the above
9. Miraculous conceptions
10. Miraculous healings
11. Supernatural satanic and demonic interaction with man
12. Cosmic signs, such as the sunlight falling back ten steps, fire falling from heaven, and so on
13. Consistent prophetic ministry from the time of Samuel until the end of the Old Testament canon

These are the kinds of things that occur throughout the Old

Testament period. Nor is this all that occurs during the Old Testament period. With the exception of Daniel, I have not even surveyed any of the other prophetic books. For example, I have omitted things like the vision Isaiah had in the year that king Uzziah died, when Isaiah was caught up into heaven and commissioned for his prophetic ministry (Isa. 6:1–13). Nor did I discuss the strange visions and happenings to Ezekiel about one hundred and forty years later. We must remember that canonical prophets were in Israel through the time of Malachi (approximately 450–400 B.C.). So at least from the time of Samuel through Malachi, there is consistent prophetic ministry to Israel. Prophetic ministry is, of course, supernatural ministry.

The book of Daniel is devastating to MacArthur's theory that the supernatural is basically confined to the periods of Moses and Joshua, and Elijah and Elisha. Daniel ministered from 605 to at least 539 B.C., well beyond the time of Elijah and Elisha. Yet proportionately Daniel's book contains more supernatural events than the books of Exodus through Joshua (the books dealing with the ministries of Moses and Joshua) and 1 Kings through 2 Kings 13 (the books dealing with the ministries of Elijah and Elisha). Every chapter in the book of Daniel has supernatural occurrences!

With the exception of the book of Daniel, and possibly the book of Genesis, the periods of Moses and Joshua, and Elijah and Elisha, do show the greatest concentration of miracles in the Old Testament period. As the previous table shows, however, you cannot find any period in Israel's history where supernatural events were not common among the people of God.

MacArthur would dispute the significance of this table. He is able to do this by a semantic sleight of hand. He defines a miracle as 'an extraordinary event wrought by God through human agency, an event that cannot be explained by natural forces.'[3] He offers no scriptural support for this definition; instead he appeals to A. H. Strong's *Systematic Theology* for support. My point is that he does not and he cannot define miracles in this way by using Scripture. The miraculous vocabulary of the Old and New Testaments simply will not permit it.

By defining a miracle as something that must occur through 'human agency,' he is able to rule out such things as angelic visitations, divine cataclysmic judgments, and cosmic signs as miracles. This would prohibit us from calling Peter's deliverance from prison by an angel in Acts 12 a miracle, nor could we call the earthquake in Acts 16 a miracle, nor could we call tearing the veil at the temple at Christ's crucifixion a miracle (Matt. 27:51). When Jesus was crucified, God raised many saints from their graves (Matt. 27:52), but since there was no 'human agency' involved here, MacArthur would not allow us to call this a miracle in the same way that he calls other New Testament raisings from the dead miracles. But most ludicrous of all, on MacArthur's view we could not call the resurrection of Jesus Christ a miracle.

What are we to call these things then? What are we to call the other phenomena in Scripture that are supernatural but not occasioned by direct human agency? MacArthur does not tell us what the Scriptures call these events. He does say, however, that miracles in Scripture are also called 'signs and wonders.'[4]

It is true that the phrase 'signs and wonders' refers to miracles done through human agency, but it is also true that 'signs and wonders' or just the word 'signs' can refer to miracles done apart from human agency. Peter, for example, refers to Jesus as 'a man accredited by God to you by miracles, wonders and signs, which God did among you through him' (Acts 2:22). But three verses before this, Peter also quotes the Joel prophecy in which God says, 'And I will show *wonders* in the heaven above and *signs* on the earth below, blood and fire and billows of smoke. The sun will be turned to darkness and the moon to blood before the coming of the great and glorious day of the Lord' (Acts 2:19–20, emphasis

mine). Here *signs* and *wonders* clearly refer to supernatural, cataclysmic judgments upon the earth done apart from human agency.

God also did many miraculous things apart from human
agency during the forty-year sojourn of Israel in the wilderness.
For instance, he led them by a pillar of fire by night, a cloud during the day, he fed them with manna, he sent plagues on them to
discipline them, and so on. Stephen refers to all of these things as
God's signs and wonders (Acts 7:36). When Daniel was thrown
into the lions' den, God sent an angel to deliver Daniel (Dan.
6:22). Afterward, king Darius praises God for this deliverance and
refers to it as one of God's signs and wonders (Dan. 6:27).[5]
MacArthur's definition of miracles, therefore, simply cannot
stand in light of Scripture.

MacArthur could, however, simply qualify the kinds of miracles he is talking about. He could allege that miracles done by
human agency are rare outside of those two periods in the Old
Testament dealing with Moses and Joshua, and Elijah and Elisha.
Even so, his point would still not be valid.

MacArthur does not want to accept as normative any of the
supernatural events from the previous table. From the book of
Samuel on, for example, there is a constant stream of prophetic
words of guidance, judgment, blessing, warning, and promise.
There are regular visions, dreams, angelic appearances, theophanies, divine afflictions and disease, divinely caused panic on
Israel's enemies, altars splitting, supernatural strength given to
the judges, and on and on. Some of these things are done through
human agency, and some are purely divine in origin.

MacArthur does not want to admit that any of these things go
on today. Yet the Scriptures teach that these very same supernatural events are a *normal* part of life in the Old Testament. This is
not to say that they are everyday events, but they occur with
some regularity in virtually every generation of believers in the
Old Testament.

This leads us to another point.

When supernatural phenomena do not occur, what is the attitude of the writers of Scripture toward their absence? When there is an absence of the supernatural in the Old Testament, the Scripture writers do not take that as normative for the people of God; rather they take it as a sign of judgment.

Psalm 74, for example, begins like this, 'Why have you rejected us forever, O God? Why does your anger smolder against the sheep of your pasture?' (v. 1). Then after describing the judgment under which Israel has fallen, the psalmist laments, 'We are given no miraculous signs; no prophets are left, and none of us knows how long this will be' (v. 9). The psalmist takes the absence of signs and prophets as the judgment of the Lord.

There is a similar lament in Psalm 77:7–10. He refuses, however, to accept the absence of the Lord's supernatural deeds as normal living conditions for the people of God. His answer to this dilemma is to remember the supernatural works of the past (v. 11). The word 'remember' very likely means to cause to remember or to extol these deeds.[6] He then refers to the Lord as 'the God who performs miracles' (v. 14). He does not say, 'the God who *performed* miracles,' but rather, 'the God who *performs* miracles.' He uses a present tense participle for the expression *performs miracles*. He means that God is still doing miracles. The fact that Israel was not experiencing these miracles was a sign of judgment, not a sign that God was no longer doing them.

The prophets speak the same way. One of the worst judgments that God could pronounce on Jerusalem was recorded by Isaiah. He said, 'The LORD has brought over you a deep sleep: He has sealed your eyes (the prophets); he has covered your heads (the seers)' (Isa. 29:10). Not to have the benefit of the ministry of the prophets and seers was regarded as a disastrous judgment from the Lord in the Old Testament.

Apparently MacArthur would have us believe that in between

his alleged two periods of miracles in the Old Testament the life of the believer consisted basically in regular Bible study and prayer, with little or no evidence of the supernatural. This scenario simply will not fit the picture given to us by the Old Testament writers.

But even if it did, MacArthur's argument would still not be valid. Even if MacArthur could prove that all supernatural occurrences in the Bible were confined to these three periods in the Scripture: the periods of Moses and Joshua, Elijah and Elisha, and Christ and the apostles, that would still not mean that the Scriptures teach miracles ended with Christ and the apostles. MacArthur would still have to prove that Scripture actually teaches that miracles would end with this third period.

The Scriptures end with the introduction of the kingdom of Christ, an introduction that is accompanied by miracles and supernatural phenomena. The only divinely inspired record we have of church life is one in which miracles and supernatural guidance are relatively common. The kingdom of Christ is introduced with miracles. Even if there had only been two periods of miracles in the Old Testament, that would not prove that the kingdom of Christ would only have a brief period of miracles. All things have changed with the coming of Christ and his kingdom. Now *all things* are possible to the one who believes.

Healing gifts are given to the whole church, and the elders of the church are to have a regular healing ministry (James 5:14–16). Whether there were one, four, or five periods of miracles in the Old Testament is irrelevant in determining whether the kingdom of Christ is meant to have miracles as a normative part of church life. This must be determined on the basis of specific statements in the New Testament. In the absence of these specific statements, MacArthur's argument collapses under the weight of all the miracles from Genesis to Revelation.

Notes

Chapter 1: The Phone Call That Changed My Life

1. The term 'cessationist' describes someone who believes that the miraculous gifts of the Holy Spirit ceased with the death of the last apostle or shortly thereafter.

Chapter 2: Surprised by the Holy Spirit

1. I still had an ignorant prejudice against charismatics and Pentecostals. I had yet to meet and fellowship with anyone from their traditions, so all my old stereotypes were still in place.

Chapter 3: Signs & Wimbers

1. When I say that I believe this ministry is available to the church today, I am not saying that all Christians in the church can experience the same level of revelatory and healing ministry that Paul Cain experiences. This 'disclaimer' is not meant to imply that Paul's gifting is totally unique in the body of Christ, although it is very exceptional. We have exceptional examples of all of the gifts of the Spirit today. For example, I believe that Billy Graham has an exceptional gift of evangelism. I would not claim that all believers can move in the same level of evangelistic ministry as Billy Graham. I do believe, however, that many can have gifts of evangelism and gifts of healing along with the other gifts. There are things the body of Christ can do that will encourage and make room for all levels of evangelistic ministry and things the body of Christ can do that will hinder evangelistic ministry at all levels. This is also true for gifts of healing and miracles as well as the revelatory gifts.

Chapter 4: The Myth of Pure Biblical Objectivity

1. There were a number of miracles in these chapters in addition to what the student himself could list. In chapter nineteen of Genesis, for example, there was

not only the destruction of Sodom and Gomorrah, but also the angels blinding the Sodomites (19:9–11) and Lot's wife turning into a pillar of salt (19:24–26). While it is true that the greatest concentration of miracles and supernatural occurrences took place during the ministries of Moses and Joshua, Elijah and Elisha, there is evidence of the supernatural consistently throughout the Old Testament. The argument using the 'three periods' is discussed fully in appendix C on pages 253–66.

2. J. I. Packer, 'The Comfort of Conservatism' in *Power Religion*, ed. Michael Horton (Chicago: Moody Press, 1992), pp. 286–87.

3. Ibid., p. 289.

4. Ibid., p. 290.

5. Edward Gross, *Miracles, Demons, and Spiritual Warfare* (Grand Rapids: Baker, 1990), p. 168.

6. Ibid., p. 170.

7. Ibid.

8. More and more theological writers are acknowledging this today. For example, Oliver R. Barclay writes, 'All of us are influenced in our thinking, by our traditions, our education and the general climate of thought of our age. These forces tend to mould our ideas more than we realize, and to make us conform to the fashion of our time, or the traditions in which we were brought up, rather than to revealed truth' ('When Christians Disagree' in *Signs, Wonders and Healing*, ed. John Goldingay [Leicester, England: Inter-Varsity Press, 1989], p. 8).

9. Even the greatest of the cessationist scholars, Benjamin Breckenridge Warfield, could not make his case on Scripture alone. He appealed both to the Scriptures and to 'the testimony of later ages' (*Counterfeit Miracles* [Edinburgh: Banner of Truth Trust, 1918; reprint 1983], p. 6).

Chapter 5: The Real Reason Christians Do Not Believe in the Miraculous Gifts

1. Strictly speaking, we do not know that all the New Testament healings were irreversible for the simple reason that we have no follow-up studies of the people who were healed. If sin or demons were the cause of an illness and the healed person did not repent, the illness could return (cf. Matt. 12:43–45 and John 5:14). Likewise, if the illness was brought on by anxiety or stress, that illness could return if the anxiety and stress were not dealt with.

2. This is John MacArthur's view. He writes, 'According to Scripture those who possess miraculous gifts could use their gifts at will' (*Charismatic Chaos* [Grand Rapids, Mich.: Zondervan, 1992], p. 215).

3. The Scriptures declare that it is God who heals, and he heals according to his sovereign will, not human will (Pss. 72:18; 103:3; 136:4; Ex. 15:26). Occasionally the book of Acts may talk about Stephen, Phillip, Peter, or Paul doing miracles, but when it uses that kind of language, it is speaking of them as agents whom God is using. The apostles themselves never took credit for a healing. They always gave glory to God. Frequently Luke describes the Lord as healing 'through' the apostles (Acts 2:43; 5:12), or simply refers to the apostles' miracles as 'God doing them' (Acts 14:3; 15:12).

4. Please do not misunderstand my Christology at this point. I believe that Jesus was and is fully omnipotent. I am saying that he voluntarily and continually allowed his omnipotence to be limited by his submission to the will of his Father (Phil. 2:5–11).

5. In chapter 13 of the book of Acts there is a much different illustration of the same principle. Here Elymas, the magician, is opposing Paul's witness to Sergius Paulus. The Holy Spirit comes on Paul and fills him. Then Paul pronounces a curse on Elymas, 'Now the hand of the Lord is against you. You are going to be blind, and for a time will be unable to see the light of the sun. Immediately mist and darkness came over him, and he groped about, seeking someone to lead him by the hand' (Acts 13:11). Does anyone seriously want to maintain that this is something Paul could do at will? If he could have, it would have been a great tool to use in all of his disputes with the Jews. This, of course, was not something he could do at will. The blinding of Elymas was the direct result of the filling of the Holy Spirit, in which God showed Paul what he was about to do, and Paul boldly proclaimed what he saw the Lord doing against Elymas.

6. This is MacArthur's suggestion in *Charismatic Chaos*, p. 215.

7. See pp. 238–41 for a complete evaluation of the suggestion that these three 'failures' on Paul's part demonstrated that he had lost his healing gift.

8. There is no universally agreed on definition for the word *charisma*. Of its seventeen New Testament occurrences, sixteen are found in Paul and one in Peter (1 Pet. 4:10). Paul's usage is so diverse that no single simple definition will do. One of the best discussions of *charisma* is found in Max Turner, 'Spiritual Gifts Then and Now,' *Vox Evangelica* 15 (1985): 7–64. Turner concludes that the various Pauline lists of gifts 'are clearly *ad hoc* and incomplete and they suggest that for Paul virtually anything that can be viewed as God's enabling of a man for the upbuilding of the church could and would be designated a *charisma*, if Paul's purpose was to underline its nature as *given* by God' (p. 31). For similar conclusions see D. A. Carson, *Showing the Spirit* (Grand Rapids: Baker, 1987), 19ff.; and Wayne Grudem, *Systematic Theology* (Grand Rapids, Mich.: Zondervan, to be published in 1994), chapter 52.

Grudem offers the following definition: 'A spiritual gift is any ability that is empowered by the Holy Spirit and used in any ministry of the church' (ibid., chapter 52). He qualifies this definition by saying, 'This is a broad definition and would include both gifts that are related to natural abilities (such as teaching, showing mercy, or administration) and gifts that seem to be more "miraculous" and less related to natural abilities (such as prophecy, healing, or distinguishing between spirits). The reason for this is that when Paul lists spiritual gifts (in Rom. 12:6–8; 1 Cor. 7:7; 12:8–10, 28; and Eph. 4:11) he includes both kinds of gifts. Yet not every natural ability that people have is included here, because Paul is clear that all spiritual gifts must be empowered "by one and the same Spirit" (1 Cor. 12:11), that they are given "for the common good" (1 Cor. 12:7), and that they are all to be used for "edification" (1 Cor. 14:26), or for building up the church' (ibid.).

9. See infra, p. 138ff.

10. Philip is not credited with doing signs and wonders, but only signs in Acts 8:6. Furthermore, Acts 8:6 gives the only *specific* examples of what constitutes signs in the book of Acts. There they are exorcisms, the healing of paralytics, lame and crippled people.

11. Grudem defines a miracle as follows: 'A miracle is a less common kind of God's activity in which he arouses people's awe and wonder and bears witness to himself.' He justifies this definition by pointing out the deficiencies in other commonly proposed definitions:

> For example, one definition of miracles is 'a direct intervention of God in the world.' But this definition assumes a deistic view of God's relationship to the world, in which the world continues on its own and God only intervenes in it occasionally. This is certainly not the biblical view, according to which God makes the rain to fall (Matt. 5:45), causes the grass to grow (Ps. 104:14), and continually carries along all things by his word and power (Heb. 1:3). Another definition of miracles is 'a more direct activity of God in the world.' But to talk about a 'more direct' working of God suggests that his ordinary providential activity is somehow not 'direct,' and again hints at a sort of deistic removal of God from the world.
>
> Another definition is 'God working in the world without using means to bring about the results he wishes.' Yet to speak of God working 'without means' leaves us with very few if any miracles in the Bible, for it is hard to think of a miracle that came about with no means at all: in the healing of people, for example, some of the physical properties of the sick person's body were doubtless involved as part of the healing. When Jesus multiplied the

loaves and fishes, he at least used the original five loaves and two fishes that were there. When he changed water to wine, he used water and made it become wine. This definition seems to be inadequate.

Yet another definition of miracle is 'an exception to a natural law' or 'God acting contrary to the laws of nature.' But the phrase 'laws of nature' in popular understanding implies that there are certain qualities inherent in the things that exist, 'laws of nature' which operate independently of God and that God must intervene or 'break' these laws in order for a miracle to occur. Once again this definition does not adequately account for the biblical teaching on providence.

Another definition of miracle is, 'an event impossible to explain by natural causes.' This definition is inadequate because (1) it does not include God as the one who brings about the miracle; (2) it assumes that God does not *use* some natural causes when he works in an unusual or amazing way, and thus it assumes again that God only occasionally intervenes in the world; and (3) it will result in a significant minimizing of actual miracles, and an increase in skepticism, since many times when God works in answer to prayer the result is amazing to those who prayed but it is not absolutely *impossible* to explain by natural causes, especially for a skeptic who simply refuses to see God's hand at work.

Therefore, the original definition given above, where a miracle is simply a *less common* way of God's working in the world, seems to be preferable and more consistent with the biblical doctrine of God's providence. This definition does not say that a miracle is a *different kind* of working by God, but only that it is a less common way of God's working, and that it is done so as to arouse people's surprise, awe, or amazement in such a way that God bears witness to himself (*Systematic Theology*, chapter 52).

12. Years after I came to see this distinction between the signs and wonders ministry of the apostles and the gifts of healing given to ordinary Christians I found this distinction made in a similar way by Professor Max Turner. He wrote,

'Either way, the "healers" have opened up ground which has been captured by their critics who urge that here, clearly, we do not have the same gift as was vouchsafed to the apostolic church. *There*, healing was instantaneous, without failure, irreversible, covering all manner of diseases, dependent on the charisma of the healer not the faith of the seeker, and so a sign to the unevangelized. But perhaps the contrast is overdrawn. We need not doubt the apostles were marked by occasionally dramatic events of healing (Acts and 2 Cor. 12:12); but, as we warned before, we need to remember that the descriptions in Acts are sometimes self-consciously of *extra*ordinary healings (*cf.* 19:11), not the "ordinary" ones. Even here, however, there is little evidence of frequent healing *independent* of seeking faith; quite the contrary. Nor do we know the apostles experienced no failures or relapses (2 Tim. 4:20; Mt. 12:45; Jn. 5:14). As for the "ordinary" gifts of healing (1 Cor. 12:10 etc.; *cf.* Jas. 5:15) they may well have been less immediate and spectacular. . . . We merely insist, on the one hand, that the idealized picture of apostolic healing drawn from some sections of Acts should not be taken necessarily as *representative* (certainly not of *charismata iamatĕŏmac;n* operating *outside* the apostolic circle, 1 Cor. 12:28f.) and, on the other hand, that serious modern testimony points to phenomena so congruent with even some apostolic experiences that only *a priori* dogmatic considerations can exclude the possibility that New Testament *charismata iamatĕŏomac;n* have significant parallels ("Spiritual Gifts Then and Now," *Vox Evangelica* 15 [1985]: 48–50.

13. I am not referring here to the Scripture-writing ministry of Paul, but to his teaching ministry. Of course, his letters reveal the depth of his teaching gift, but they only give us a very small percentage of the totality of his teaching.

14. I should qualify the phrase 'what I was seeing and hearing.' I have to admit that during the time I believed that the Bible taught that miraculous gifts had ceased, I never looked or searched sincerely for actual cases of healings. This is also true of most of the cessationists I know. Many frequently claim that they have never 'seen' a medically documented healing involving the gifts of the Spirit. The truth is, most of them have never searched for one with any diligence. They cannot bring themselves to waste the time because they *already know* that there are not any medically documented healings that would support the contemporary use of the miraculous gifts of the Spirit.

Once I tried to get a friend, who was also a theological professor, to investigate a miracle that had taken place through the ministry of another seminary professor. The seminary professor who had been used to do the miracle was a conservative evangelical, who is held in high esteem across the body of Christ, and who had begun to believe in the miraculous gifts.

A healing had occurred in the eyes and ears of a little boy. I called the boy's father (they lived in another state) in order to verify the miracle. The father said it was true and that he had medical documentation.

When I told the story to my friend, the cessationist professor, I urged him to call and investigate. He did not even want the phone number. When I questioned his reluctance to investigate, he told me that he did not doubt that the miracle had occurred, but he doubted that God had done it! So there was no need for him to investigate.

The facts of the case were:

1. A seminary professor, who held historic orthodox theology,
2. asked God in Jesus' name
3. to do a miracle on a little child
4. from a Christian family,
5. and the miracle was performed immediately.

Even with these facts, which my friend would not dispute, it was easier for him to believe that Satan had done the miracle rather than Jesus! The cessationist mindset often precludes any sincere investigation.

15. I have heard many reports of apostolic healing in various places around the world, but I have not verified them. Just to cite one, Carl Lawrence, who was a missionary in Southeast Asia for almost twenty years, reports that miracles are so common in the house churches in China that a whole book could be written on the miracles that have taken place there in recent years (*The Church in China* [Minneapolis: Bethany House Publishers, 1985], p. 73 n. 7). He even describes a number of raisings from the dead that can be documented (pp. 75ff.). I believe that there is a great deal of healing taking place today which no one has taken the trouble to document. The fact that someone may not have witnessed a miracle says nothing about the occurrence or even the frequency of miracles. It is merely a statement about that particular person's experience.

16. For example, in two widely read recent scholarly studies of New Testament prophecy, both David Hill (*New Testament Prophecy* [1979], p. 191) and David Aune (*Prophecy in Early Christianity and the Ancient Mediterranean World* [1983], p. 338) conclude that it was the leadership of the church that abandoned the gift of prophecy rather than God withdrawing the gift.

17. The problem is not only that there are very scanty historical sources for the first fourteen- or fifteen-hundred years of church history, but that even these sources have received insufficient attention in scholarly research. Turner comments, 'The first lament is that there is, to my knowledge, *no* critical history of any of the three gifts [healing, prophecy, and tongues] we chose to discuss; though this is not to say we lack for semi-popular or highly-partisan surveys' (*Vox Evangelical* 15 [1985]: 41). Indeed, few people really possess the necessary linguistic skills or the critical abilities to evaluate many of the original sources. I have read a number of anticharismatic reviews of church history wherein the authors confidently

assert that there is no reliable evidence in history for the existence of the gifts after the death of the apostles. Yet the majority of these very authors possess neither the ability to read the original historical sources in Greek and Latin, many of which are still untranslated, nor the critical skills to evaluate these sources.

18. *Showing the Spirit*, p. 166.

19. Warfield, *Counterfeit Miracles*, pp. 38ff.

20. Ibid., pp. 37–38.

21. Ibid., p. 38.

22. For example, Turner ('Spiritual Gifts Then and Now,' pp. 41–42) observes that Warfield's 'book swings violently from a confessionalist, and somewhat naive evidentialist, treatment of miracles in the apostolic age, to an extreme skepticism towards *any* claims of miracles in the church in the *post*-apostolic period, quite clearly dependent on Conyers Middleton. Had he shown the same openness— some would say credulity—towards post-apostolic claims that he evinced when discussing New Testament miracles, which of the miracles of the saints would not have received his defence, if not indeed his approbation?! And, had he turned the degree of skepticism manifest in his treatment of post-apostolic writers onto the New Testament accounts, what scant few miracles of the apostles (or of the Lord himself) would have escaped his sharp wit and criticism!'

23. For example, see Ronald Kydd, *Charismatic Gifts in the Early Church* (Peabody, Mass.: Hendrickson Publishers, 1984); Cecil M. Robeck, Jr., 'Origin's Treatment of the Charismata in 1 Corinthians 12:8–10' in *Charismatic Experiences in History*, ed. Cecil M. Robeck, Jr., (Peabody, Mass.: Hendrickson Publishers, 1985), pp. 111–25; Donald Bridge, *Signs and Wonders Today* (Leicester, England: Inter-Varsity Press, 1985), pp. 174ff.; Paul Thigpen, 'Did the Power of the Spirit Ever Leave the Church,' *Charisma* 18: 2 (1992): pp. 20–29; Morton T. Kelsey, *Healing and Christianity* (New York: Harper and Row, 1973), pp. 129–99; James Edwin Davison, 'Spiritual Gifts in the Roman Church: I Clement, Hermas and Justin Martyr' (Ph.D. diss., University of Iowa, 1981); and Cecil Robeck, Jr., 'The Role and Function of Prophetic Gifts for the church at Carthage, AD 202–258' (Ph.D. diss., Fuller Theological Seminary, 1985).

Chapter 6: Responding to Spiritual Abuses

1. In John MacArthur's recent book, *Charismatic Chaos*, he leads his readers to believe that these kinds of abuses, and even worse, are characteristic of the majority of groups that practice the gifts of the Spirit. MacArthur's exposure to the charismatic movement and to the other groups that practice the gifts of the Spirit seems to have come largely through watching the brand of charismatic/

Pentecostal religion promulgated on the religious television channels and through the bizarre examples his researchers were able to dig up as they combed through charismatic/Pentecostal literature *looking* for the bizarre. As far as I know, he does not fellowship regularly nor minister among the various groups and movements that practice the gifts of the Spirit. I do fellowship and minister among these groups. I have spent the last seven years traveling widely across the world, speaking in both small and very large gatherings from among these kinds of Christians. I have a much greater exposure at the grass roots level than either MacArthur or his researchers. I have also read more widely among this kind of literature than MacArthur or his researchers. My experience has brought me to the opposite conclusion than that of MacArthur and his researchers. While these abuses do occur, they do not occur with great regularity in the majority of the churches where the gifts of the Spirit are practiced. And they are corrected by responsible leaders when they do occur. It is, of course, always possible to drag out bizarre cases where some people or groups do hold legitimately bizarre doctrine. These represent a very small minority of the charismatic movement, however, and responsible leaders within the charismatic movement have always spoken out against them.

2. This is not to say that doctrine is unimportant when evaluating miraculous events. It does suggest, however, that God will allow considerably more deviation in doctrinal matters than many contemporary groups are willing to allow.

3. This is John MacArthur's approach in *Charismatic Chaos*. Throughout the book MacArthur cites one example after another of contemporary charismatic abuse. Rather than interact seriously with the Scriptures and the *theological* arguments of his charismatic brothers, he contents himself with enumerating the most bizarre examples of charismatic abuse in chapter after chapter of his book.

To cite one example of this practice, chapter 7 of *Charismatic Chaos* is titled 'How Do Spiritual Gifts Operate?' (see pp. 152–70). MacArthur never answers his own question! Instead, he cites one abuse after another, naming offenders such as Benny Hinn, Kenneth Hagin, Fred Price, Maria Woodworth-Etter, John and Carol Wimber, Norvil Hayes, and the first-century Corinthian Christians. This chapter would have been better titled 'How Spiritual Gifts Don't Operate.' MacArthur let himself get so carried away in this chapter that he actually wrote, 'Nowhere does the New Testament teach that the Spirit of God causes Christians to fall into a trance, faint, or lapse into frenzied behavior' (p. 158). Are we reading the same Bible? The Lord caused Peter to fall into a *trance* on Simon's roof (Acts 10:10), and Paul to fall into a *trance* while praying in the temple (Acts 22:17). As for 'fainting,' John fell like a dead man at the feet of the Lord Jesus in Revelation 1:17. And as for 'frenzied behavior,' the 120 were doing something besides speaking in foreign languages, which caused many to think that they were drunk (Acts 2:13–15)! *Charismatic Chaos* is filled with these kinds of unscriptural assertions and biblical errors. They do not lend credibility to MacArthur's objectivity as a reliable critic of the charismatic movement.

In regards to the multitude of abuses listed by MacArthur, he *assumes* that charismatic doctrine itself produces these abuses. Yet he misses the point. No one debates that there are abuses in charismatic churches. The real question is the relationship between these abuses and charismatic doctrine. For the most part, these abuses do not spring from wrong doctrines, but from wrong applications of right doctrines.

4. It is also interesting that he felt no freedom to confess his sin in his own anticharismatic church nor to any of his cessationist friends.

5. MacArthur writes as though sexual immorality is more common in the charismatic wing of the church (*Charismatic Chaos*, pp. 21, 167, and 253).

6. J. I. Packer, 'The Comfort of Conservatism' in *Power Religion*, ed. Michael Horton (Chicago: Moody Press, 1992), p. 286. In this same article Packer draws attention to the criticism that E. J. Carnell received 'when he described American fundamentalism as evangelicalism gone cultic' (p. 293).

7. Authoritarian fundamentalism can plague both charismatic and noncharismatic churches. The issue here does not deal with the gifts at all. It concerns a forced conformity to an individual group or movement's distinctive interpretations and practices which, in turn, are given the same authority as the Scriptures themselves in actual practice.

Chapter 7: Scared to Death by the Holy Ghost

1. As quoted by Vinson Synan, *The Holiness-Pentecostal Movement in the United States* (Grand Rapids, Mich.: Eerdmans, 1971), pp. 95–96.

2. Ibid., p. 106.

3. *Journals from October 14, 1735 to November 29, 1745*, vol. 1 of *The Works of John Wesley*, 3d ed. (Grand Rapids, Mich.: Baker, 1991), p. 204.

4. Ibid., p. 210.

5. Jonathan Edwards, 'An Account of the Revival of Religion on North Hampton in 1740–42, as Communicated in a Letter to a Minister of Boston' in *Jonathan Edwards on Revival* (Carlisle, Pa.: The Banner of Truth Trust, 1984), p. 150.

6. Ibid, p. 151.

7. Ibid., pp. 153–54.

8. Gross, *Miracles, Demons, and Spiritual Warfare*, p. 91.

9. *Theophany* is the term used to describe God's appearance to an individual or

a group. Theologians generally regard the Old Testament theophanies as an appearance of the preincarnate Christ rather than an appearance of God the Father, since no one has ever seen God the Father (John 1:18).

10. The visionary experience in Daniel 10:1ff. is interesting. Only Daniel could see the vision, but the men with Daniel experienced such dread from the presence of God that they ran away (Dan. 10:7).

11. It is doubtful that the word 'tremble' is used as a figure of speech here. Who would want to argue that a genuine experience of the presence of the Lord would not normally produce trembling?

12. Gross, *Miracles, Demons, and Spiritual Warfare*, p. 91.

13. Jonathan Edwards, 'The Distinguishing Marks of a Work of the Spirit of God' in *Jonathan Edwards on Revival* (Carlisle, Pa.: The Banner of Truth Trust, 1984), p. 127.

14. Ibid., p. 91.

15. Ibid., p. 118.

Chapter 8: Were Miracles Meant to Be Temporary?

1. Calvin lamented that his Catholic opponents did 'not cease to assail our doctrine and to reproach and defame it with names that render it hated or suspect. They call it "new" and "of recent birth." They reproach it as "doubtful and uncertain." They ask what miracles have confirmed it' (*Institutes of the Christian Religion*, Prefatory Address, 3).

For a helpful discussion of this period, see John Ruthven, *On the Cessation of the Charismata: The Protestant Polemic of Benjamin B. Warfield* (Ph.D. diss., Marquette University, 1989). See especially chapter two, 'Historical Antecedents to B. B. Warfield's Cessationist Polemic,' pp. 21–62. Sheffield Press will publish this work in the fall of 1993.

2. The two texts most commonly used to serve this function are Ephesians 2:20 and Hebrews 2:3–4. Ephesians 2:20 is considered in more detail on page 248. The cessationist interpretation of Hebrews 2:3–4 is evaluated in note 6 of this chapter.

3. Calvin was not as narrow regarding the purpose of miracles as his posterity would become. In the *Institutes* he saw miracles: proving the deity of Jesus because unlike the apostles Christ did miracles by his own power (1.13.13); confirming the gospel preached by the apostles (PA 3); and he used the miracles of Moses to argue that miracles confirmed Scripture and vindicated the authority of God's servants (1.8.5).

The Reformers' emphasis on the authenticating function of miracles crystallized into its final form in Benjamin Warfield's *Counterfeit Miracles*. Warfield saw the *distinctive* or *primary* purpose of miracles as the authentication of the apostles as trustworthy teachers of doctrine (pp. 6, 21, 23). Ultimately then the purpose of miracles is to authenticate the inscripturated revelation of God (pp. 25–26). In my opinion, this was and is the best possible way to attempt to prove from the Scriptures that miracles and the miraculous gifts of the Spirit were confined to the New Testament period.

4. The majority of New Testament scholars do not think this verse or the last twelve verses of Mark's Gospel were written by Mark himself. They think that the original ending to Mark's Gospel was lost and that these verses were added later by someone other than Mark. Nevertheless, these last twelve verses were written very early in the history of the church, for they are found in several manuscripts of Tatian's *Diatessaron* (A.D. 170). They were also quoted by Irenaeus (who died in A.D. 202) and Tertullian (who died in A.D. 220). At the very least, therefore, these verses reflect what the early church thought about the purposes of miracles, even if these verses are not considered part of the original Scriptures.

5. There is one use of the verb 'to bear witness,' *martureo*, in which it is said of the Gentiles at Cornelius' house that God 'showed [that is, bore witness] that he accepted them by giving the Holy Spirit to them, just as he did to us' (Acts 15:8). Here the point, however, is not that he allowed Cornelius and the Gentiles to work miracles to authenticate them as special servants, but rather that his giving the Holy Spirit to them demonstrated that they were believers on a par with the Jewish Christians.

6. The word translated as 'confirmed,' *bebaioo*, is also used of Christ's confirming the promises of God to the patriarchs (Rom. 15:8) and of God strengthening his servants (1 Cor. 1:8; 2 Cor. 1:21; Col. 2:7; Heb. 13:9). But it is never used of miracles confirming a servant.

Hebrews 2:3–4 is frequently used by cessationists to prove that miracles ceased with the apostles. The author of Hebrews asks us:

> How shall we escape if we ignore such a great salvation? This salvation, which was first announced by the Lord, was confirmed to us by those who heard him. God also testified to it by signs, wonders and various miracles, and gifts of the Holy Spirit distributed according to his will.

The author of Hebrews is not limiting this text to the apostles. He does not say that the message was confirmed by the apostles, but that the message was confirmed 'by those who heard' the Lord.

The apostles were not the only ones who heard the Lord. Others heard him also, and others did miracles and received miraculous gifts of the Spirit. In other words, the writer of the book of Hebrews seems to be saying that neither he, nor his audience, heard the Lord directly nor saw his miracles directly.

They first heard the message about the Lord Jesus through 'those who had heard him' directly. When they heard this message, God confirmed it by working signs and wonders through the group that preached to them. It could have been the apostles who preached to them, but it also could have been others who had originally heard the Lord.

The text certainly leaves open the possibility that God will confirm with miracles the message about the Lord Jesus when it is preached by others who did not hear Jesus directly.

7. 'Signs, wonders, and miracles' are in the dative case and are probably meant to be taken as datives of accompaniment.

8. He would have used the nominative case rather than the dative case. See Ralph P. Martin, 2 *Corinthians* (Waco, Tex.: Word Books, 1986), p. 436.

9. The word in 2 Corinthians 12:12 translated 'perseverance,' *hupomone*, implies suffering as well. He also appeals to revelations from the Lord in defense of his apostleship (2 Cor. 12:1–10.)

10. Philip Edgcumbe Hughes, *Paul's Second Epistle to the Corinthians*, The New International Commentary on the New Testament (Grand Rapids: Eerdmans, 1962), p. 457. He cites 2 Corinthians 1:12; 2:17; 3:4ff.; 4:2; 5:11; 6:3ff.; 7:2; 10:13ff.; and 11:6, 23ff.

11. Alfred Plummer, *Second Epistle of St. Paul to the Corinthians* (Edinburgh: T & T Clark, 1915), p. 359. He cites 2 Corinthians 3:2 and 1 Corinthians 2:4; 9:2).

12. Martin, *2 Corinthians*, p. 434.

13. Ibid., p. 434–36.

14. Ibid., p. 438.

15. This is what The Westminster Confession of Faith teaches:

> The authority of the holy Scripture, for which it ought to be believed and obeyed, dependeth not upon the testimony of any man or church, but wholly upon God (who is truth itself), the Author thereof; and therefore it is to be received, because it is the Word of God (1.4).

In support of this statement the Westminster divines appealed to 2 Peter 1:19, 21;2 Timothy 3:16; 1 John 5:9; and 1 Thessalonians 2:13. Calvin made the same point in the *Institutes* (1.7.5).

16. Again, consider the teaching of The Westminster Confession of Faith:

We may be moved and induced by the testimony of the church to an high and reverent esteem of the holy Scripture; and the heavenliness of the matter, the efficacy of the doctrine, the majesty of the style, the consent of all the parts, the scope of the whole (which is to give all glory to God), the full discovery it makes of the only way of man's salvation, the many other incomparable excellencies and the entire perfection thereof, are arguments whereby it doth abundantly evidence itself to be the Word of God; yet, notwithstanding our full persuasion and assurance of the infallible truth, and divine authority thereof, is from the inward work of the Holy Spirit, bearing witness by and with the Word in our hearts (1.5).

On this point the Westminster divines appealed to 1 John 2:20, 27; John 16:13–14; 1 Corinthians 2:10–12; and Isaiah 59:21. Calvin made this same point in the *Institutes* (1.7.5).

17. Thomas Edgar, *Miraculous Gifts* (Neptune, N.J.: The Loizeaux Brothers, 1983), pp. 263–64.

18. *Counterfeit Miracles*, p. 21.

19. Warfield dismisses this explanation as unscriptural (ibid., p. 21), and calls it 'helpless' since

the reason which it gives for the continuance of miracles during the first three centuries, if valid at all, is equally valid for their continuance to the twentieth century. What we shall look upon as the period of the planting of the church is determined by our point of view. If the usefulness of miracles in planting the church were sufficient reason for their occurrence in the Roman Empire in the third century, it is hard to deny that it may be sufficient for the repetition of them in, say, the Chinese Empire in the twentieth century. And why go to China? Is not the church essentially in the position of a missionary church everywhere in this world of unbelief? When we take a really "long view" of things, is it not at least a debatable question whether the paltry 2000 years which have passed since Christianity came into the world are not a negligible quantity, and the age in which we live is not still the age of the primitive church? (Benjamin B. Warfield, Counterfeit Miracles [Edinburgh: The Banner of Truth Trust, 1918; reprint edition 1972], p. 35).

The Anglicans to whom Warfield replied held the same theory as Edgar, only they saw the miracles ceasing at the end of the third century rather than at the end of the first as Edgar does. Warfield's objections are still valid regardless of where one puts the cessation of miracles.

20. Ibid.

21. This subject is referred to today in academic disciplines as 'narrative theology.' The advances in recent scholarly discussions of narrative theology ought to eliminate forever this argument that we cannot use the Gospels and the book of Acts as sources of doctrine.

Chapter 9: Why Does God Heal?

1. The Hebrew writers simply took this word and put it in the abstract plural *rah^{d}mim*, when they wanted to express God's compassion.

2. The most common verb used in the Greek New Testament to refer to God's compassion is *splanchnizomai*. This verb is used twelve times. Once it is used of the Samaritan's compassion for the wounded man (Luke 10:33). The other eleven uses refer to God's compassion. In two separate parables Jesus uses this verb to refer to God's compassion in saving and forgiving sinners (Matt. 18:27 and Luke 15:20). The remainder of the uses of this verb all refer to compassion as the major motivation for Jesus' healing and miracles. So in nine out of eleven occurrences where this verb is used of God's compassion it refers to the compassion of the Lord Jesus Christ as his motivation for healing!

What is the meaning of *splanchnizomai* when it refers to God's compassion? The nominal form of this word originally referred to the inner parts of a man, the heart, liver, and so on. It could be used of the inward parts of a sacrificial animal, but it became common to use this word in reference to the lower parts of the abdomen, the intestines, and especially the womb (*Theological Dictionary of the New Testament*, eds. Gerhard Kittel and Gerhard Friedrich [Grand Rapids, Mich.: Eerdmans, 1971] 7:548).

Some theologians have felt that this term was too rough or graphic to be used in reference to God's compassion. Using the word for 'intestines' to refer to God's compassion is akin to our using the word 'guts' for courage in modern English, as when we say, 'He really has guts.' However, I think the New Testament writers meant to do exactly this. They were impressing on the readers the power and the force of God's compassion. They may also have had in mind a physical feeling associated with compassion. Sometimes a sharp pain in the abdomen will accompany intense feelings of compassion or pity for those we love. The choice of such a graphic word served to impress the New Testament Christians that God's compassion for them was rooted in his deep love for them and his sensitivity to their pain.

3. There was a similar connection in the Old Testament between the miraculous and the manifestation of God's glory (cf. Numbers 14:22).

4. Mary Garnett, *Take Your Glory, Lord: William Duma His Life Story* (POB 50, Roodepoort 1725, South Africa: Baptist Publishing House, 1979), p. 40ff.

5. Technically, their faith led Jesus first to forgive the man's sins and then, as proof that his sins were forgiven, he healed the man.

6. When we ask for healing or anything else, we must always ask in the spirit of 'if you are willing.' I know that sometimes people use this phrase to mask their unbelief, but it really is the only attitude that is appropriate when we approach 'the King eternal, immortal, invisible, the only wise God,' with a request.

Chapter 10: Why God Gives Miraculous Gifts

1. MacArthur writes, 'Charismatics believe that the spectacular miraculous gifts were given for the edification of believers. Does God's Word support such a conclusion? No. In fact, the truth is quite the contrary.' I do not understand how MacArthur can conclude that there is no scriptural support for the edifying purpose of the miraculous spiritual gifts. He never discusses the relevant scriptural texts (e.g., 1 Cor. 12:7; 14:3–5, 26) that overturn his theory.

2. This list is not meant to be exhaustive. We are probably to understand that all New Testament churches had the gifts in operation.

3. The word *zeloo* is capable of several different translations. It can mean 'to strive after something,' 'to desire,' to 'exert oneself earnestly,' to be 'deeply attracted to something,' or to 'manifest zeal' (W. Bauer, *A Greek-English Lexicon of the New Testament and Other Christian Literature*, eds. W. F. Arndt and F. W. Gingrich, rev. F. W. Gingrich and F. W. Danker [Chicago: The University of Chicago Press, 1979], p. 338). The NIV translates *zeloo* with 'eagerly desire,' the NASB 'earnestly desire,' and the KJV with 'covet earnestly.'

MacArthur alleges, 'Nothing in Scripture indicates that the miracles of the apostolic age were meant to be continuous in subsequent ages *nor does the Bible exhort believers to seek any miraculous manifestations of the Holy Spirit*' (*Charismatic Chaos*, p. 117, emphasis mine). This is an incredible assertion. Paul does exhort believers to seek miraculous manifestations of the Holy Spirit in 1 Corinthians 12:31; 14:1, 39. MacArthur does not even bother to seriously interact with these texts. They only way MacArthur could make such an assertion is to claim that in 1 Corinthians 12:31 Paul must not have had in mind the gifts listed in 1 Corinthians 12:8–10. But surely this would be an arbitrary claim. Second, he must deny that when Paul exhorts believers to seek prophecy he is referring to supernatural prophecy. MacArthur must define Paul's use of prophecy primarily as preaching (which, in fact, he does, ibid., p. 69). This, of course, is in direct conflict with the supernatural, revelatory character of prophecy described by Paul in 1 Corinthians

14:24–25 and especially 14:26. No modern exegetical or scholarly study would support MacArthur in such a arbitrary assertion.

(MacArthur does admit that supernatural prophecies were sometimes given before the New Testament was complete to instruct the churches in matters not covered by Scripture, but he limits this type of prophecy to the apostolic era [ibid., p. 69]).

4. Some have suggested that 1 Corinthians 14:18 could be translated, 'I thank my God that I speak in tongues more than all of you put together.' See Archibald Robertson and Alfred Plummer, *First Epistle of St. Paul to the Corinthians* (Edinburgh: T & T Clark, 1911), p. 314.

5. Fee comments that this edifying function of tongues 'has sometimes been called "self-edification" and therefore viewed as pejorative. But Paul intended no such thing. The edifying of oneself is not self-centeredness, but the personal edifying of the believer that comes through prayer and praise' (*1 Corinthians*, p. 657).

6. The analogy of the body is foreshadowed by Isaiah, who refers to the prophets of Israel as 'your eyes' (Isa. 29:10).

7. For a detailed discussion of this passage, see Wayne Grudem, *The Gift of Prophecy in the New Testament & Today* (Westchester, Ill.: Crossway Books, 1988), pp. 227–40. Grudem concludes that the only plausible explanation of 'the perfect' in 1 Corinthians 13:10 is that it must refer to the time of Christ's return.

Richard Gaffin, who is both a skillful exegete and a cessationist concludes that

> the coming of 'the perfect' (v. 10) and the 'then' of the believer's full know-
> ledge (v. 12) no doubt refer to the time of Christ's return. The view that they
> describe the point at which the New Testament canon is completed cannot be
> made credible exegetically (*Perspectives on Pentecost* [Phillipsburg, N.J.: Presby-
> terian and Reformed Publishing Company, 1979], p. 109).

8. When the Old Testament speaks of 'seeing' God 'face to face,' the reference is to seeing the angel of the Lord, who is the preincarnate Christ. God the Father did not permit anyone in the Old Testament to see his face (Ex. 33:20; see also John 1:18).

9. The translation of the New International Version, 'fully known' accurately reflects the meaning of the verb *epiginosko*.

Chapter 11: Why God Doesn't Heal

1. This story appeared in the *Baptist Standard*, February 7, 1993, page 24. One of the ironic things about this healing is that Duane Miller was a former

Assemblies of God pastor but had left that denomination because he disagreed with their theology of speaking in tongues and divine healing.

2. Later in the text Luke says that Jesus forgave the paralytic's sins when he saw their faith (5:20). Before there was any mention of faith, however, Luke tells us that the power of the Lord was already present for healing.

3. When I speak of driving away the presence of God, I am not speaking of his ontological presence. God is, of course, omnipresent. I am using the term 'presence' here to refer to his beneficial presence, his conscious or felt presence in which blessing is brought to his children.

4. I am not using the term 'apostasy' in the technical sense that it has in some theological systems. I am using it in the general sense of 'falling away' or 'backsliding.' I do not wish at this point to enter the debate over how much or what kind of sin it is possible for true Christians to commit. Most of the texts I use in this section refer to genuine believers, although some of the scriptural examples could refer to those who are unbelievers masquerading as believers in the church.

5. Psalm 74 is attributed to Asaph, one of David's choir directors. However, this probably means that it was written by one of Asaph's descendants (cf. *The NIV Study Bible*, p. 860).

6. It is not clear in this psalm whether the judgment is on the nation as a whole or only on the individual psalmist. There are elements which could indicate that the distress is merely personal and other elements which seem to argue that the distress is national in scope.

7. This is why we should not hastily condemn miracles in a group with wrong doctrine as though their miracles were worked by satanic power. The Galatian church had divine miracles (Gal. 3:5) even though they were in the process of abandoning the gospel (1:6; 3:1). God was still giving them time to repent. I believe, however, that if they had refused to repent, God would have eventually removed his divine presence and power so that no more godly miracles would have occurred in the Galatian churches.

8. Isaiah 29:10.

9. See appendix A, p. 219.

10. James Boice actually alleges that this is what Jesus meant in Matthew 12:39–42 ('A Better Way: The Power of the Word and Spirit' in *Power Religion*, ed., Michael Horton [Chicago: Moody Press, 1992], pp. 125–26). See appendix A, pp. 219–21, for a refutation of this interpretation.

Chapter 12: Pursuing the Gifts With Diligence

1. Gross, *Miracles, Demons, and Spiritual Warfare*, p. 69.

2. Henry Scougal, *The Life of God and the Soul of Man* (Harrisonburg, Va.: Sprinkle Publications, 1986 reprint), p. xvii.

Chapter 13: A Passion for God

1. C. S. Lewis, *Reflections on the Psalms* (New York: Harcourt, Brace & World, 1958), p. 51.

2. Exodus 15:20; 2 Samuel 6:16; and Judges 11:34. Cf. 1 Samuel 18:6–7; Psalms 30:11; 150:4; and Jeremiah 31:4, 13.

3. *Reflections on the Psalms*, p. 52.

4. Jonathan Edwards, *The Religious Affections* (Carlisle, Penn.: The Banner of Truth Trust, reprint 1984), p. 29.

5. Ibid., p. 49.

6. Ibid., pp. 49–50.

7. Ibid., pp. 31ff.

8. *Reflections on the Psalms*, p. 57.

9. *The Oxford English Dictionary*, 'passion,' III.6.

Chapter 14: Developing Passion & Power

1. For the technical details and background to John 12:1–8 see Rudolf Schnackenberg, *The Gospel According to St. John*, trans. Cecily Hastings, et al. (New York: The Seabury Press, 1980), II: pp. 365–70.

2. In Romans 5:5 Paul says that the Holy Spirit gives to each of our hearts a personal revelation of God's lavish love for us. If it takes the work of the Holy Spirit to make us *feel* the love of God, how much more is the ministry of the Holy Spirit required in order to *produce* love for God in our hearts?

3. This story is told in detail by Mahesh Chavda in *Only Love Can Make a Miracle* (Ann Arbor, Mich.: Servant Publications, 1990).

Appendix A: Other Reasons Why God Heals & Works Miracles

1. Cf. Norman Geisler, *Signs and Wonders* (Wheaton, Ill.: Tyndale House Publishers, 1988), p. 144; and John Woodhouse, 'Signs and Wonders and Evangelical Ministry' in *Signs and Wonders and Evangelicals* (Homebush West, NSW, Australia: Lancer Books, 1987), p. 26.

2. A sign from heaven would not necessarily be incontrovertible, since even the Devil was apparently able to make fire fall from heaven (cf. Job 1:16).

3. The other New Testament passages that bear on this subject are 1 Corinthians 1:22, where Paul states that the Jews seek for signs, and three passages in John (2:18; 4:48; and 6:30). For a fuller discussion of these texts see Gerd Theissen, *The*

Miracle Stories of the Early Christian Tradition, trans. Francis McDonagh (Philadel-
phia: Fortress Press, 1983), pp. 295–97. On the two requests for signs in the Synoptic Gospels, Theissen comments, 'Rejection of the demand for signs is not a
rejection of signs (Mark 8:11ff., par.). On the contrary, refusal of a sign is a punishment for unbelief, which would be nonsense if it were accepted that signs were
valueless' (ibid., p. 296). On Jesus' statement in John 4:48, 'Unless you people see
miraculous signs and wonders, you will never believe,' Theissen comments,
'Believing without seeing—it is the problem of every later generation. This is not
criticism of belief in miracles, but criticism of a skepticism which refuses to believe
what it cannot see' (ibid., p. 297). The request of Jesus for a sign in John 6:30 is
not met with the harsh rebuke of the Synoptic Gospels. Apparently this request
was not uttered in the same spirit as that of the Pharisees in Matthew 12:38 and
16:1.

It is also common for writers to cite a text where miracles do not lead to faith
(e.g., Matt. 11:20–24) as evidence of the very limited value of miracles in the New
Testament times or in the present time. Theissen replies to this argument, 'The fact
that the miracles in Chorazim and Bethsaida do not lead to repentance is not evidence against this [i.e., the high value that the New Testament places on miracles]:
does the word automatically lead to repentance? (ibid., p. 297).

In addition to the hardness of heart of the religious leaders, the New Testament
also mentions others who would not believe no matter how great a miracle is presented to them (cf. Luke 16:19–31). Because of these kinds of texts, some people
who are hostile to God's present-day healing ministry have concluded that
miracles have no authenticating value at all! The fact that the Pharisees did not
believe in the face of miraculous evidence does not mean that miracles have no
authenticating value. It simply means that there are some people whose hearts are
so hardened that no matter what kind of evidence they encounter, they will not
believe.

It is not uncommon for theologians to demean the authenticating function of
the miraculous on other grounds. In 1741 Jonathan Edwards wrote the following
eloquent paragraph:

> Therefore I do not expect a restoration of these miraculous gifts in the
> approaching glorious times of the church, nor do I desire it. It appears to me
> that it would add nothing to the glory of those times, but rather diminish
> from it. For my part, I had rather enjoy the sweet influences of the Spirit,
> showing Christ's spiritual divine beauty, infinite grace, undying love, draw-
> ing forth the holy exercises of faith, divine love, sweet complaisance, and
> humble joy in God, one quarter of any hour, than to have prophetical visions

and revelations the whole year. It appears to me much more probable that God should give immediate revelations to his saints in the dark times of prophecy, than now in the approach of the most glorious and perfect state of his church on earth. It does not appear to me that there is any need of those extraordinary gifts to introduce this happy state, and set up the kingdom of God through the world, I have seen so much of the power of God in a more excellent way as to convince me that God can easily do without ('The Distinguishing Marks of a Work of the Spirit of God,' in *Jonathan Edwards On Revival* [Edinburgh: Banner of Truth Trust, Reprint 1984], pp. 140–41).

This is not a view that Jesus or the New Testament can share. Jesus said, 'But the witness which I have is greater than that of John; for the works which the Father has given Me to accomplish, the very works that I do, bear witness of Me, that the Father has sent Me' (John 5:36 NASB). John the Baptist did no miracles (John 10:41). In contrast, Jesus' testimony was confirmed by his miraculous works. This makes the testimony of Jesus greater than that of John. In other words, Jesus taught that a message confirmed by miraculous works has a greater confirmation than one that is not confirmed by the miraculous.

5. Cf. Isaiah 42:1–9 and 49:1–13.

6. Gaffin argues that miracles 'disclose the essence of the kingdom, but that they are nevertheless not of its essence' (*Perspectives on Pentecost*, p. 45). He uses the raising of Lazarus as an example of the relationship of miracles to the kingdom. He states,

> This event doesn't simply point away to regeneration or inner-renewal and cleansing from sin, rather it shows that Jesus' claim in the Gospel ('I am the resurrection and the life,' v. 25) has to do with the *whole* man, that salvation in Christ concerns the restoration of sinners in their psychosomatic wholeness, body as well as soul. Lazarus' resurrection points to the glorified, spiritual resurrection to be received by believers at Christ's return. But—and this is the point—through the miracle Lazarus does not receive that glorified body; eventually he dies, is buried, and with other dead believers awaits the resurrection. . . . In this sense, then, the variously distributed workings of the Spirit, of which the healing of Jesus and the apostles are an instance, are provisional and, in some instances, function as signs. (Ibid.)

For the sake of argument, I would be happy to grant that all earthly healings and all earthly blessings are provisional. I would also be happy to grant that all miracles have a sign function among other purposes. When viewed in the light of eternity, this present form of the kingdom is provisional. Evangelism, for example, will not be necessary in the eternal state. But that does not mean evangelism is not an essential part of the kingdom in its present form. If the rule of Jesus is essential to the kingdom of God—and it is—how can one deny that the power to rule over the enemies of God, chief among whom is the Devil, is also essential to the kingdom of God. This view is echoed by Grundmann in *TDNT* 2:302, 'The miracles of Jesus are part of the invading dominion of God which Jesus brings with His own person in proclamation and act. They are the dominion of God overcoming and expelling the sway of demons and Satan.'

7. Max Turner has argued this same point: 'It is more worrying that Warfield and those who relied on him, failed to perceive that, for the New Testament writers, the healings were not externally attesting signs, but part of the scope of the salvation announced (*cf.* section 4.2 above), which reached beyond the merely spiritual to the psychological and physical. The dawning of salvation, viewed holistically, was the beginning of the reversal of Satan's oppression (Lk. 4:18–21; 7:20f.; Acts 10:38 etc.). As such, the healings were still regarded as having legitimating function with respect to Jesus and to the apostles (around whom they clustered with especial intensity), but essentially the healings belonged as part of the firstfruits of the kingdom of God, and so as part of the message of salvation which the church announced. So, if there are sick in the church, James can expect (at least as a rule of thumb) that the elders prayer of faith will bring healing (Jas. 5:15). The relationship which healing sustains to the kerygma of the dawning kingdom of God suggests that the New Testament writers did not envisage the two ever being separated' ('Spiritual Gifts Then and Now,' *Vox Evangelica* 15 [1985: 38]).

Appendix B: Did Miraculous Gifts Cease With the Apostles?

1. Benjamin B. Warfield, *Counterfeit Miracles* (Edinburgh: The Banner of Truth Trust, 1918, reprint 1972), pp. 235–36.

2. Ibid., p. 6.

3. Peter Masters, *The Healing Epidemic* (London: The Wakeman Trust, 1988), pp. 69–70.

4. In Philip's case the word *wonders* is not used, but it is apparent from the context that his ministry is no less miraculous than Stephen's or the apostles.

5. The book of Acts does not mention any miraculous powers given to the other five men on whom the apostles laid hands. According to Acts 6:1–6, the purpose of the laying on of hands was not to impart miraculous powers but to set aside these seven men to take charge of the food ministry and make sure that all were treated fairly.

6. The term 'narrative literature' refers to those portions of Scripture which tell

stories, such as the book of Kings in the Old Testament or the Gospels and Acts in the New Testament. Narrative literature is interpreted differently than poetry (the Song of Solomon), or hymnic literature (the Psalms), or wisdom literature (Proverbs and Ecclesiastes), or didactic literature (the New Testament epistles), or prophetic literature (Revelation), and so on.

7. Masters, *The Healing Epidemic*, p. 69. I do not understand why Masters persists in calling Barnabas an apostle's 'deputy' when the Scripture plainly calls him an apostle (Acts 14:14).

8. Luke uses the same Greek expression to describe Paul's being filled with the Holy Spirit and the apostles' being filled in Acts 2:4. Warfield protests that, 'Acts 9:12–17 is no exception, as is sometimes said; Ananias worked a miracle on Paul but did not confer miracle-working powers. Paul's own power of miracle-working was original with him as an Apostle, and not conferred by anyone.' Yet Ananias *is* an exception to Warfield's theory that only the apostles and those whom the apostles laid hands on received the miraculous charismata. Ananias is exercising both the gift of healing and prophecy without any apostle having laid hands on him. Furthermore, when did Paul get miracle-working power if it was not at the same time that he was filled with the Spirit?

9. Masters attempts to discount the example of Ananias healing Saul in Acts chapter 9, but his reasons for doing so are not convincing at all.

10. According to Peter Masters, Paul is not referring to miracles that God was doing through members of the Galatian churches, but rather Paul is referring to miracles that he did in his recent visit to the Galatian churches (*The Healing Epidemic*, p. 134). If this view were true, Paul would not have used the present tense of the participle to describe this experience in Galatia. If Paul were referring to miracles that he did while he was in Galatia, he would have said, 'Does the one who gave you his Spirit and *worked* miracles among you do so because you observe the law, or because you believe what you heard?' But Paul does not use a past tense. In fact, he uses the present tense of a participle, which indicates that this activity is going on at the time of his writing; that is, God is presently working miracles among the Galatian churches in Paul's absence.

Some might allege that here it says that God works miracles, not that men gifted by God work miracles. In the New Testament, however, God is always the ultimate subject where miracles are concerned. For example, just prior to listing the charismata, Paul writes that God 'works [*energon*] all of them in all men' (1 Cor. 12:6). At the time Paul wrote Galatians, it would have been much more normal according to New Testament practice to imagine that Galatians 3:5 refers to the gift of miracles in operation. Burton argues that Paul's language 'implies that the apostle has in mind chiefly the charismatic manifestation of the Spirit' (Ernest De Witt Burton, *The Epistle to the Galatians* [Edinburgh: T & T Clark, 1921], p. 151). Lightfoot draws attention to the similarity of the participle *energon* in Galatians 3:5 with the *energemata* used to describe the gift of working miracles in 1 Corinthians 12:10 and concludes that 'as in the epistle to the Corinthians, St. Paul assumes the possession of these extraordinary powers by his converts as an acknowledged fact' (J. B. Lightfoot, *The Epistle of St. Paul to the Galatians* [Grand Rapids: Zondervan, reprint 1957], p. 136). Thus the epistles demonstrate that there was a wide distribution of the miraculous gifts of the Spirit across the New Testament church. They were not confined to the apostles and their very close associates.

11. Warfield, *Counterfeit Miracles*, pp. 21–22.

12. See p. 234.

13. Timothy also received an additional spiritual gift through the laying on of Paul's hands (2 Tim. 1:6). Some would allege that these two passages refer to the same gifting. I know of no firm evidence, however, that would indicate that this is so. Furthermore, there is no evidence at all that Paul laid hands on all those who had spiritual gifts at Corinth (1 Cor. 12–14), at Rome (Rom. 12:6), Thessalonica (1 Thess. 5:20), Ephesus (Eph. 4:11), and Galatia (Gal. 3:5). Therefore, Warfield's argument is not only an argument from silence but also is contradicted by the specific facts of the New Testament.

14. Gross, *Miracles, Demons and Spiritual Warfare*, p. 49.

15. Gross, *Miracles, Demons and Spiritual Warfare*, p. 46.

16. Notice that Luke makes no explicit mention of spiritual gifts in connection with John and Peter's ministry to the Samaritans (Acts 8: 14–25). The emphasis is clearly not on receiving gifts but on receiving the Holy Spirit. The Holy Spirit is mentioned five times in six verses (vv. 14–19), but the gifts are not explicitly mentioned once in Acts 8:14–25.

17. Max Turner, 'Spiritual Gifts Then and Now,' pp. 37–38.

18. Gross, *Miracles, Demons and Spiritual Warfare*, p. 48.

19. Some have also attempted to use 2 Corinthians 12:7–10 as another example of the failure of Paul's healing gift. However, all we know for sure about the problem in 2 Corinthians 12:7–10 is that a demonic tormentor was behind it (v. 7). We do not know whether the tormentor was causing an illness or some other kind of opposition to Paul's ministry, for example, persecution from the Judaizers. Consequently, this passage is irrelevant to the discussion of whether or not Paul's healing gift remained with him until the end of his life.

20. Geisler, *Signs and Wonders*, pp. 136–37.

21. Ibid., p. 137.

22. Ibid., p. 136.

23. Ephesians, Philippians, Colossians, and Philemon are called the 'prison epistles.' Their dates are not exact. Some have thought they were written from Ephesus between A.D. 53–55, others from Cessarea between A.D. 57–59, but the general consensus seems to be that they were written from Rome between A.D. 60–61. 1 Timothy and Titus are believed to have been written between A.D. 63–65 after Paul had been released from his first Roman imprisonment. 2 Timothy is believed to have been written at the end of Paul's life, during his last Roman imprisonment between A.D. 66–67.

24. In fact, in Ephesians Paul does mention the gift of prophecy by referring to the fact that prophets are given to the church (Eph. 4: 11), a text that Geisler conveniently overlooks. When he was formulating his argument, he was careful not to mention that we have no record of prophecy during this time period of A.D. 60–68.

25. Notice that Luke began the book of Acts by referring to his Gospel as 'all that Jesus *began* to do and to teach' (Acts 1:1, emphasis mine). The Gospel of Luke is the beginning of Jesus' acts and teachings, and the book of Acts is a continuation of the deeds and teachings of Jesus.

26. MacArthur has a similar way of handling the Scriptures. He writes of Paul that,

> Though he at one time seems to have had the ability to heal others at will (Acts 28:8), as Paul neared the end of his life he showed no evidence of such a gift. He advised Timothy to take a little wine for his stomach's sake, a common way of treating illness in that day (1 Tim. 5:23). Later on, at the very end of his career, Paul left a beloved brother sick at Miletus (2 Tim. 4:20). He surely would have healed him if he could.
>
> In the early pages of Acts, Jerusalem was filled with miracles. After the martyrdom of Stephen, however, no more miracles were recorded in that city. Something was changing. (*Charismatic Chaos*, pp. 125–26)

Does MacArthur seriously want us to believe that Scripture teaches that the miraculous gifts of the Holy Spirit were being withdrawn after the seventh chapter of Acts? Paul is not even converted yet, and we are supposed to believe that the gifts of the Spirit are being withdrawn from the apostles who stayed in Jerusalem! This is an unbelievable insensitivity to the literature of the New Testament. It is also an abuse of the New Testament to support one's own prejudicial interpretation.

Beginning with the martyrdom of Stephen, Luke introduces what have become known as the 'road narratives.' In each of these road narratives there is movement away from Jerusalem. In chapter eight, for example, the Ethiopian eunuch is converted on a road moving away from Jerusalem. In chapter nine Paul is converted on a road away from Jerusalem. And in chapter ten Peter travels on a road leading away from Jerusalem to bring the gospel to the Gentiles. Yes, of course, 'something is changing,' but it is not a divine withdrawal of apostolic miracles. Luke is showing with consummate skill the beginning of a fulfillment of the Lord's prediction of judgment on Jerusalem. These things have been well known in the scholarly studies of Acts for years now. To attempt to use the movement away from Jerusalem in the book of Acts as indication that healing and miracles are leaving at approximately A.D. 35, no more than two years after the death of the Lord, is absolutely incredible.

27. Furthermore, the whole idea that God withdrew Paul's healing gift before the end of his life *may* contradict Paul's statement in Romans 11:29: 'For the gifts [*charisma*] and the calling of God are irrevocable' (NASB).

28. For example, Wayne Grudem, *The Gift of Prophecy*, pp. 275–76; and D. A. Carson, *Showing the Spirit*, pp. 88ff. Grudem agrees 'apostle' is an office, not a spiritual gift.

29. Someone might object, however, that Paul does refer to apostles as spiritual gifts because in Ephesians 4:11 he names apostles, prophets, evangelists, pastors, and teachers as examples of 'gifts' mentioned earlier in Ephesians 4:8. However, the word translated 'gift' in Ephesians 4:7 is not the word that Paul consistently uses elsewhere for spiritual gifts. In fact, in Ephesians 4:11 Paul is describing not spiritual gifts (*charismata*) but five different ministries whose function is to equip the saints to do the work of ministry.

30. Gordon D. Fee, *The First Epistle to the Corinthians*, New International Commentary on the New Testament (Grand Rapids, Mich.: Eerdmans, 1987), p. 620.

31. Some dispute that this verse clearly sets forth James as an apostle, however, the Greek text virtually demands that we view James as an apostle. See Grudem, *The Gift of Prophecy*, p. 272.

32. It is not as likely, however, that he is viewing Timothy as an apostle in 1 Thessalonians 2:7. See Grudem, ibid., pp. 272–75.

33. There are, however, several different interpretive possibilities for this text. See Fee, *First Corinthians*, pp. 731–32. Epaphroditus (Phil. 2:25), some anonymous brothers, and possibly Titus (2 Cor. 8:23) are also called apostles. However, most people feel that this is a nontechnical use of the term apostle, simply meaning 'messenger.'

34. This observation was made long ago by Robertson and Plummer, *First Epistle of St. John to the Corinthians*, 2d ed. (Edinburgh: T & T. Clark, 1914), p. 279.

35. In what has become one of the classic essays on New Testament apostleship, Karl Rengstorf maintained that 'with personal encounter with the risen Lord, personal commissioning by Him seems to have been the only basis of the apostolate' (*TDNT* 1:431).

36. Some, however, have argued that the prophets mentioned in Ephesians 3:5, as well as Ephesians 2:20, are to be identified with the apostles. See Wayne Grudem, *The Gift of Prophecy*, pp. 46ff.

37. MacArthur, *Charismatic Chaos*, pp. 123–25. Thomas Edgar claims that 1 Corinthians 15:8 is also an argument for the ceasing of the apostles. Paul was enumerating a list of people who had seen the Lord Jesus after his resurrection when he wrote of himself in verse eight, 'And last of all he appeared to me also, as to one abnormally born.' Edgar takes this to mean that Paul was the last one to see the risen Lord Jesus and, therefore, the last of all the apostles (*Miraculous Gifts* [Neptune, N.J.: Loizeaux Brothers, 1983], pp. 60–62). Even if this were the correct interpretation of 1 Corinthians 15:8, it would not mean that Jesus could not appear to people after the apostle Paul and appoint other apostles. All it would mean is that at the time of the writing of 1 Corinthians 15:8, Paul was the last one to have seen the Lord Jesus. This is not the only interpretation possible, however, nor even probable (see Fee, *First Corinthians*, pp. 732–34).

38. MacArthur, *Charismatic Chaos*, p. 124.

39. Ibid., p. 125.

40. Gross, *Miracles, Demons, and Spiritual Warfare*, p. 53.

Appendix C: Were There Only Three Periods of Miracles?

1. MacArthur, *Charismatic Chaos*, pp. 112–14. It was Warfield who popularized this argument. He was, however, more careful than MacArthur in stating the argument. He maintained that there were four periods of revelation, not three. He included the time of Daniel as the fourth period. See B. B. Warfield, "Miracles" in *A Dictionary of the Bible*, 4th ed., J. D. Davis ed. (Grand Rapids: Baker, 1954), p. 505.

2. MacArthur heard a tape of a message in which I made this point. He took issue with my interpretation in the following way:

> Deere is so determined to find biblical support for an ongoing ministry of signs and wonders that he misreads Jeremiah 32:20. . . . Deere believes Jeremiah was saying signs and wonders continued in Egypt and Israel after the Exodus and that Jeremiah was acknowledging their existence even in his

day. What Jeremiah actually wrote, of course, was that God had made a name for himself through the signs and wonders he performed in Egypt, and that his name was known "even to this day" both in Israel and among the Gentiles. Anyone familiar with Old Testament history knows that the miracles of the Exodus were unique, and the Israelites always recalled them as evidence of their God's greatness. (*Charismatic Chaos*, p.113)

Basically, MacArthur has criticized my usage of Jeremiah 32:20 by simply asserting that virtually everyone knows that Jeremiah was referring to signs and wonders of the past rather than to signs and wonders of his day.

Apparently MacArthur thought that this assertion was sufficient both as an explanation of Jeremiah 32:20 and as a refutation of my use of it. He did not refer to the Hebrew text underlying the expression "even unto this day" to see if it could bear the meaning he had assigned to it. Nor did he explore any contextual reasons that might have led him back to a more literal interpretation of what Jeremiah actually wrote. Nor did he cite any scholarly studies or any other support that could justify his rejection of the literal meaning of Jeremiah 32:20.

Although in MacArthur's opinion I may not qualify as "anyone familiar with Old Testament history," I would still like to suggest that Jeremiah's statement should be taken literally. The reasons for doing so are as follows. First, this is exactly what a literal interpretation of the Hebrew text means. The phrase translated "even unto this day," when used of customs or other activities, refers to the continuation of that activity at least up to the time of the speaker or writer (cf. Josh. 9:27, 13:13; 15:63; 16:10; 23:8–9, and B.D.B., p. 401 for many other examples). The NIV has translated the Hebrew text in its normal sense when it says of signs and wonders that God has "continued them to this day." Second, contextually the spirit of prophecy is still in the land at the time of Jeremiah's writing. Prophecy is both a sign and a wonder according to the Bible. Consider Isaiah's statement,

> Behold, I and the children whom the LORD has given me are for signs and wonders in Israel from the LORD of hosts, who dwells on Mount Zion. (Isa. 8:18 NASB)

In light of the prophetic tradition, Jeremiah's own presence and ministry in the land is a sufficient condition for a literal understanding of "even unto this day."

Third, there is the ministry of Daniel (605 B.C. to 537 B.C.), chronologically very close to Jeremiah (626 B.C. to after 586 B.C.), which is certainly filled with signs and wonders. Daniel's ministry would justify, if not demand, a literal interpretation of "even unto this day."

MacArthur does not interact with these reasons or any other linguistic, contextual, or historical reasons for understanding Jeremiah's words in their normal meaning. Instead, motivated by a theological prejudice that already predetermined what Jeremiah can or can not mean, he simply para-phrases Jeremiah's words into a vague theological axiom that only halfway resembles the words of the original text.

3. MacArthur, *Charismatic Chaos*, p. 106.

4. Ibid., p. 107.

5. Jesus also refers to cataclysmic judgments done apart from human agency as signs (Luke 21:11, 25).

6. The K^ethib of the MT has *zakar* in the *Hiphil* stem. In the *Hiphil, zakar* means "to bring to mind" or "to mention," and can be used even in the sense of praising or extolling the Lord and his works (see Francis Brown, S. R. Driver, and Charles A. Briggs, *A Hebrew and English Lexicon of the Old Testament* [Oxford: Clarendon Press, 1907], p. 271).

Surprised by the Voice of God

by Jack Deere

This book is written for ordinary Christians who want to hear God's voice above the clamour of everyday life. The still, small voice of God that spoke to Elijah in the cave is far more powerful than tradition or circumstance. But how do we tell when it is God speaking to us, and not our emotions, or the opinions of others, or even dark spiritual forces?

Jack Deere brings together inspiring stories from people who have learned to trust God's voice today, his own experiences in teaching and pastoral ministry, and mature biblical teaching—all of which can help us to understand the Bible and to hear from God both for ourselves and for those to whom we minister.

'Jack Deere has done it again. If anything, this volume is more compelling than the previous work, *Surprised by the Power of the Spirit.*'

—R T KENDALL

'Packed with gripping illustration, this classic has been written by a theologian to help the common man. It is full of practical wisdom and biblical insight. Those who "covet to prophesy", or to understand more about prophecy, will want to sell their beds to buy this book. Once started, the reader will be impelled to read right through.'

—DAVID PYTCHES

'A refreshing and powerful word on the ministry of the prophetic. No one desiring to hear God's voice speaking today can afford to ignore this book.'

—LYNDON BOWRING